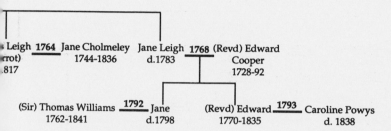

Leigh **1764** Jane Cholmeley   Jane Leigh **1768** (Revd) Edward
rrot)   1744-1836   d.1783   Cooper
817   1728-92

(Sir) Thomas Williams **1792** Jane   (Revd) Edward **1793** Caroline Powys
1762-1841   d.1798   1770-1835   d. 1838

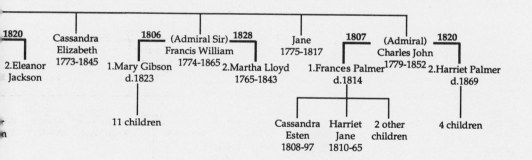

1820   Cassandra   **1806** (Admiral Sir) **1828**   Jane   **1807** (Admiral)   **1820**
          Elizabeth   Francis William   1775-1817   Charles John
2.Eleanor   1773-1845   1.Mary Gibson 1774-1865 2.Martha Lloyd   1.Frances Palmer1779-1852 2.Harriet Palmer
Jackson   d.1823   1765-1843   d.1814   d.1869

                            11 children   Cassandra   Harriet   2 other   4 children
                                                           Esten   Jane   children
                                                            1808-97   1810-65

JANE AUSTEN

—————JANE AUSTEN—————

REAL AND IMAGINED WORLDS

OLIVER MacDONAGH

YALE UNIVERSITY PRESS

NEW HAVEN & LONDON

1991

Set in Linotronic Bembo by SX Composing Limited, Essex, England
Printed and bound in Great Britain by The Bath Press, Avon.

Library of Congress Cataloging-in-Publication Data

MacDonagh, Oliver.
    Jane Austen : real and imagined worlds / Oliver MacDonagh.
      p.   cm.
    Includes bibliographical references and index.
    ISBN 0-300-05084-4   4. Austen, Jane, 1775-1817 –
Criticism and interpretation.
I. Title.
[PR4037.M28   1991]   90-26432
823′.7—dc20   CIP

For my colleagues, and dear friends,

in the Department of History, 1973-90

JANE AUSTEN COUNTRY

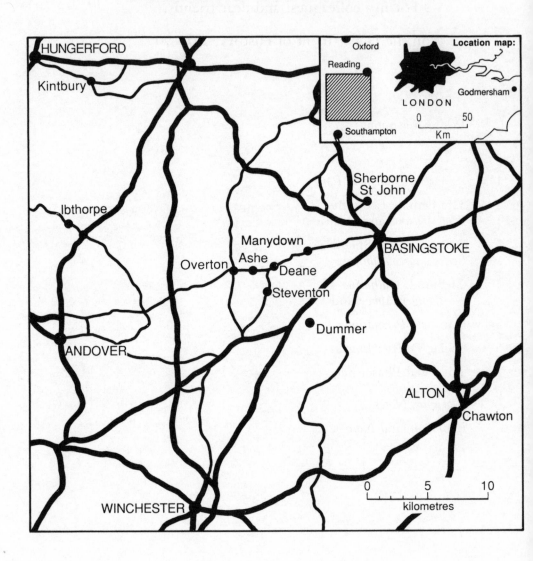

CONTENTS

NOVELS ARE RARELY listed in historians' bibliographies, and this is as it should be. Readers of a historical work should, in principle, be able to learn as much as the author from his or her listed sources, and learn essentially the same sort of thing. But the historical author scarcely knows what he or she has learnt from a work of fiction. A few things may be attributable directly – an epitomizing phrase, a vivid illustration, a character who constitutes an archetype. But generally the effects of novel-reading on a historian's thought are too amorphous and diffused to be defined; they may vary widely, moreover, from historian to historian. Yet they may also have suggested many of the themes or emphases of the historical book, or at any rate how these should be treated.

One can however get rather closer with one particular sort of novel – the contemporaneous work of some past epoch which also aims to depict accurately the world about. Here historians have some access to the felt reality of the time of composition – the degree of the access depending, of course, on the novelist's area of experience and degree of social intelligence and integrity. Jane Austen was the first and is probably, within her chosen area, the finest 'historian's novelist', in this particular sense.

One purpose of my book is, therefore, to draw attention to the illumination of English history, in the quarter-century 1792-1817, which her novels may provide. The other is to try to illuminate the novels themselves by historians' evaluations of the period. The methodologies interact, one hopes – with energy and counter-energy setting one another off successively. But they are essentially two plain, simple and well-tried procedures. The justification, such as it is, for building a book about them must lie altogether in the performance. It is this which makes me tremble sometimes at my temerity.

This is triply an amateur book. First, it is a work of love. Not that I am a besotted Janeite. I freely allow that there may be a score of greater novelists, and even greater English novelists, than she. No one else, however, casts the same enchantment. It depends, I suppose, on what enslaves one; and while others – countless others – may be fettered for different reasons, it is her alloy of precision and elegance which captures me. I say this to explain how I, a professional historian, come to attempt a book upon her writing. Perhaps a mathematician could better justify an outburst that springs from admiration for such qualities. But historians too must (or should) subscribe to the creeds of exactitude, economy and grace.

Secondly, I am no 'professional' in the field of Austen personal material. Rather, I depend on the long line of testifiers and recollectors, and of editors and collators of correspondence, memoranda, diaries, family papers and literary drafts, which stretches from the first edition of Henry Austen's *Biographical Notice*, published in 1818, to Deirdre Le Faye's much revised and enlarged version of the Austen–Leighs' *Life and Letters of Jane Austen* and Jo Modert's *Jane Austen's Manuscript Letters in Facsimile*, published in 1989 and 1990 respectively. I am a simple debtor to the fruits of all this labour, produced over more than 180 years.

Thirdly, I am untrained – and largely unlettered – in literary criticism. So conscious am I of this that I have tried to obtrude as few as possible of my own judgements of literary quality upon the reader. But we all know how even the just man fares; and here and there consciously, and I daresay more often self-deceivingly, I have fallen to a temptation. In general, however, so far as this aspect of the book is concerned, I have striven hard to remember my place as an uninvited guest worker in an advanced and highly complex system of production. I have also striven to write so as to interest 'the general reader' equally with the historian and student of literature.

The order of the chapters is to some degree arbitrary, but I have taken as my guide what I suppose Jane Austen would have regarded as the order of importance of their subject-matters in her own life. In each case I have selected one large topic and, most often, the novel or fragment of a novel which seems to me to throw most light upon it. In two instances I have used more than one piece of Jane Austen's work to underpin a chapter.

To study Jane Austen's Anglicanism, I have chosen *Mansfield Park*; to study her economic condition, knowledge and assumptions, *Sense and Sensibility*; to study her experience and ideals of the family,

Persuasion; to study the petty societies in which she lived and her reactions to their limitations and inducements, *Emma*; and to study both the final phase of her life and her relationship to the contemporary world in general during one particular portion of her 'times', *Sanditon*.

In the case of her situation as a poor gentlewoman at the turn of the eighteenth century, I have selected three works, her early epistolary novel *Lady Susan*, the unfinished *The Watsons* and *Pride and Prejudice*, as – so it seems to me – the most revealing. Similarly, I have chosen three works, the early fragment *Catharine, or The Bower*, *Northanger Abbey* and, again, *Pride and Prejudice*, to explore Jane Austen's ideas of girlhood, growing up generally, and female education and preparation in particular.

For what may be, alas, the last time, I must thank Mrs Pamela Crichton and Mrs Beverly Gallina most warmly for their comradeship in an enterprise and inestimable help in getting a book of mine up to the publisher's starting line. I trust that I need not express my other customary gratitude in such valedictory terms. May there be Prefaces still to come in which I can try to express again my deep appreciation of my wife's kind forbearance with it all.

O. MacD.

Canberra
November 1990

CHAPTER 1

RELIGION:
Mansfield Park

Perhaps the most celebrated error about *Mansfield Park* is that Jane Austen meant its theme to be ordination. I write this with some pain, for by collating texts and dates I laboriously discovered the error for myself, only to learn, too late, that the world had already known it for a dozen years or more.

And yet, although the original mistake was gross – the letter preceding that in which Jane Austen told her sister Cassandra that she would write next on ordination had made it clear that *Mansfield Park* was already half complete[1]* – it may also have been inspired. There is one sense in which ordination, as the very pivot of organized religion, can be regarded as the novel's leading theme. 'Ordination' need not be confined to the narrow usage of ceremonial appointment to the Christian ministry. On the one hand, the primary meaning of the word is classification (generally social in character) and arrangement into ranks. On the other, the taking of Anglican orders in 1813 (when *Mansfield Park* was finished) raised many questions of ecclesiastical discipline – residence, pluralism and ritual; of livelihood – the variation, sources and ownership of clerical income; of the nature of the parish and its duties, and the crisis presented by urbanization and manufacturing industry; of religion of the heart, conversion and enthusiasm; and, though only in a premonitory and tentative form as yet, of the sacramental and special or 'holy' nature of the priesthood. It is with these religious meanings of ordination that I am primarily concerned, although, of course, no late Georgian would have distinguished them altogether from social order and stable rank.

We should note particularly that the spiritual and ecclesiastical issues of 1813 foreshadowed the great debates and endeavours of the Victorian Church. Conversely, they also signalled the profound

---

* Superior figures refer to the Reference Notes at p. 169.

changes which the Church of England had begun to undergo in the
final decades of the eighteenth century. As it happens, both the mid-
eighteenth century and the Victorian Church have received considerably more historical attention than the intervening decades of transi-
tion.[2] Thus *Mansfield Park* may throw a sudden, intense light – however needle-thin or subjective – on one great turning-point in English
history. It may also be itself revealed at a greater depth, or at any rate
another level, if it is scrutinized as a religious novel. In short, I propose trying another suit of clothes, a clerical suit, upon the book. If it
fits even tolerably it may tell us something about not only Jane Austen herself but also the nature of what might be termed 'middle'
Anglicanism, in the closing years of the Napoleonic wars. It will also
indicate, I think, a strangely anticipatory quality in the novel.
Looked at in an ecclesiastical light, *Mansfield Park* seems to leap forward – or half forward – to the literature of principle and the Church
of conscience, each of which was to flourish so profusely in mid-
nineteenth-century England.

                                        I

First, let us assemble the few surviving indications of Jane Austen's
own religion, considering in turn her family, her known experiences
and her private observations.

   One salient feature is that her life spanned the era of incipient
church reform. The years 1775-1817 were marked by profound
changes in Anglican expectations of their clergy, and to a lesser extent in clerical practice itself. Evangelicalism was at once a cause and
an effect of this transformation. But the transformation transcended
Evangelicalism, narrowly defined. It was also a counterpart of, and
interconnected with, the associated administrative, political, and university reform movements of the late eighteenth century, each of
which took a decided shape in the 1780s. Characteristically, the
Church lagged a little behind the rest. In its case the 'centre of
gravity' of the change was probably one to two decades later.

   Jane Austen's own family provides, to a degree, an illustration of
these developments. Her father, George Austen, appears to have
passed for an exemplary clergyman in the late eighteenth century.
Yet he was not ordained until the age of twenty-nine, and accepted
orders then – at least the chronology would suggest as much – so that
he could accept, practically simultaneously, a proctorship at Oxford

and a family living. For the first three years of his rectorship of
Steventon, he was an absentee. He did not come into residence until
his marriage in 1764. Meanwhile, to augment his income, his uncle
had bought him the reversion to whichever of the two adjoining parishes, Ashe or Deane, should fall in first; and when Deane became
vacant in 1773, he must have supplied its duties, if at all, by a curate
until his eldest son, James, could succeed there as his *alter ego* after he
came down from Oxford. Doubtless to raise more money, the
rectory at Deane was let from 1773 until James needed it for a home
when he married, and became curate there, in 1792; and again in the
elder Mr Austen's final years after he had passed over the duties and a
certain proportion of the income of Steventon to James. Thus
George Austen was a pluralist (if only in mild form) for most of his
clerical life, as well as a non-resident in its opening and closing
phases. He was, moreover, only a part-time rector in the sense that
he pursued other avocations. He tutored and boarded at home for
several years as many as four or five of the sons of the rich or related,
and farmed – he was an eager and active agriculturalist – probably
during the entire period of his residence at Steventon.

We know nothing certainly of his theological views and tone, but
the impression gained is of a sound median High-Churchman. His
clerical children however bore some of the marks of a later generation. It is true that James, Jane's eldest brother, was also a sort of
pluralist and, at a lower clerical level, a non-resident. In 1791, he became vicar (effectively, curate) of the parish of Sherborne St. John,
near Basingstoke, while still holding the curacy of Overton, more
than ten miles away. Indeed, he continued to hold Sherborne St.
John after becoming curate and eventually rector of Steventon itself.
He was also presented in 1792 to yet another living, at Cubbington,
Warwickshire, by his uncle Thomas Leigh; this he maintained by
employing a curate to perform its duties.[3] None the less, James was
noted as a particularly strict and earnest priest, who actually rejected
presentation to another living from scruples about simony – his
grand-uncle's acquisition of a second living for his father had borne a
decidedly simoniacal air![4] Henry, George's fourth son, intended for
the church but escaping into, first, the Oxfordshire militia and then
private banking, and finally accepting orders after being declared in-
solvent in 1815, proved as perpetual curate of Overton to be a stern
and fiery Evangelical. In the wider family circle, Jane's cousin, the
Revd Edward Cooper, was a decided puritan, while another clerical
cousin, the Revd George Cooke, a celebrated tutor of Corpus

Christi, Oxford, and the teacher of both Keble and Thomas Arnold, was recalled as 'an impressive preacher of earnest awakening sermons'.[5] 'Impressive', 'earnest' and 'awakening' are all of course revealing words. Each was important in the code language which signalled the Evangelical.

It is true, of course, that the commonplace search for money and security for a large family aspiring to keep its place in the upper middle class provides much of the explanation of George Austen's clerical conduct. It is also true that it can be replicated in the records of the early Victorian period – for a very small minority, one need hardly say, as clerical incomes of £800 to £1,000 per annum, family livings, and the opportunities to practise pluralism or simony or even (since few incumbents could afford two roofs) non-residence were comparatively rare.[6] Nevertheless, the shift in popular expectations and accepted standards in the church between the 1780s and the 1830s was marked and clear; and *Mansfield Park* both stands at the crossroads in time, and must have been informed by the author's intimate knowledge of this revolutionary or evolutionary process.

Although we know little certainly of her spiritual life, there can at least be no reasonable doubt that Jane Austen was a conscientious and believing churchwoman. Her private writings suggest moreover – though merely as an impression – that her religious seriousness increased as she aged, and in particular in the final decade of her life. Her attendance at divine service was always regular; she said, and even composed, domestic prayers; she read sermons, devotedly. Her admiration of Charles the Martyr might suggest a species of proto-tractarianism. But this would be anachronistic. Her love of Bishop Sherlock's *Sermons*[7] was probably the true index of the nature of her High or tory Anglicanism. For Sherlock and his school it was not the protestantism of the Church of England but its latitudinarian (or Arian or deist) wing which was abhorrent. As her clergyman brother, Henry, an enemy of all popish things, carefully attested, 'her opinions accorded strictly with those of our Established Church'.[8] To Henry we also owe the only considerable comment upon her religious disposition. 'One trait only remains to be touched on', he wrote towards the end of his 'Notice' of 1817,

> It makes all others unimportant. She was thoroughly religious and devout; fearful of giving offence to God, and incapable of feeling it towards any fellow creature. On serious subjects she was well-instructed, both by reading and meditation.[9]

Henry is not to be trusted altogether. Jane herself warned against his 'Brotherly vanity & Love'.[10] But however superficial or marmoreal, this particular judgment on religion can scarcely have done more than exaggerate or simplify the reality.

But much the best, if also a most fragmentary and oblique, source for Jane Austen's views and nature is her letters. Unfortunately, these interfamilial writings say little on the heavier matters of life, and least of all on its spiritual dimension, which only 'enthusiasts' (to use the contemporary term) would ordinarily speak of outside church walls. Moreover, it is arguable that, if anywhere, Jane would have canvassed religious subjects in her letters to Cassandra, and Cassandra destroyed many – perhaps the bulk – of these, and almost certainly those which were most intimate or personal. None the less, a handful of religious threads survives, and it may be possible to guess at the fabric and pattern of which they once formed part.

Apart from an early note of condolence to a relative, as coldly chiselled as any lapidary inscription of the day – 'But the very circumstance which at present enhances your loss, must gradually reconcile you to it the better; – the Goodness which made him valuable on Earth, will make him Blessed in Heaven'[11] – the first significant reference to religion in the correspondence comes in 1808. A letter of 24 October describes the visit to Southampton of two of Jane Austen's nephews whose mother had just died after childbirth. Jane told Cassandra that 'as far as I can judge they are both very properly impressed by what has happened'. On the preceding day, a Sunday, she had taken them to church where '*I saw Edward was much affected by the sermon, which, indeed, I could have supposed purposely addressed* to the afflicted. . . . In the evening we had the Psalms and Lessons, and a sermon at home, to which they were very attentive'.[12] Shortly afterwards, having read accounts of Sir John Moore's irreligious death in Spain, she told Cassandra that 'tho' a very Heroick son, he might not be a very necessary one to her [his mother's] happiness. . . . I wish Sir John had united something of the Christian with the Hero in his death'.[13]

But the most telling references to religion, for our purposes at least, are those clustered in 1813–14, during the final stages of the composition of *Mansfield Park*, and soon after its publication. The first of these is interesting for its implicit leaning towards the sturdy Protestant and John Bullish element in Anglicanism. 'It must be a real enjoyment to you', Jane wrote to her sailor brother, Francis, in the Baltic in mid–1813,

since you are obliged to leave England, to be where you are, seeing
something of a new Country, & one that has been so distinguished
as Sweden. . . . Gustavus-Vasa, & Charles 12th, & Christina, &
Linneus – do their Ghosts rise up before you? – I have a great respect for former Sweden. So zealous as it was for Protestan[t]ism!
– And I have always fancied it more like England than many
Countries; – & according to the Map, many of the names have a
strong resemblance to the English.[14]

A letter of fourteen months later to her sister-in-law's sister, Martha Lloyd, contains two significant passages. The first throws a shaft
of light upon her personal piety.

I have seen West's famous Painting [*His Rejection by the Elders*], and
prefer it to anything of the kind I ever saw before. I do not know
that it *is* reckoned superior to his 'Healing in the Temple' but it has
gratified *me* much more, and indeed is the first representation of
our Saviour which ever at all contented me.[15]

The second is more generally interesting and suggestive:

they consider it [an American war] as certain, and as what is to
ruin us. The Americans cannot be conquered, and we shall only be
teaching them the skill in War which they may now want. . . . If we
are to be ruined, it cannot be helped – but I place my hope of better
things on a claim to the protection of Heaven, as a Religious
Nation, a Nation in spite of much Evil improving in Religion,
which I cannot beleive the Americans to possess.[16]

Finally a letter of 18 November 1814 to her niece, Fanny Knight,
discussing Fanny's suitor, John Plumtre, contains the clearest and
perhaps the best-known of the religious comments in the correspondence. 'And as to there being any objection from his Goodness', Jane
wrote,

from the danger of his becoming even Evangelical, I cannot admit
that. I am by no means convinced that we ought not all to be Evangelicals, & am at least persuaded that they who are so from Reason
and Feeling, must be happiest & safest. Do not be frightened from
the connection by your Brothers having most wit. Wisdom is
better than Wit, & in the long run will certainly have the laugh on
her side; & don't be frightened by the idea of his acting more
strictly up to the precepts of the New Testament than others.[17]

The four religious references of 1813-14 seem to carry, however faintly, these particular implications: that Jane Austen's Christianity was Christocentric in the orthodox pious-Protestant sense; that she conceived of religion as also national in character; that her Anglicanism and her chauvinism were mutually supportive and interpenetrating; that she rejoiced in what seemed to her the increasing religiosity and advance in public morality in her homeland; that she was – or at any rate believed one ought to be – seriously devout; and that, while she herself disliked and eschewed, she also respected and even envied the Evangelical school in the Church of England, whose salvation seemed the more secure for the totality of their conversion.

II

It is to the unadulterated eighteenth-century Church that we are introduced in the second chapter of *Mansfield Park*. Edmund Bertram, the second son, is destined for the family living, and doubtless for a life of pluralism by Sir Thomas's ownership of a second living nearby at Thornton Lacey. It is implied that probity, level-headedness and the absence of disinclination are quite enough to warrant ordination in such happy circumstances: 'the character of Edmund, his strong good sense and uprightness of mind, bid most fairly for utility, honour, and happiness to himself and all his connections. He was to be a clergyman'.[18] Only the accident that his brother's extravagance had led to the sale of the next incumbency of Mansfield rendered immediate pluralism after his ordination impracticable.

In the book's first canvass of religion, Mary Crawford expresses the thoroughgoing secular version of these proceedings, though it is also coloured by her own predilection for fortune, boldness and éclat. Family livings she allowed, but as the asylum of the youngest of a long line of boys rather than the featherbed of an able second son. '"Do you think", asks Edmund, "the church itself never chosen then?". "*Never* is a black word. But yes, in the *never* of conversation which means *not very often*, I do think it"' (p. 92). In short, for Mary, already the devil's disciple, taking orders is a mere matter of adopting a career, and, at that, choosing the lowest occupation which was compatible with respectability. As for ordination for religion's sake, without a living, '"that is madness indeed, absolute madness"'(p. 109).

Then comes the first adumbration of a new order. Edmund attempts a twofold defence of his choice. He admits that the prospect of a good living (or good livings) may have biased him – but, he argues, not improperly.

> 'There was no natural disinclination to be overcome, and I see no reason why a man should make a worse clergyman for knowing that he will have a competence early in life. I was in safe hands. I hope I should not have been influenced myself in a wrong way, and I am sure my father was too conscientious to have allowed it. I have no doubt that I was biassed, but I think it was blamelessly.'
> (p. 109)

The concept of spiritual vocation is – so far – absent from Edmund's exposition, as it is indeed from Fanny Price who at this point compounds Edmund's argument with '"Nobody wonders that they [men] should prefer the line where their friends can serve them best, or suspects them to be less in earnest in it"' (p. 109). Edmund's conscience may be tender; but it is for his own sincerity that he argues here, supporting it (like Edward Ferrars in *Sense and Sensibility*) by a sort of *nihil obstat* reasoning and the threadbare question, how otherwise can the Church be 'filled'?

Though Edmund's second defence is essentially Erastian, it is not wholly lacking in spiritual intimations. He presents the clergyman as social moulder.

> 'I cannot call that situation nothing, which has the charge of all that is of the first importance to mankind, individually or collectively considered, temporally and eternally – which has the guardianship of religion and morals, and consequently of the manners which result from their influence. No one here can call the *office* nothing.'
> (p. 92)

The manners which the clergy influence are not the mere externalities of taste or refinement, but – a key conflation of Edmund's – '"*conduct* . . . the result of good principles; the effect, in short, of those doctrines which it is their duty to teach and recommend"' (p. 93). It is not precisely social control which Edmund here envisages, but rather a form of social husbandry. Fittingly enough perhaps, he sees it as practicable only in the countryside. In the large places, not only are the clergy lost '"in the crowds of their parishioners"' but also vice and godlessness congregate. The greatest rising problem of the contemporary church, urbanization, is recognized but apparently without alarm – or hope. Edmund believed that it was by example, as well as tending, that the clergy would influence the rest, and in a great darkness a penny candle cannot reach far: '"as the clergy are, or are not what they ought to be"', Edmund concludes, '"so are the rest of the nation"' (p. 93). But he has, it would seem, already excluded the metropolis from the nation.

At first sight, this defence of taking orders might seem to march in step with Sir Thomas Bertram's celebrated exposition of the village pastor's role, much later in the book.

> 'But a parish has wants and claims which can be known only by a clergyman constantly resident, and which no proxy can be capable of satisfying to the same extent. Edmund might, in the common phrase, do the duty of Thornton, that is, he might read prayers and preach, without giving up Mansfield Park; he might ride over, every Sunday, to a house nominally inhabited, and go through divine service; he might be the clergyman of Thornton Lacey every seventh day, for three or four hours, if that would content him. But it will not. He knows that human nature needs more lessons than a weekly sermon can convey, and that if he does not live among his parishioners and prove himself by constant attention their well-wisher and friend, he does very little either for their good or his own.'
>
> (pp. 247-8)

Edmund immediately agrees that his father has grasped thoroughly the duty of a parish priest. But this should not lead us to miss the generational difference between the two. Sir Thomas's exegesis lacks all spiritual reference. The phraseology seems to reduce even the ecclesiastical element to formality. So far as we are told, the lessons which Sir Thomas's conscientious, resident rector will provide are lessons in propriety and good will. He is the forerunner of the district officer and the social worker. A parish, as Sir Thomas said, '"has wants and claims which can be known only by a clergyman constantly resident"'. In his earlier discourse, however, Edmund had added another dimension altogether. Conduct may have held the centre of the stage here, too. But the notions of salvation, of eternity and of theological instruction were at least minor characters in the cast.

But perhaps the dramatic metaphor is unfortunate for Edmund. For it is precisely at this point that he and Henry Crawford divide, in religion as well as many lesser things. Here as ever, Crawford is neither as shallow nor as irresponsive as his sister. He can see ordination positively – as opening a way to display aesthetic satisfaction and the manipulation of other minds – whereas for her it merely led

straight, idle, greedy and inglorious to the grave. But Crawford's
extraordinary sensitivity and celerity of mind serve only to underline
his greater subversiveness. He treats the church (as he treats all else)
as a stage for role-playing, for experimentation in personality, entirely without regard to ordained order or harmony, or to religion in
its proper, literal sense of 'that which binds'.

The passage between himself and Edmund after his reading from
Henry VIII and his exordium on the beauties of the Anglican liturgy
makes this clear. The preacher, Crawford declares,

> 'who can touch and affect such an heterogeneous mass of hearers,
> on subjects limited, and long worn thread-bare in all common
> hands; who can say any thing new or striking, any thing that rouses
> the attention, without offending the taste, or wearing out the
> feelings of his hearers, is a man whom one could not (in his public
> capacity) honour enough. I should like to be such a man'. (p. 341)

The self-exploration and self-realization for which Crawford strove,
and the sublimity of his irreligion, are revealed by his insistence upon
a sophisticated '"audience"' (the very word he uses is significant),
who would be capable, as he says, '"of estimating my composition"'. The preacher as actor is to be further emphasized by the rarity
of the performance: '"once or twice in the spring, after being
anxiously expected for half a dozen Sundays together; but not for a
constancy; it would not do for a constancy"' (p. 341). It was of
course the repudiation of 'constancy' which caused Fanny Price in-
voluntarily to shake her head, and thus become drawn into a brief
but critical exchange, which is emblematic of the conflict between
restlessness and control which underlies a great deal of the novel.
Before all this, however, Edmund has spoken, not (note) of preaching, but of scripture reading, and in a vein totally antithetical to
Crawford's, despite their apparent general agreement. It is interesting that Edmund stresses the change – the '"improvement"', to use
his specific term – which the Church has undergone during the past
generation. One manifestation of this change is more theologically
informed and more spiritually engaged congregations. Another is
clergy concerned to convey the meaning of the word God. Thus,
although Crawford and Edmund may seem to be *ad idem* in looking
for rhetorical effectiveness, Crawford's hope is that the preacher's
vanity will be fed, Edmund's '"that distinctness and energy may
have weight in recommending the most solid truths"' of religion
(p. 340).

The same contrast is drawn in more material terms in the discussion on the Thornton Lacey parsonage which accompanied the game of Speculation at Dr Grant's. Edmund is not averse to spending a little money on his future home, but only to render the house and premises more comfortable at moderate expense. Crawford, however, is at once seized by the fact that the house already *appears* to be something more, far more, than a mere parsonage, far more than the material expression of a mere ' "few hundreds a year"'. The fact that the Thornton Lacey parsonage would pass for what it was not – as a county family's home proclaiming a rental of £2,000 or £3,000 per annum – led him to propose such 'improvement' as would render it '"the residence of a man of education, taste, modern manners, good connections.... [with] such an air as to make its owner be set down as the great land-holder of the parish, by every creature travelling the road"' (p. 244). Again, Edmund accepts plain clericality, but Crawford wishes to sink it in a grandiose stage set, in the creation of an illusion and a fresh part to play.

Edmund is indubitably on the side of the angels, but not at the extremity of the host, even in terms of Jane Austen's narrow range. This is Fanny's station. The spiritual spectrum of *Mansfield Park* would seem to run, Fanny, Edmund, Sir Thomas, Mary and Crawford, the last two being separated by their relative moral capacities and depth of mind. It is Fanny who strikes the only note of religious emotion in the book – pinchbeck though it may be in the feeble Gothicism of '"nothing awful here [Sotherton chapel]"'.[19] It is Fanny who makes the only reference to the interior workings of spiritual reflection – puerile though it may be to argue that Dr Grant's conduct would be still more gross were it not for '"that knowledge of himself, the *frequency*, at least, of that knowledge which it is impossible he should escape"' (p. 112) as a preacher of the gospel. It is Fanny who, first and most clearly of all in the novel, categorizes Crawford's liaison with Maria in sternly religious terms, in the language of guilt, sin and punishment.

> The horror of a mind like Fanny's, as it received the conviction of such guilt... can hardly be described. At first, it was a sort of stupefaction; but every moment was quickening her perception of the horrible evil.... Miss Crawford's... eager defence of her brother, her hope of its being *hushed up*, her evident agitation, were all of a piece with something very bad; and if there was a woman of character in existence, who could treat as a trifle this sin of the first

magnitude, who could try to gloss it over, and desire to have it un-
punished, she could believe Miss Crawford to be the woman!
(pp. 440-1)

But although there is no question that Fanny's religious understanding and practice are superior to all the rest – just as, consequen-
tially, her principles and moral perceptions are the finest – even she is
not wholly immune from the corruption of the world's slow stain.
We have seen already that, in Edmund's defence, she proclaims a
prudential, not to say worldly, view of holy orders. In the end, she
succumbs to the accumulated pressure to take a part in the half-
improper drama, *Lovers' Vows*. In the end (the author makes it clear),
she would also have succumbed to Henry Crawford, had he been
constant, and his sister yielding – to Edmund's suit. Thus Fanny is
no saint or ranter. But she is awarded the character of earnest, strict
and struggling Christian. It is made clear that within limits, very
close limits of course, her principles can be overborne, though it is
also made quite clear that her inner citadel is inviolable.

By conduct, reticences and sentiments alike, Edmund stands
decidedly to the left of Fanny in the spiritual spectrum of *Mansfield
Park* – if a word-play equating 'rightness' with 'rectitude' is acceptable. But this should not blind us to the essential seriousness of his
religion. 'Seriousness' is the *mot juste*. Although it was the very shib-
boleth of the Evangelicals in the early nineteenth century, it was not
their special or peculiar sectly property, but rather a word used to
connote conscientious religious practice in general. Possibly this
usage is attributable to William Law's *Serious Call to the Devout Life*,
long an established 'classic' of the Church of England. It is surely significant therefore that Edmund's very opening observation on religion – like a motto at a chapter head – at once rebukes and excuses
Mary Crawford for not being '"serious even on serious subjects"'
(p. 87). As we have seen, the serious breaks through, however
quietly, in each of his disquisitions on the manning of the Church
and the disposition of its goods and duties; and his is the opposite
Janus-face to Crawford's, the face of duty as against self-indulgence,
in each of their clerical discussions. Thus, the stage is long set for the
denouement in which he at last realizes the depth of the religious gulf
which separates him from Mary Crawford: '"it had not entered my
imagination to conceive the difference could be such as she had now
proved it"' (p. 457). Characteristically perhaps, he begins his
account of the crisis by calling Maria's adultery a '"crime"'. But he

ends by naming it a sin:

> 'she spoke of the crime itself, giving it every reproach but the
> right, considering its ill consequences only as they were to be
> braved or overborne by a defiance of decency and impudence in
> wrong; and, last of all, and above all, recommending to us a com-
> pliance, a compromise, an acquiescence, in the continuance of the
> sin, on the chance of a marriage which, thinking as I now thought
> of her brother, should rather be prevented than sought'. (p. 458)

With her usual acuity, caricaturing yet penetrating to the reality,
Mary Crawford discerns Edmund's fundamental bias in her parting
words:

> 'At this rate, you will soon reform every body at Mansfield and
> Thornton Lacey; and when I hear of you next, it may be as a cele-
> brated preacher in some great society of Methodists, or as a mis-
> sionary into foreign parts.' (p. 458)

There *was* one notable if vicarious conversion, though not quite at
Thornton Lacey or as a consequence of Edmund's preaching. By the
book's end, Sir Thomas has come painfully to realize that his
daughters' tragedy was rooted in the heartlessness, the mere outward
appearances, of their religion. A chain of phrases bears this out:
'principle, active principle, had been wanting'; 'of the necessity of
self-denial and humility, he feared they had never heard from any
lips that could profit them'; they 'had been instructed theoretically in
their religion, but never required to bring it into daily practice'
(p. 463). This seems to me pivotal in the novel. Painfully, Sir
Thomas (and to a lesser extent, Edmund) has learnt the living meaning of seriousness, in religion, in principle, in duty.

The lesson of the book is reinforced by Mary Crawford's un-
changed spirit. In fact, she ends deepened and hardened in her levity.
Her first letter to Fanny at Portsmouth rejoices in the luck that
Edmund's clericality can remain undisclosed, now that the clergy no
longer wear distinctive dress (p. 416); her second, in the prospect of
Edmund's succession to the baronetcy. '"It [his ordination] was a
foolish precipitation last Christmas, but the evil of a few days may be
blotted out in part. Varnish and gilding hide many stains. It will be
but the loss of the Esquire after his name"' (p. 434). This is the petty
form of her brother's ineradicable superficiality (in the strict sense of
concern for surfaces) in religion, a horrible travesty of the divine. In
the end, Crawford is shown to be not even the seed which springs up

momentarily in shallow soil. Fittingly, he emerges as merely the *appearance* or *illusion* of such a seed. His temporary 'reformation' is really grounded in self-indulgence. It knows nothing of 'principle, active principle' or of 'the necessity of self-denial and humility'.

But we must not forget that in terms of formal Anglicanism the range of *Mansfield Park* is very narrow. There is nothing to establish that Fanny is an enthusiast or even a positive Evangelical. There is nothing to establish that the Crawfords are positive latitudinarians or even non-attenders on the Sabbath. The religion of the heart and act, with which the book is implicitly absorbed, did not require any departure from or even much new emphasis in the received and commonplace teaching of the Church of England. By its very origin and nature, Anglicanism was a median religion. By upbringing, disposition and reflection alike, Jane Austen was (our shreds of evidence suggest) a median member of the Church of England in her day. 'Median' is far from 'lukewarm'. Hooker and Butler, to look no further, were archetypes of the median, finders of the middle yet unfenced ground. In the nature of things, this ground shifted its location imperceptibly from epoch to epoch. Clerical discipline; improvement, moral and behavioural; the priest as gospel-preacher; the 'duties' of the parish and their failure in the city; the challenge of the Wesleyans and 'New Reformation' – these were the burning issues for the serious in 1812-13; and to each, the response in *Mansfield Park* is, almost classically, moderate. Root-and-branch reform of structures is never canvassed; but individual rectitude and earnestness in one's station are most strongly urged. The clergyman remains central to the order and government of the countryside; but both in and beyond this he is to be a true dispenser of the Word of God. Fullblown Evangelicalism and emotional indulgence in religion are implicitly rejected but not the great doctrines which infuse them – sin, hell, atonement and redemption.

We cannot doubt that Mr Watson in *The Watsons* spoke for Jane Austen herself, when he repudiated the preener and the ranter equally in praising a sermon delivered '"without any Theatrical grimace or violence"'. Mr Howard had preached '"with great propriety & in a very impressive manner... much better calculated to inspire Devotion.... Mr H. read like a scholar & a gentleman"'.[20] This is the early-nineteenth-century beau ideal of true-believing, excess-hating, mean-loving Anglican clericality, to be celebrated once again in *Mansfield Park*.

III

Unlike Maria Bertram, I shall not try to cross the ha-ha or climb the iron gate into the pleasure ground: I shall not attempt literary criticism here. The preliminary wilderness of history, deceptive as Sotherton's own, is daunting enough. But I cannot forbear from pointing out that at least four of the acknowledged master scenes in the novel are 'calibrated' on the measures of seriousness and ordination. First, the afternoon of illicit companionships and vain pursuits at Sotherton, with all its bold imagery of bounds-breaking and passing from the ordered to the unrestrained, is both preceded and inaugurated by a lengthy exposition of the clerical role and responsibility. The Church, as Edmund specifically says, is the ordained guardian of the public morality which is here, symbolically, defied. As we have seen, he lays it down that as the clergy '"are, or are not what they ought to be, so are the rest of the nation"' (p. 93). The second set piece is Crawford's characteristically sudden, whim-driven return to Mansfield. Incapable of guessing at, let alone comprehending such a mode of judgment as Fanny's, he at once launches into a delighted reminiscence on the interrupted theatricals, '"such an interest, such an animation, such a spirit diffused!...I never was happier"': '"... never happier than when behaving so dishonourably and unfeelingly!"', Fanny responds in silence, '"Oh! what a corrupted mind!"'. This critical scene of moral antithesis reaches its climax, its ultimate expression, in ordination. Crawford jeeringly assumes that the gentleman-rector will be non-resident, sybaritic, moneyed and idle – Christmas and Easter services, '"I suppose, will be the sum total of sacrifice"' – and proposes an expedition to mock Edmund Bertram's first sermon. Edmund is saddened by Crawford's un-witting self-revelation. '"No, he can feel nothing as he ought"' is Fanny's wondering, appalled reaction (pp. 225-7).

In a third tableau, the game of Speculation at Mansfield parsonage, Jane Austen uses sport for theme-unfolding, as she was to do again with the child's alphabet in *Emma*. Crawford vainly attempts to seduce Fanny into avarice and aggression; Mary proclaims, '"No cold prudence for me"' (p. 243). Again, the crescendo of the scene is cast in religious terms. The adroit speculator, Crawford, proposes to use a good clerical house and income to produce much larger secular displays. Mary, 'not born to sit still and do nothing', as she says herself, hopes 'to shut out the church, sink the clergyman, and see only the respectable, elegant, modernized, and occasional residence of a man of independent fortune'. To these, Edmund opposes a sturdy, ordinary ecclesiasticism, Sir Thomas, a correct but severe statement of clerical duty, in terms of service as against aggrandizement. It was time, as Mary Crawford in her chagrin put it to herself, 'to have done with cards if sermons prevailed' (p. 248).

Fourthly, as we have seen, the final demonstration of Crawford's role-playing, the reading of *Henry VIII* in which he becomes the king, queen, Buckingham, Wolsey and Cromwell rapidly in turn, also culminates in ordination (pp. 337-43). In effect, Crawford proposes to transfer this plastic, centre-less activity to the very part of clergyman itself. Edmund tacitly resists. For him, the intrinsic message of the gospel and the priest's capacity to communicate it livingly to his people were the points at issue. Mere pulpit ostentation seemed a grotesque irrelevance. It is the inconstancy of which Crawford implicitly boasts which outrages Fanny. That he would play the clergyman occasionally and for applause epitomized not only the actor's versatility but also his ultimate amorality and emptiness of being.

IV

But to scramble back to history proper: what lights does the ecclesiastical or spiritual historian gain from the lancet windows of *Mansfield Park*? First, the clerical profession was on the threshold of important structural changes in 1813. The statistical information is incomplete but it does seem likely that the number ordained to the Anglican ministry had been more or less static for over a century. It was also close to the total number of parishes throughout this time. Almost all the ordained were graduates of the ancient universities, and the great majority of them comparatively or truly poor. Dramatic changes were at hand. A steady climb in the number of clergy was beginning, and would continue until 1901; and this increase was to be not merely absolute but even relative to population in England and Wales down to 1870. Moreover, the expansion was one of prestige, training and generally income too, in the first half of the century at least. The university population more than doubled between 1810 and 1850, and though the proportion taking orders may have declined, it still accounted for the great bulk of Oxford and still more of Cambridge graduates. The church was even growing in fashion after 1830. The aristocratic and squirearchical element was of course always small, but it was probably larger, even proportionately, in the next two or three decades than ever before or later. Internally, there was a corresponding advance in the enforcement of residence, in the increasing provision of curates (and thereby career training and ladders in many cases), in educational requirements, and even in the creation and augmentation of stipends.[21]

In turn, much of the new order would soon disappear, and other elements were to grow markedly in the future. The climacteric was probably the 1860s. But in *Mansfield Park* we have one depiction of a clerical world on the very eve of the revolution which produced this extraordinary phase. It is a view from the top of this world, and also the view of a country clergyman's daughter, whose experience – Bath excepted – was practically confined to the south-eastern corner of the island, and almost all of whose adult life was lived in wartime in the peculiar circumstances of high agricultural demand and buoyant tithes. But this was her familiar world from birth to death; and depending on the capacities of the observer, and the rarer he or she is in terms of time or condition, the more is the evidence to be prized.

Of special interest to the historian is the fact that while *Mansfield Park* contains no reference to – let alone recommendation of – structural or organizational changes in the Church, these are implicit in its values. Edmund's preparation for ordination had been casual and perfunctory. Apart from the years of tedium in the college chapel, it apparently consisted of what might be fitted into a week's visit to his friend at Peterborough (pp. 88, 255). Similarly, Dr Grant, having bought the Mansfield living, retained it after he removed to London to the Westminster stall gained by the 'interest on which he had almost ceased to form hopes' (p. 469). We may perhaps take it for granted that Edmund succeeded him as pluralist and let Thornton Lacey, unless he in turn sold the second living for the lifetime of some clerical speculator. All of this was recounted as if these were the most ordinary, even inevitable, proceedings. They were probably so regarded by the author. Jane Austen could not or at any rate did not think outside the customary categories. Yet the sacerdotal doctrine which *Mansfield Park* preaches is implicitly corrosive of the *ancien régime*. The insistence on residence was ultimately incompatible with pluralism. The serious performance of parish duties was ultimately incompatible with a traffic in livings based on the accident of possessing capital; so too were even hereditary rights to presentation and the use of political or social 'interest' for clerical advancement. The absence of training for the priesthood was ultimately incompatible with Edmund's call for a counterpart to educated laity and effective clerical exegesis of the scriptures (pp. 339–40). The very word 'improvement', as used by three of the novel's main protagonists, is a touchstone. The Crawfords speak the mid–eighteenth-century language at its worst. For Mary, 'improvement' in religion means less obligatory devotion (pp. 86–7); for Henry, grander rectories and rhetorical excursions (pp. 243–4, 341). But for Edmund, it is conduct rooted in religion (pp. 339–40). An ecclesiastical framework built or maintained in the spirit of the first two cannot long endure, at least in its entirety, as the spirit of the third advances.

There is one other dimension to be considered. In 1813, the church was still generally regarded, as in *Mansfield Park*, as a plain profession. It was moreover still clearly the leader of professions. Only law presented any challenge; and the English Bar was both relatively lower in prestige than, say, the Irish or the Scottish, and weighed down by a mass of disreputable attorneyism and counsel out of work. Again, we are on the brink of a revolution, or at least an unsettlement. Clerical orders were about to become infused by two additional and contradictory concepts. The first was the concept of service (as with the higher military and civil services), with stipend certain and duties illimitable, as against an occupation with rewards proportionate to individual exertion and success. The other was the concept of vocation or divine calling, according to the ideal of the Roman priesthood. Moreoover, not merely law but also medicine, engineering and a number of similar occupations were soon to be regularized, rendered meritocratic and, in effect, unionized in a way that holy orders never could; and in so doing they would rapidly come to overshadow and outbid the church as a profession.[22]

But *Mansfield Park* was not written for posterity. Nor was it much in tune with the novels of its day. Almost contemporaneously the Honourable Mr Listless in *Nightmare Abbey* welcomed 'modern books':

> There is, as it were, a delightful north-east wind, an intellectual blight breathing through them; a delicious misanthropy and discontent, that demonstrates the nullity of virtue and energy....[23]

Mansfield Park was far from 'modern' by such a formula. It was none the less a prophetic work, anticipating the high Victorian themes of duty, principle and religion. This is no more than we should expect in a work which seems to have been seriously designed in the most serious of senses. That 'impressive preacher of earnest awakening sermons', Mr Cooke, considered *Mansfield Park* (as Jane Austen told Cassandra) '"the most sensible novel he has ever read", and the manner in which I treat the clergy delights them [the Cookes] very much'.[24] At the same time, its Anglican breadth and balance have a perennial air, as again we should expect from medianism erected into a principle of theological interpretation. One of the anti–hero's nightmares in David Lodge's *Changing Places* is troops of protesting undergraduates parading under the banner 'Fanny Price is a fink'.[25] Barbaric though the language may be, are not these phantasmagorical student demonstrators bearing an unconscious witness to the spirit of William Law, after all?

CHAPTER 2

THE FEMALE ECONOMY:
The Watsons, Lady Susan and *Pride and Prejudice*

WITH THE POSSIBLE exception of its conclusion, *Lady Susan* was composed in 1793-4, when Jane Austen was approaching, and just past, her eighteenth birthday and in the flush of confidence and youth. *The Watsons* was written some eleven years later, and apparently abandoned upon her father's death in January 1805.[1] In the course of 1801-4, she had been uprooted from her home in Hampshire, and lost the one man whom her sister Cassandra believed she might happily have married. It was with this diminished hope and in the encircling gloom that she sat down to produce *The Watsons*. She was then twenty-eight years of age, and facing lifelong spinsterhood and the loss, sooner or later, of the support of her father's income. The respective treatments of a theme common to the two works, the female economy, seem to reflect the profound change of mind from a girl on the edge of womanhood to that of a woman on the edge of middle age. A little over a decade later Jane Austen was to use this very theme in contrasting the Anne Elliot of 1806 and 1814, the Anne Elliot of nineteen and twenty-seven years of age.

It is impossible to say where *Pride and Prejudice* fits along the time-scale of Jane Austen's maturity. The original version, *First Impressions*, was, according to her sister Cassandra, written in 1796-7.[2] It was apparently still intact in 1799.[3] But when between 1799 and 1812 Jane Austen rewrote *First Impressions* we do not know, any more than we know the extent of her revision. Substantially, however, the consideration of the female economy in *Pride and Prejudice*, as it was published eventually in 1813, seems to stand midway between the standpoints of the other works.

I

Without going to the length of regarding the villainess of *Lady Susan*, Lady Susan Vernon, as a heroine disguised, we can certainly speak of her role as heroic in the same sense as Lucifer's in *Paradise Lost*. Lady Susan is uniformly malevolent, invariably choosing the heartless, selfish or evil course, though masking it generally by the opposite pose. Yet the very invariability of her malignity anaesthetizes the reader's hostility. Just as the 'baddy' of the old Western became insensibly the mere obverse of Alan Ladd or Gary Cooper, so Lady Susan's constancy in wickedness, the very monotony of her choice of the worst line of conduct, renders her little more than a conventional foil, in terms of serious morality. Moreover, we know from the beginning that she is bound for ultimate frustration or defeat. Perverse though it may be, our sympathies go out, in part at least, to the ordained losing cause: *victrix causa deis placuit sed victa Catoni*. Lady Susan's poverty and comparative isolation, her lack of effective allies and the audacity of her battle against the odds, turn us a little further towards her side. Most telling of all, she is physically and intellectually attractive in a high degree. Even her inveterate enemy, Mrs Catherine Vernon, confesses, on first meeting her,

> I have seldom seen so lovely a Woman as Lady Susan. She is delicately fair, with fine grey eyes & dark eyelashes; & from her appearance one would not suppose her more than five & twenty, tho' she must in fact be ten years older. I was certainly not disposed to admire her, tho' always hearing she was beautiful; but I cannot help feeling that she possesses an uncommon union of Symmetry, Brilliancy and Grace . . . her Countenance is absolutely sweet, & her voice & manner winningly mild. I am sorry it is so, for what is this but Deceit? Unfortunately one knows her too well. She is clever & agreable, has all that knowledge of the world which makes conversation easy, & talks very well, with a happy command of Language, which is too often used I believe to make Black appear White.[4]

How are readers – in particular, how are women readers – to distance themselves altogether, as they are ostensibly meant to do, from such exterior perfections?

It is true that Lady Susan is given the sentiments and the demeanour of a monster when it comes to her treatment of her sixteen-year-old daughter, Frederica. Here she is consistently cruel and ill-

wishing, relentlessly determined to force a hated wastrel, Sir James
Martin, upon her child. But this element in the characterization
seems arbitrary, even baseless. In general, Lady Susan's moral
defects and ill behaviour are attributable to her unbridled vanity and
pursuit of self-interest. Nothing in the book suggests that she might
be jealous of Frederica or that she would gain anything from marrying her to Sir James beyond the thwarting of another woman. The
nearest that Jane Austen comes towards providing a credible explanation of Lady Susan's hostility towards her daughter is, I think,
that professed in letter 19, from Lady Susan to her companion in in-
iquity, Mrs Johnson. Frederica, she writes contemptuously,

> is busy pursueing the plan of Romance... actually falling in love.
> ... I never saw a girl of her age, bid fairer to be the sport of Man-
> kind. Her feelings are tolerably lively, & she is so charmingly art-
> less in their display, as to afford the most reasonable hope of her
> being ridiculed & despised by every Man who sees her.   (p. 274)

Perhaps this provides us with the secret of Lady Susan's appeal for
readers. She is the champion of women in the everlasting tourna-
ment between the sexes. Every man whom she encounters in the
novel is subdued. Even the decrepit Mr Johnson's deep antagonism
towards her might not have survived a meeting face to face. The enslavement of the young and silly Sir James may have been no great
achievement in itself. But Lady Susan actually reduces him to a state
in which he is ready to marry either her daughter or herself, as she
dictated. The libertine Manwaring's was evidently a valuable scalp in
her belt. The fact that Lady Susan was herself susceptible to his
charm and 'person' – let alone his wife's desperate eagerness to marry
him and frenzy at losing him – establish him as a successful lady-
killer. Even Lady Susan once confesses that 'were he at liberty, I
doubt if I could resist even matrimony offered by *him*' (letter 39,
p. 308). Yet it is he who cannot keep away from Lady Susan, not she
who cannot keep apart from him.

Again, she had grievously offended her brother-in-law, Charles
Vernon, by intriguing (vainly) against his marriage to Catherine De
Courcy, and also by denying him the opportunity to buy Castle Vernon which (seemingly because of her extravagance) her late husband
was forced to put upon the market. She could not, as she herself put
it, 'endure that my Husband's dignity should be lessened by his
younger brother's having possession of the Family Estate' (letter 4,
p 249). None the less, when the elder Vernon died, she had no diffi-

culty in restoring herself in Charles's estimation, or in securing from him immediately both an income and a pressing invitation to stay at his home, Churchill. 'Disposed however as he always is', wrote Mrs Charles Vernon sourly, 'to think the best of everyone, her display of Greif & professions of regret, & general resolutions of prudence were sufficient to soften his heart, & make him really confide in her sincerity' (letter 3, p. 247).

Lady Susan's supreme trophy (a conquest made twice over) was, however, Reginald De Courcy, Mrs Vernon's brother. He comes to Churchill fully armed against Lady Susan's charms, writing to Mrs Vernon beforehand:

> As a very distinguished Flirt, I have always been taught to consider her; but it has lately fallen in my way to hear some particulars of her conduct at Langford [Manwaring's home] which proves that she does not confine herself to that sort of honest flirtation which satisfies most people, but aspires to the more delicious gratification of making a whole family miserable. By her behaviour to Mr Manwaring, she gave jealousy & wretchedness to his wife, & by her attentions to a young man [Sir James] previously attached to Mr Manwaring's sister, deprived an amiable girl of her Lover. . . .
>
> What a Woman she must be! I long to see her, & shall certainly accept your kind invitation [to Churchill], that I may form some idea of those bewitching powers which can do so much – engaging at the same time & in the same house the affections of two Men who were neither of them at liberty to bestow them – & all this, without the charm of Youth . . . by all that I can gather, Lady Susan possesses a degree of captivating Deceit which must be pleasing to witness & detect. (letter 4, pp. 248-9)

Thus it was in a mood of amused contempt, ready to flirt with her as an agreeable wanton, as a woman 'entitled neither to Delicacy nor respect', that Reginald met Lady Susan at Churchill. But she immediately discerned and resented his 'low' opinion, and countered it by sober, gentle and refined comportment, and a winning manner. Inside a fortnight, Reginald had been overcome. It was not perhaps surprising that he should have been affected by (in his own words) 'such Loveliness & such Abilities'. But, astonishingly, she had also induced him to absolve her from responsibility for her misbehaviour in the past, and to attribute this instead 'to her neglected Education & early Marriage, . . . she was altogether a wonderful Woman' (letter 8, p. 256).

De Courcy was a very good match; he was heir to a 'considerable' entailed estate, with an infirm and ailing father into the bargain. Mrs Johnson, who retailed this crucial information to Lady Susan, advised her strongly to snap him up. At first Lady Susan was undecided. Reginald, though inferior to Manwaring, was not unattractive; but she would never lower herself to bestow 'affection on a Man who had dared to think so meanly' of her. She leaves us in no doubt however that she is determined on establishing her supremacy in the duel of the sexes, and she believes (as she tells Mrs Johnson) that marriage to De Courcy is within her reach.

> I have made him sensible of my power, & can now enjoy the pleasure of triumphing over a Mind prepared to dislike me, & prejudiced against all my past actions. . . .
> It has been delightful to me to watch his advances towards intimacy, especially to observe his altered manner in consequence of my repressing by the calm dignity of my deportment, his insolent approach to direct familiarity. My conduct has been equally guarded from the first, & I never behaved less like a Coquette in the whole course of my Life, tho' perhaps my desire of dominion was never more decided. I have subdued him entirely by sentiment & serious conversation. . . . (letter 10, pp. 257-8)

Reginald assured his frightened father that for all his new-found admiration of Lady Susan's abilities and character, he had no thought of marrying her: 'Our difference of age [apparently, about ten years] must be an insuperable objection' (letter 14, p. 263). But Mrs Vernon, who, being female, could immediately discern the truth in such affairs, put little trust in his resolution. She told her mother that while she rejoiced with all her heart that her father was 'made easy by it [Reginald's letter] . . . between ourselves, I must own that it has only convinced *me* of my Brother's having no *present* intention of marrying Lady Susan – not that he is in no danger of doing so three months hence' (letter 15, p. 266). Mrs Vernon's fears appear to have been well founded, for in the very next letter in the series Lady Susan enlarges on the cumulative effect of her 'eloquence' in deepening Reginald's 'Consideration & Esteem', as well as on her own growing appreciation of his cleverness and conversability (letter 16, p. 268).

Her conquest is endangered however when the ill-used Frederica Vernon turns up at Churchill, having fled her boarding-school in terror lest she be forced into an immediate marriage to Sir James. Lady Susan now finds herself in double jeopardy. First, Frederica may expose her cruelty to her, in particular, in forcing Sir James upon an unwilling daughter. Lady Susan is not over-worried that Frederica will denounce her outright; she considers her daughter to be much too cowed for that. But she fears lest Frederica's depressed and pathetic bearing may evoke an ultimately fatal enquiry into its cause, or that Frederica may inadvertently reveal something of her real predicament. Secondly, Frederica is a potential rival for Reginald's regard. Mrs Vernon found her most winning and

> very pretty, tho' not so handsome as her Mother, nor at all like her. Her complexion is delicate, but neither so fair, nor so blooming as Lady Susan's – & she has quite the Vernon cast of countenance, the oval face & mild dark eyes, & there is peculiar sweetness in her look when she speaks either to her Uncle or me, for . . . we behave kindly to her. . . .   (letter 17, p. 270)

It was not however Frederica's beauty which Lady Susan feared – she believed that this affected Reginald little. It was her evident, slavish partiality for him, and the response which this might eventually awaken.

Sir James Martin's untoward arrival at Churchill suddenly undermines Lady Susan's entire position, for it leads to Frederica's throwing herself on De Courcy's mercy, as her last hope of escaping her odious suitor: 'if *you* do not take my part', ran her frenzied note to Reginald, '& persuade her [Lady Susan] to break it off, I shall be half-distracted. No human Being but *you* could have any chance of prevailing with her' (letter 21, p. 279). The consequent *éclaircissement* – aided no doubt by Frederica's appeal as damsel in distress – ended in a complete rupture between Reginald and Lady Susan, and his quick decision to leave Churchill immediately. But no sooner did the indomitable 'Mistress of Deceit' (as Mrs Vernon called her) learn of Reginald's imminent departure than she determined to bring him to heel again. With supreme confidence in her abilities, Lady Susan coolly told Mrs Vernon, 'I should not be surprised if he were to change his mind at last, & not go' (letter 23, p. 284).

So it proved. Once summoned to her presence, Reginald was rapidly overcome. At the price of feigning ignorance of Frederica's abhorrence of Sir James, and of promising to abandon the projected marriage, she re-conquered him immediately. Her motive was domination; her pride had revolted against his 'fancied sense of superior Integrity which is peculiarly insolent'. Now she exulted in her power.

Oh! how delightful it was, to watch the variations of his Countenance while I spoke, to see the struggle between returning Tenderness & the remains of Displeasure. There is something agreable in
feelings so easily worked on.... And yet this Reginald, whom a
very few words from me softened at once into the utmost submis-
sion, & rendered more tractable, more attached, more devoted
than ever, would have left me in the first angry swelling of his
proud heart, without deigning to seek an explanation!

Humbled as he now is, I cannot forgive him such an instance of
Pride; & am doubtful whether I ought not to punish him, by dis-
missing him at once after this our reconciliation, or by marrying &
teizing him for ever (letter 25, p. 293).

Lady Susan was not however entirely satisfied with her victory –
though she herself described it thus – because she had surrendered
'the very article by which our quarrel was produced'. She was therefore still resolved on marrying Frederica to Sir James. On Mrs Johnson's strong urging, she decided to accept Reginald as her own husband, and soon procured from him the necessary proposal. But this
meant, for her, only the postponement and not the abandonment of
her plan for disposing of her daughter. Indeed, the 'romantic nonsense' and the 'idle Love' for Reginald which Frederica had earlier ex-
hibited rendered Lady Susan all the more determined (p. 294).
Having settled so much with great dispatch, she felt that she had
earned herself some dissipation, and left Churchill for London at last.
She also felt that she had earned herself a holiday from De Courcy.

Unfortunately, she was hoist with her own petard; she proved the
victim of her own irresistibility. Both Manwaring (maddened by
jealousy) and De Courcy (marriage to whom she wished to stave off
as long as possible, unless his father should conveniently vacate the
baronetcy, by dying) came to London in pursuit of her. Not prepared to end the delightful attentions of Manwaring, she stumbled in
her efforts to conceal them from Reginald. Accidental meetings with
Mr Johnson and Mrs Manwaring revealed all her former perfidy to
him, and he threw her off in fury and disgust.

This was the end. It might not have been had Reginald met Lady
Susan face to face. *She* did not despair of making yet another recovery if only she could confront him once again; and Mrs Vernon
was far from thinking him secure. But he prudently confined his outrage to the written page, and its second expression led Lady Susan to
round on him in turn. There was now nothing left for her but to

marry Sir James herself, clearing the way for Frederica to capture De Courcy. By the stage of denouement, Jane Austen had – perhaps from loss of patience or interest[5] – begun to burlesque her own creation (as she was to do again in the concluding paragraphs of *Northanger Abbey*), and the final conquest of Reginald by Frederica owes as much to his sister's and his mother's labours on her behalf as to Frederica's own appeal. She had to wait 'till such time as Reginald De Courcy could be talked, flattered & finessed into an affection for her – which... might be reasonably looked for in the course of a Twelvemonth. Three Months might have done it in general, but Reginald's feelings were no less lasting than lively' (conclusion, p. 313).

Despite the ultimate thwarting of Lady Susan's full design, the novel as a whole seems to celebrate female power. Its leitmotif is Lady Susan's obsession with subduing men. Nor has she any intention of submitting to reciprocal enslavement. Although she is sexually attracted to Manwaring, this is a mere occasional indulgence and in no way her motivating force. It is dominion, virtually for its own sake, which she desires, and it is by 'feminine' weapons that she masters her 'opponents'. The conditions of combat restrict Lady Susan's weapons to charm of face, form and manner. The potent swords of youth and money are missing from her armoury. Contrariwise, Frederica is still worse armed, possessing only girlishness, prettiness and (for what they are worth) 'principles'. Yet she too conquers – with the aid of two female managers, Mrs Vernon and Lady De Courcy.

Perhaps there is a little more to it than this. Lady Susan is an extraordinarily intelligent woman, and Frederica displays her partiality for a man so openly as to bring into play what Jane Austen more than once implies are powerful engines – masculine 'gratitude' and vanity. 'I must confess', she wrote of Henry Tilney's and Catherine Morland's love affair,

> that his affection originated in nothing better than gratitude, or, in other words, that a persuasion of her partiality for him had been the only cause of giving her a serious thought. It is a new circumstance in romance, I acknowledge, and dreadfully derogatory of an heroine's dignity; but if it be as new in common life, the credit of a wild imagination will at least be all my own.[6]

None the less it was a testimony to female power that, with comparatively meagre advantages, the fortune-less Lady Susan and her

fortune-less daughter, at the ages of thirty-five and sixteen respectively, can secure highly eligible, rich, young bachelors. It is a
further tribute to that power – or at least to the superior perspicacity
of females – that almost every man but not a single woman in the
novel is imposed on by Lady Susan. In particular, Mrs Vernon sees
through every manœuvre which deceives her brother; and even the
headmistress of Frederica's school very quickly takes Lady Susan's
measure. In general, the males prove themselves easy dupes. They
appear to hold all the cards – the land and cash, the social initiatives,
liberty of movement and action, and lax codes to govern their moral
conduct. But in practice the women can deploy a countervailing
force with little difficulty – even if it has to be at the cost of employing artifice and cunning, or being pitied.

II

The Watsons strikes quite a different note. Money is scarcely a consideration in the marriages and affairs of *Lady Susan*. In this fragment
of a novel it is almost everything. Emma Watson at the age of nineteen is returned to her home because the aunt who had practically
adopted her – Mrs Turner, a rich widow – had bought herself
another husband. The new husband, Captain O'Brien, had taken his
bride to live in Ireland, and Emma was regarded as *de trop*. '"I was
not so ungrateful Sir"', Emma replied to a suggestion that it was by
her own choice that she did not accompany her aunt '"into *that*
Country"', '"as to wish to be any where but with her. – It did not
suit them, it did not suit Capt. O'brien that I sh^d be of the party"'.[7]
The home to which Emma returned is presided over by an ailing impoverished widowed parson, whose other three daughters, Emma's
elder sisters, Elizabeth, Penelope and Margaret, are also as yet unmarried. Matrimony was their only hope of escape from current
penury and future ruin or near-ruin. Dowerless, they were pursuing
it with varying degrees of ruthlessness.

The eldest of the girls, Elizabeth, aged twenty-eight, is honest and
down-to-earth. At the very beginning of the fragment, she tells
Emma that Penelope had robbed her of a likely husband several years
before.

'Yes, Emma, Penelope was at the bottom of it all. – She thinks
everything fair for a Husband; I trusted her, she set him [her lover,
Mr Purvis] against me, with a veiw of gaining him herself, & it

ended in his discontinuing his visits & soon after marrying somebody else. – Penelope makes light of her conduct, but *I* think such
Treachery very bad.'   (p. 316)

It is clear that Penelope, currently in Winchester in pursuit of a well-
to-do elderly clergyman or physician ('Dr' Harding could mean
either) is a relentless and unscrupulous man-hunter. '"There is
nothing she w^d not do to get married – she would as good as tell you
so herself."' Elizabeth was capable of love. She confessed that losing
Purvis '"has been the ruin of my happiness"'. None the less, she is
determined to marry if she can. She may have little stomach for
matrimony any longer, '"but"', as she tells Emma simply,

'you know we must marry. – I could do very well single for my
own part – A little Company, & a pleasant Ball now & then,
would be enough for me, if one could be young for ever, but my
Father cannot provide for us, & it is very bad to grow old & be
poor & laughed at. – I have lost Purvis, it is true but very few
people marry their first Loves. I should not refuse a man because
he was not Purvis –.'   (pp. 316-17)

Morally and emotionally, Emma is too fastidious – as yet at any
rate – to acquiesce in such arguments of female expediency. An exchange follows in which Elizabeth and she, though politely and considerately, set out the respective cases for principle and prudence.
Penelope, Emma declares,

'must have too masculine & bold a temper. – To be so bent on
marriage – to pursue a Man merely for the sake of situation – is a
sort of thing that shocks me; I cannot understand it. Poverty is a
great Evil, but to a woman of Education & feeling it ought not, it
cannot be the greatest. – I would rather be Teacher at a school (and
I can think of nothing worse) than marry a Man I did not like.' – 'I
would rather do any thing than be Teacher at a school' – said her
sister. '*I* have been at school, Emma, & know what a Life they
lead; *you* never have. – I should not like marrying a disagreable
Man any more than yourself, – but I do not think there *are* many
very disagreable Men; – I think I could like any good humoured
Man with a comfortable Income. – I suppose my Aunt brought
you up to be rather refined.'   (p. 318)

Emma, the heroine of *The Watsons*, unselfish, sensitive and candid,
would have been duly rewarded by the affections and hand of the
Revd Mr Howard, a well-bred and agreeable clergyman in his early

thirties, had the book been finished. This would have meant that both parties had rejected a much more materially advantageous marriage. Lord Osborne, 'a very fine young man', albeit with 'an air of Coldness, of Carelessness, even of Awkwardness' about him, would eventually propose – in vain– to Emma. His widowed mother, 'tho' nearly fifty... very handsome, &... [with] all the dignity of Rank' (p. 329), would make it clear to Howard – again in vain – that she would welcome his advances. So much is vouched for by Cassandra Austen, who later told her nieces that Jane intended Emma

> to decline the offer of a marriage from Lord Osborne, and much of the interest of the tale.... to arise from Lady Osborne's love for Mr Howard, and his counter-affection for Emma, whom he was finally to marry.[8]

But Emma's is the solitary case of 'true love' in the novel, and serves to underline the pragmatic or mercenary motives governing the conduct of all her sisters and indeed most of the other characters. Elizabeth seeks marriage as a fate, for fear of worse; Penelope schemes for it ceaselessly, reckless of the cost to others. Emma's third sister, Margaret, is also striving to entrap a husband, although her inherent silliness leads her to construct faulty snares. Margaret's current quarry, Tom Musgrave, an easy-tongued, good-looking coxcomb with the comfortable income of £800 to £900 per annum, is practised in eluding, as well as inviting, such a hunt. Vanity leads him, as highly eligible, to arouse female expectations which he has no intention of meeting. '"He generally pays attention to every new girl"', Elizabeth tells Emma, '"but he is a great flirt & never means anything serious.... Most of the girls hereabouts are in love with him, or have been... he is always behaving in a particular way to one or another"' (pp. 315-16).

Robert Watson, Emma's elder brother, an attorney in Croydon, is as contemptuous as Musgrave of women's sense, and takes a thoroughly materialistic view of marriage. '"A pretty peice of work your Aunt Turner has made of it!"', he tells Emma on the first occasion that they are alone together,

> 'By Heaven! A woman should never be trusted with money. I always said she ought to have settled something on you, as soon as her Husband died.' 'But that would have been trusting *me* with money,' replied Emma, '& *I* am a woman too. –' 'It might have been secured to your future use, without your having any power over it now.... He might have provided decently for his widow,

without leaving every thing that he had to dispose of, or any part of it at her mercy.' – 'My Aunt may have erred' – said Emma warmly – 'she *has* erred – but my Uncle's conduct was faultless. I was her own Neice, & he left to herself the power and the pleasure of providing for me.' – 'But unluckily she has left the pleasure of providing for you, to your Father, & without the power. – That's the long & the short of the business. After keeping you at a distance from your family for such a length of time as must do away all natural affection among us & breeding you up (I suppose) in a superior stile, you are returned upon their hands without a sixpence.' 'You know,' replied Emma struggling with her tears, 'my Uncle's melancholy state of health. – He was a greater Invalid than my father. He c^d not leave home.' 'I do not mean to make you cry,' – said Robt rather softened – & after a short silence, by way of changing the subject, he added – 'I am just come from my Father's room, he seems very indifferent. It will be a sad break-up when he dies. Pity, you can none of you get married! – You must come to Croydon as well as the rest, & see what you can do there. – I beleive if Margaret had had a thousand or fifteen hundred pounds, there was a young man who w^d have thought of her.'(pp. 351-3)

Robert's own wife is commonplace in looks and nature, but was also his employer's daughter, endowed with a snug fortune of £6,000. 'Mrs Robt was not less pleased with herself for having had that six thousand pounds', and Robert is every whit as pleased with his matrimonial bargain even if 'In her person there was nothing remarkable; [and] her manners were pert and conceited' (p. 349).

Thus the worldly marriage predominates in *The Watsons*, and with it a female economy in which the odds heavily favour those young women whose fathers can and will pay money for their matrimonial settlement. It is implied that the four Watson girls are attractive physically or in manner. Elizabeth and Emma are spoken of, by either the author or some character in the fragment, as good-looking. Even the petulant Margaret, we are told, 'was not without beauty; she had a slight, pretty figure, & rather wanted Countenance than good features'. It seems to have been her insecurity which marred her looks, for it was 'the sharp & anxious expression of her face [which] made her beauty in general little felt' (p. 349). Although Penelope neither appears nor is described directly in the fragment, it is a fair inference, from what others say about her, that she is lively and has appeal for men. Yet it seems likely that, of the four fortuneless sisters, only Emma would have found a husband. Contrariwise, we can have little doubt that the Watsons' friend, Mary Edwards, would have ended up with one. She had a fortune, and her parents' prime concern was the discouragement of unworthy suitors. The underlying assumptions of *The Watsons* are, therefore, nearly opposite to those of *Lady Susan*, where beauty, wit or *naïveté* seem to be enough to win a woman more or less whichever man she fancies. In *The Watsons* the generality of women receive according to what they possess materially. Emma is the solitary bright deed in a naughty world.

III

It would be interesting to know whether Charlotte Lucas was a character in *First Impressions*, written before *The Watsons*, or added afterwards in a subsequent revision. In *Pride and Prejudice* Charlotte stands in opposition to Elizabeth Bennet as the proponent, even if *faute de mieux*, of 'career' marriage for women. Although 'sensible, intelligent'[9] and Elizabeth's chosen friend, she deliberately angles for a match with the sycophantic bore Collins, 'solely from the pure and disinterested desire of an establishment... marriage had always been her object; it was the only honourable provision for well-educated young women of small fortune, and however uncertain of giving happiness, must be their pleasantest preservative from want' (pp. 122-3). She is not so hardened in prosaicness as to be quite free of shame in communicating the success of her endeavour to Elizabeth. On Elizabeth's cry of anguished astonishment, she

> gave way to a momentary confusion here on receiving so direct a reproach; though, as it was no more than she expected, she soon regained her composure, and calmly replied, 'Why should you be surprised, my dear Eliza? – Do you think it incredible that Mr Collins should be able to procure any woman's good opinion, because he was not so happy as to succeed with you?'

Charlotte proceeds to cover over the awkwardness of the revelation by attributing Elizabeth's exclamation to surprise at Mr Collins proposing marriage to a second woman within three days of being rejected by the first. She then expounds the classic female defence of the loveless match:

> 'But when you have had time to think it all over, I hope you will be satisfied with what I have done. I am not romantic you know. I

never was. I ask only a comfortable home; and considering Mr
Collins's character, connections, and situation in life, I am convinced that my chance of happiness with him is as fair, as most
people can boast on entering the marriage state.'

Elizabeth makes no further protest, but privately her censure of
Charlotte knew no measure. She had 'sacrificed every better feeling
to worldly advantage'; she had 'disgraced' herself; 'Charlotte the
wife of Mr Collins, was a most humiliating picture!'. Moreover, it
was impossible for Charlotte to be even 'tolerably happy in the lot
she had chosen' (pp. 124–5).

Jane Austen does not however allow this somewhat dramatic view
of 'career' marriage a complete walk–over. It is evident from the later
description of life in her new home at Hunsford that Charlotte is
pleased with her bargain. Granted, this owes a great deal to her skill
in diverting her husband from her side. She encourages him, literally, to cultivate his garden, which draws him outside for many hours.
She also sees to it that he has the better parlour for his study because
this faces the road and affords him the amusement of watching such
spectacles as the highway offers. Elizabeth 'soon saw that her friend
had an excellent reason for what she did, for Mr Collins would un-
doubtedly have been much less in his own apartment, had they sat in
one equally lively; and she gave Charlotte credit for the arrangement'
(p. 168). Similarly, Collins's blunders and pomposity should have repeatedly put his wife to the blush, 'but in general Charlotte wisely
did not hear' (p. 156). Thus between closing her parlour door and her
ears sufficiently often on her husband, Mrs Collins manages to
extract a great deal of happiness from her new condition. Her delight
is her pleasant home and domestic responsibilities. Her house

> was rather small, but well built and convenient; and every thing
> was fitted up and arranged with a neatness and consistency of
> which Elizabeth gave Charlotte all the credit. When Mr Collins
> could be forgotten, there was really a great air of comfort through-
> out, and by Charlotte's evident enjoyment of it, Elizabeth sup-
> posed he must be often forgotten.   (p. 157)

When Elizabeth leaves Hunsford, she is cast into 'melancholy' at the
thought of abandoning Charlotte to such a companion as Mr Collins, but has to admit that Charlotte herself seemed quite content –
for the present, at any rate. 'Her home and her housekeeping, her
parish and her poultry, and all their dependent concerns, had not yet
lost their charms' (p. 216).

Charlotte had lived up to her creed. At the outset, she had laid down to Elizabeth the supreme importance of securing the man whom one marked out as prey; thereafter, 'there will be leisure for falling in love as much as she [the woman] chuses'. Prior knowledge of one's future partner's character was unnecessary, if not actually dangerous.

> 'Happiness in marriage is entirely a matter of chance. If the dispositions of the parties are ever so well known to each other, or ever so similar before-hand, it does not advance their felicity in the least. They always continue to grow sufficiently unlike afterwards to have their share of vexation; and it is better to know as little as possible of the person with whom you are to pass your life.'
>
> (pp. 22-3)

Perhaps such defiant perversity was not meant to be taken at face value. Certainly, Elizabeth Bennet did not believe that Charlotte was wholly serious, still less that she would ever act on such an outrageous principle. But Charlotte did precisely what she advocated. She chose Mr Collins 'with her eyes open' (p. 216). She even took pains to identify with him, after their marriage, so far as practicable. Her first letters from her new home to Elizabeth took their tone from him: it 'was Mr Collins's picture of Hunsford and Rosings rationally softened' (p. 147). Charlotte even pandered to Lady Catherine de Bourgh in the interest of his advancement. At least, so Elizabeth explained to herself Charlotte's repeated calling on Lady Catherine; she 'recollected that there might be other family livings to be disposed of' (p. 169). Similarly, Charlotte took it as a point in favour of Mr Darcy's suit, when he sought Elizabeth, that he 'had considerable patronage in the church' (p. 181). She had now to calculate Mr Collins's advantage as well as her own, or rather the two had become identical.

The merging of individuals in a new joint interest both emphasized and symbolized the social character of marriage. Charlotte's ultimate justification lay in her obedience to the social law which laid down that middle-class young women without resources tended to be lonely, purposeless and very poor if they could not attain such a union. Even the soft-judging Jane Bennet recognizes the force of this particular law when she expostulates at Elizabeth's unbridled condemnation of Charlotte's engagement, and warns of the ill-consequences of wholesale indulgence in high principle.

'My dear Lizzy, do not give way to such feelings as these. They

will ruin your happiness. You do not make allowance enough for
difference of situation and temper. Consider Mr Collins's respectability, and Charlotte's prudent, steady character. Remember that
she is one of a large family; that as to fortune, it is a most eligible
match; and be ready to believe, for every body's sake, that she may
feel something like regard and esteem for our cousin.'   (p. 135)

Pragmatic marriage is therefore allowed to make something of a
case for itself in *Pride and Prejudice*. This form of female settlement is
not as pervasive in the novel as in *The Watsons* – if the surviving fragment of the latter may be taken as indicative of the intended whole.
No less than Elizabeth, Jane Bennet makes a romantic marriage, and
we may perhaps infer that even Kitty Bennet, under the influence of
her elder sisters, will eventually adopt their principles. Correspondingly, it is the novel's villain, George Wickham, who becomes the
exemplar of the market view of marriage. He has tried to sell his
charm to Georgiana Darcy for her £30,000, and turns his attentions
from Elizabeth to Mary King when he comes to believe that Mary
has a fortune. Finally, he allows himself to be bribed – rather cheaply
– into making an honest woman of Lydia Bennet. Yet although
romantic marriage is clearly the ideal in *Pride and Prejudice*, pragmatic
marriage is presented as common practice, if not in fact the com-
monest. In defending it, Charlotte Lucas had a particularly poor case
to argue. She could make no pretence of prior affection for Mr Collins, and tacitly admitted that any woman of sense would find his
company 'irksome'. But was the alternative – penurious, occupa-
tionless and perhaps unloved spinsterhood, at best fitting into the
interstices of relations' lives – a better fate? It was not too easy to re-
fute Charlotte's doctrine of matrimony as *pis aller*. The heroic sacrifice of lifelong security and utility for the sake of delicacy of feeling
was doubtless to be applauded, but hardly to be universally expected.

IV

Jane Austen's first love affair (that we know of) was with Tom
Lefroy, a recent graduate of Trinity College, Dublin, currently reading law at the Inns of Court in London. She was then just twenty
years of age, with Lefroy some three weeks younger. His twentieth
birthday, on 8 January 1796, was the first subject alluded to in her letter of the next day to Cassandra. In the remainder of that letter she

returned three times to the theme of Tom Lefroy. She wrote of a couple who had danced twice together at a private ball held the preceding night that

> *they* do not know how *to be particular.* I flatter myself, however, that they will profit by the three successive lessons which I have given them.
>
> You scold me so much in the nice long letter which I have this moment received from you, that I am almost afraid to tell you how my Irish friend [Lefroy] and I behaved. Imagine to yourself everything most profligate and shocking in the way of dancing and sitting down together. I *can* expose myself, however, only *once more*, because he leaves the country soon after next Friday, on which day we *are* to have a dance at Ashe [the home of his aunt, Mrs Lefroy] after all. He is a very gentlemanlike, good-looking, pleasant young man, I assure you. But as to our having ever met, except at the three last balls, I cannot say much; for he is so excessively laughed at about me at Ashe, that he is ashamed of coming to Steventon, and ran away when we called on Mrs Lefroy a few days ago.[10]

Later in the letter Jane wished that her brother Charles, who was evidently due to call at Kintbury, in Oxfordshire, where Cassandra was staying, had been at the ball, 'because he would have given you some description of my friend, and I think you must be impatient to hear something about him'. Finally, after an interruption in the writing, she reported,

> After I had written the above, we received a visit from Mr Tom Lefroy and his cousin George. The latter is really very well-behaved now; and as for the other, he has but *one* fault, which time will, I trust, entirely remove – it is that his morning coat is a great deal too light. He is a very great admirer of Tom Jones, and therefore wears the same coloured clothes, I imagine, which *he* did when he was wounded.[11]

Jane Austen maintained her 'flip' tone in her second (and last) letter to Cassandra touching on Lefroy's visit. Again she referred to him in three different places, half-mockingly or self-mockingly. She would refuse the expected offer from him 'unless he promises to give away his white coat'; she would confine herself to him in future, but did not 'care sixpence' for him; and her tears flowed at 'the melancholy idea' of the day 'on which I am to flirt my last with Tom Lefroy'.[12]

All this may be variously interpreted but the most likely explanation seems to be that Jane was enamoured of Lefroy. Her repeated return in the course of her letters to the subject of their affair suggests as much. The bantering tone enabled her at once to apprise Cassandra that she had an admirer and to protect her own pride and privacy should it all come to nothing. According to Lefroy tradition, it was 'she who did all the running'.[13] This is compatible with her letter of 8 January to Cassandra; but that Tom Lefroy was to a degree responsive is clear both from the 'particularity' of their behaviour, and his testimony in later years that, albeit with only a boy's love, he had been in love with her.[14]

The crux of the matter may well have been that Lefroy was still a 'boy' when it came to serious commitment. His own family was poor; he was dependent on a wealthy uncle for his education; and he had still several terms ahead of him as a law student before he could be called to the Irish Bar. He was in fact destined to marry young, when he was twenty-three years old; but this met with Lefroy approval because his bride was the only daughter and heiress of an affluent baronet, Sir Jeffry Paul of Silversprings, Co. Wexford. To enter into an engagement with Mary Paul in 1797 was a very different proposition from entering into an engagement with the fortuneless Jane Austen in 1796. Tom Lefroy's aunt, Mrs Anne Lefroy, with whom he was staying, took fright when his affair with Jane appeared to have taken a serious turn. Alarmed lest a very improvident match would alienate the uncle who supported him, Mrs Lefroy induced Tom to return to London 'as soon as possible'.[15]

Tom's departure from Ashe on or about 20 January 1796 ended the matter for him. Not so with Jane; more than two and a half years were to pass before she had further news of him, and her eagerness to glean it and sharp reaction at the time make it all too clear that he was still green in her memory. She wrote to Cassandra:

Mrs Lefroy did come last Wednesday [14 November 1798], and the Harwoods came likewise, but very considerately paid their visit before Mrs Lefroy's arrival, with whom, in spite of interruptions both from my father and James [Jane Austen's brother], I was enough alone to hear all that was interesting, which you will easily credit when I tell you that of her nephew she said nothing at all, and of her friend [Mr Blackall] very little. She did not once mention the name of the former to *me*, and I was too proud to make any enquiries; but on my father's afterwards asking where he was,

I learnt that he was gone back to London in his way to Ireland, where he is called to the Bar and means to practise.[16]

Professor Honan's judgment that Jane Austen had, in her inexperience, tried to squeeze more out of the situation than its possibilities allowed[17] seems just. At the beginning of 1796, she was apparently still living, in fancy at least, in the world of *Lady Susan*. In this world, women generally got their way in matters of the heart; men responded simply to their attractions; money and livelihood were not determinants in marriage. By the end of 1798 she had undergone contrary lessons. During her visit to Steventon of 14 November, Mrs Lefroy made it clear not only that nothing more was to be hoped for from Tom Lefroy, but also that another possible suitor, Revd Samuel Blackall, a Fellow of Emmanuel College, Cambridge, was withdrawing from the field. We know little about Blackall, but it is evident from Jane Austen's comments that he had earlier shown an interest in her. Mrs Lefroy (with whom he had stayed while in the neighbourhood, and who may have then hoped to make a match of it between them)[18] showed Jane Austen a letter which she had received from him 'a few weeks ago'. He concluded (Jane wrote) with

> a sentence to this effect: 'I am very sorry to hear of Mrs Austen's illness. It would give me particular pleasure to have an opportunity of improving my acquaintance with that family – with a hope of creating to myself a nearer interest. But at present I cannot indulge any expectation of it.' This is rational enough; there is less love and more sense in it than sometimes appeared before, and I am very well satisfied. It will all go on exceedingly well, and decline away in a very reasonable manner. There seems no likelihood of his coming into Hampshire this Christmas, and it is therefore most probable that our indifference will soon be mutual, unless his regard, which appeared to spring from knowing nothing of me at first, is best supported by never seeing me.
>
> Mrs Lefroy made no remarks on the letter, nor did she indeed say anything about him as relative to me. Perhaps she thinks she has said too much already.[19]

Jane Austen may have been taking a small private revenge when nearly fifteen years later she read of Blackall's marriage to the daughter of a 'late' West Indian planter, and wrote to one of her brothers:

I should very much like to know what sort of Woman she is. He was a piece of Perfection, noisy Perfection himself which I always recollect with regard... I would wish Miss Lewis [now his wife] to be of a silent turn & rather ignorant, but naturally intelligent & wishing to learn; – fond of cold veal pies, green tea in the afternoon, & a green window blind at night.[20]

Had Blackall been a prosy don, with a hankering after meat pies and tea? It is probably too much to hope that he particularly disliked the colour green.

V

On 25 November 1802 Cassandra and Jane Austen arrived at Manydown, the home of their friends, the Biggs, for a visit. A week later, on 2 December, the son of the house, Harris Bigg Wither, proposed marriage to Jane Austen and was accepted. The proposal was altogether unexpected. Harris, twenty-one years of age and some six years Jane's junior, had conducted no preliminary courtship. He was a large, gauche, moody young man afflicted with a bad stammer. In offering marriage to Jane he may have wished to confirm his independence of his father; but there is no reason to doubt that his primary motivation was attraction of the ordinary male kind to Jane. Neither is there, however, any reason to believe that Jane was correspondingly attracted to Bigg Wither. He may have had his amiable side; certainly, his level-headed sisters appear to have been fond of him. But before this visit Jane had known him only as an awkward schoolboy.

Why did she accept his offer? First, Bigg Wither belonged to the long-established gentry and was heir to extensive Hampshire estates. By Austen standards he would be rich, and socially and possibly politically significant, when he succeeded his father. Secondly, Manydown was only six miles from Jane Austen's former home, Steventon. To live there would be to return to her beloved childhood surroundings, to dwell in the country once again and to escape from abhorrent Bath, where she had now been settled for eighteen months. Thirdly, as her niece Caroline wrote, 'My aunts had very small fortunes; and on their father's death, they and their mother would be, they were aware, but poorly off – I believe most young women so circumstanced would have gone on trusting to love after marriage'.[21] Professor Honan puts it succinctly: Bigg Wither's proposal 'offered her [Jane] a chance of wedlock as against becoming a

socially outcast and burdensome spinster, an appalling handicap to
her brothers and worry for Cassandra and their mother'.[22] Fourthly,
Bigg Wither was 'eminently eligible' according to contemporary
standards. To secure him would be both a societal and a feminine
triumph; as it is put in *Persuasion*, 'It is something for a woman to be
assured, in her eight- and twentieth year [only a fortnight away for
Jane Austen at the time of the proposal] that she has not lost one
charm of earlier youth'.[23] Moreover there was 'the pleasure it [the
marriage] would give all her family and his' to be considered.[24] Her
chief mentor, Cassandra, approved; her sister-in-law Mary 'thought
the match a most desirable one';[25] and Bigg Wither's sisters, Alethea
and Catherine, were among Jane Austen's oldest and dearest friends.

Within twenty-four hours of her acceptance Jane Austen broke off
her engagement. Presumably a night of agonized reflection had
brought home to her the enormity of what she had done. It can
scarcely have been the likely 'family' consequences of the marriage
which appalled her, although the prospect, when she came to consider it, of leaving her close home circle may have had some influence
on her decision. Much more potent (one would guess) were the pic-
tures of married life with Harris which sprang to mind, as she
thought things through to the actualities, during the course of her internal debate. Certainly the revulsion must have been powerful for
Jane Austen to have committed such a *bêtise* as to jilt Bigg Wither out
of hand. Her courage in facing him, and 'explaining herself' in person to him so quickly, might be applauded later on. But at the
moment of rupture it must have seemed to his family an aggravation
of the slight, and to hers evidence of want of consideration and responsibility towards the Austen men on whom she depended for her
support.

How closely did Jane Austen's behaviour in this contretemps re-
semble that of Charlotte Lucas in *Pride and Prejudice*? Bigg Wither
may have been no Mr Collins; but such impressions of him as we can
form do not suggest a lover who was attractive in either bearing or
person. Jane Austen's reasons for agreeing to enter into a loveless
match were less cold-blooded than Charlotte's, in that she wished to
return to a familiar happy place and neighbourhood; but it was essentially security and provision that she too sought. Again, although
Jane Austen did not set out to trap a husband after the manner of
Charlotte Lucas, this scarcely constitutes a fundamental distinction
between her acceptance of Bigg Wither and Charlotte's closing with
Mr Collins's proposal. As Jane reasoned herself into choosing Harris

and Manydown at the expense of (to apply Elizabeth Bennet's phrase) 'every better feeling',[26] her arguments must have approximated to those attributed to Charlotte in *Pride and Prejudice*.

This is but one side of the coin. The other is Jane Austen's rapid reversal of course. Her niece Catherine's supposition (based on letters from Jane since destroyed) that she acted 'in a momentary fit of self-delusion'[27] seems a reasonable gloss on her behaviour. On the night of her betrothal, she 'found she was miserable & that the place & fortune that would certainly be *his*, could not alter the *man*';[28] realized that she was playing with others' lives and felicity as well as her own; made her retraction at the earliest moment next morning; and fled immediately – first to her brother James at Steventon and then to her parents in Bath – lest Harris importune her further. We cannot say categorically that she woke up on 3 December 1802 with all the principles of an Elizabeth Bennet and a corresponding determination to live up to them. There may have been various alloys in her change of mind. But essentially she was choosing, in the end, the system of marriages of integrity or love instead of marriages of prudence and material and social advancement.

The Bigg Wither case shows that the choice of marriage system was clear-cut only in theory. In actual cases it might be nicely balanced. Had Jane Austen given more weight to the opprobrium which attached to breaking an engagement, or had her family been harsh instead of indulgent in dealing with its daughters, she might well have ended as Harris's wife – with the possible consequence (according to one speculation) of no novels but a line of extremely intelligent little Bigg Withers. In affairs of the heart, every girl was not born into the world either a little Liberal or a little Conservative. Doubtless there were predispositions one way or other. But personal circumstances might also count heavily, might indeed be decisive, for even a true believer in the 'love match' when the crisis came.

Jane Austen was well aware of this. She leaves her reader in no doubt as to which is a woman's better course or fortune. In *Lady Susan* it is scarcely an issue. There, as we have seen, women's ability to attract is presented as virtually all-powerful. In *The Watsons* the prudential marriage looms so large as to seem virtually the expected thing. One would need more elaboration of Emma Watson's qualities than the fragment provides to understand how, even with all her prettiness, candour and good understanding, she is able to arouse the keen attentions of three men, Mr Howard, Tom Musgrave (though mere novelty might have been enough for him) and Lord Osborne, practically on first acquaintance. In *Pride and Prejudice* however the scales are more evenly balanced. Elizabeth Bennet's strength of character, self-honesty and acute intelligence make her a worthy and believable protagonist of the marriage of affection and respect. But the unhappy example of Elizabeth's parents showed that even the disinterested pursuit of youth and beauty might end disastrously, where talents were unequal and characters discordant. Moreover, although Jane Austen loads the dice against Charlotte Lucas's philosophy of marriage by making a fool her lot, and even implicitly condemns her action, she does allow Charlotte to set up a rational and substantial defence of her chosen creed.

Nor should we forget that none of the matches in Jane Austen's novels which receive her approbation was an imprudent one. Tilney, Darcy, Bingley, George Knightley, Colonel Brandon and Edmund Bertram could all support a wife comfortably, or more; and Emma Woodhouse is an heiress into the bargain. Edward Ferrars and Captain Wentworth can also set up good establishments by the time they marry; but it should be noted that Jane Austen does not endorse their marrying until they are financially invulnerable. Even after their engagement, neither Elinor Dashwood nor Edward Ferrars was 'quite enough in love to think that three hundred and fifty pounds a-year would supply them with the comforts of life'; they would wait until £850 per annum, 'an income quite sufficient for their wants', was 'secured to them'.[29] As for Anne Elliot, even after her ecstatic reunion with Wentworth she did not condemn Lady Russell for the advice which had originally separated them. 'It was, perhaps, one of those cases', she said, 'in which advice is good or bad only as the event decides'; and she still maintained that she herself had been right to follow it. 'I should have suffered more in continuing the engagement than I did even in giving it up, because I should have suffered in my conscience.' She acknowledged the prudential basis of her decisions when she added that she would have delightedly renewed the engagement in 1808 had Wentworth then come to her with his 'few thousand pounds, and posted into the Laconia'.[30]

Thus, Jane Austen's view of the contemporary female economy seems to come down to three interrelated propositions: that both head and heart should possess a power of veto when it came to marriage; that the two were not however of equal potency – the head might sometimes be overridden, the heart, never; but that it was not always easy to estimate each force correctly, or to abide by the answer after one had cast one's sum.

CHAPTER 3

RECEIVING AND SPENDING:
Sense and Sensibility

I ENTITLE THIS chapter 'Receiving and Spending' rather than 'Getting and Spending' because not a single developed character in *Sense and Sensibility* works for his or her income; all live on rents, mortgages, dividends or interest. Even Edward Ferrars commences his labours as a clergyman only as the book ends. None the less it is notorious that *Sense and Sensibility* is firmly founded in contemporary economic reality. Jane Austen knew the exact value of money, as gained, lost and used by her particular class.

This is not to claim for her any knowledge of economics beyond that of the ordinary educated person. As G. H. Treitel says in another connection (that of law), it was the 'accuracy of her observation rather than any expert knowledge [that] saved her from errors'.[1] Besides, she wrote for people who shared her background of everyday information, for whom further explanation was unnecessary. When, for example, she indicated in passing that Edward Ferrars had advanced from twenty-three to twenty-four years of age, she took it for granted that her audience would understand its significance. This change would enable him to take the incumbency of Delaford: under the Clergy Ordination Act of 1801, a man must be twenty-four years old before he could be ordained to the Anglican priesthood or hold a living in the Church of England.[2] Similarly with John Dashwood's stricture on Colonel Brandon's want of business sense:

> and for the next presentation to a living of that value [£200 per annum] – supposing the late incumbent to have been old and sickly, and likely to vacate it soon – he might have got I dare say – fourteen hundred pounds. And how came he not to have settled that matter before this person's death? – *Now* indeed it would be too late to sell it, but a man of Colonel Brandon's sense! – I wonder he should be so improvident in a point of such common, such

natural, concern![3]

Her readers did not need to be told that the contemporary courts
steered a way between selling an advowson (the right to be presented
to an ecclesiastical living) *before* and selling it *after* the incumbency fell
vacant. The first was treated as legal, the second as contravening the
Simony Acts and leading to the forfeiture of the right.[4] The law
governing these particular forms of income and property was especially within the province of a parsonical family such as the Austens.
But Jane Austen clearly – and doubtless rightly – assumed that it
would also be common knowledge in the circles which she
addressed. Directly or indirectly, clerical livings touched the interests
of many within these circles; and few of the rest would have been
ignorant of the elementary rules governing the buying, selling and
possession of so important a constituent of the middle- and upper-
class economies.

At any rate, Jane Austen was accustomed from childhood to hear
money matters discussed in informed and detailed fashion; and the
lessons she learnt were driven home by her own comparative
poverty. It was natural that such knowledge should suffuse her imaginary as well as her real world. In *Sense and Sensibility* it may also
have served the deliberate artistic purpose of adding substantiality to
her characters and their milieux.

I propose therefore to consider, first, the economic knowledge
which Jane Austen acquired, then, the economic knowledge which
the novel displays, and finally some of the implications of the relationship between the two.

I

The Revd George Austen was in substantially the same financial
situation as the Revd Edward Ferrars at the conclusion of *Sense and
Sensibility*, with an income of £800 to £900 per annum, the possession
of a commodious parsonage and some acres to be grazed and tilled.
But we do not know whether Edward's income was ever to be subjected to the offset of children, let alone so numerous a family as Mr
Austen's eight offspring – six of them boys, into the bargain. Mr
Austen was remarkably successful in finding careers for his sons, that
is, for the five who needed them, for his second boy, George, was
mentally defective and maintained elsewhere throughout his life.
The Revd George showed extraordinary skill in operating various

eighteenth-century mechanisms for securing respectable occupations for fortuneless young men. One was the closed scholarship system of the older universities. He himself had secured the scholarship and later fellowship at St. John's College, Oxford, reserved for old Tonbridgians; and he saw to it that his eldest son, James, made good his claim (through the maternal line) to the scholarship, and later fellowship, at the same college awarded to Founder's Kin. George Austen also sent his fourth son, Henry, to St. John's, Oxford, where he too was awarded a scholarship, although of the ordinary college kind. The expectation was of course that both James and Henry would eventually make their careers as clergymen of the Church of England. A fine student and teacher in his own right, Mr Austen himself prepared both of them for university.

The third Austen boy, Edward, benefited from another mode of attaining a competence or better – 'adoption' by a well-to-do but childless relation. This type of provision was surprisingly common. The family that 'adopted' Edward and whose surname he eventually assumed, the Knights, had been maintained by several similar importations during the preceding century. Adoption was not yet recognized in English law, so that the newcomers had no indefeasible legal rights before succeeding. But for all practical purposes they stood next in line for more or less substantial inheritances. A third avenue open to the sons of poor gentlemen was the Navy. A naval cadetship, at the age of twelve or so, provided a comparatively inexpensive entry to a profession; luck, assiduity and influence (which Mr Austen possessed in moderate degree) must take care of the subsequent career. Mr Austen's youngest boys, Frank and Charles, were both sent to the Portsmouth Naval College. Thereafter, their father pulled every string he could to secure their early advancement in the service. As things turned out, all that either needed was a start. Their own abilities then saw them, after various vicissitudes, to the top.

Thus, given the smallness of his resources, Mr Austen managed to settle his sons extraordinarily well. But however he economized it was a far from costless business. Scholarships by no means covered all undergraduate expenses at Oxford; Mr Austen allowed his eldest son £10 to £30 per annum until he came into his fellowship, and diverted some of his clerical income to him after he was ordained. Henry may have needed considerably more support at Oxford. Certainly, in addition to sums similar to those given James, he received a cheque for £60 from his father in 1792.[5] In the next year, he threw up Oxford and orders, and accepted instead a commission in the militia;

this too cost money initially, though much less than the regular army would have done. Meanwhile, Frank and Charles had to be fitted out for naval college (admission to which carried free board and tuition but nothing more), and maintained partially for a time, even after they were midshipmen.[6]

As may be readily deduced, all such provision left little money for the Austen girls, either for marriage portions or to maintain them creditably. After 1797 Cassandra possessed a little capital of her own, £1,000 bequeathed to her by her fiancé, the Revd Thomas Fowle, who had died on service in the West Indies. Evidently it was in reference to the investment of this sum that Jane wrote to Cassandra on 18 December 1798, 'It is a great satisfaction to us to hear that your Business is in a way to be settled, & so settled as to give you as little inconvenience as possible'.[7] By the standard computation of the day, of a 5 per cent return on long-term investments – which Jane Austen used consistently in her calculations in *Sense and Sensibility* – this should have earned Cassandra £50 per annum. Jane had nothing of her own beyond the pin-money allowed her by her father, which was probably only £20 a year. Twenty pounds was Cassandra's annual allowance, to judge by Jane's communication of 28 December 1798, written when Mr Austen had been rendered temporarily euphoric by good news: 'If you will send my father an account of your Washing & Letter expences &c, he will send you a draft for the amount of it, as well as for your next quarter [£5, to be paid on 1 January]'.[8] It is unlikely that there would have been any differentiation between the sisters' pin-money.

The principal charge on Jane's allowance was materials for, and small items of, clothes. Only gloves, stockings and the like were purchasable. 'I wish', she wrote once, 'such things [as gowns] were to be bought ready-made'.[9] Dresses and other outer garments needed dressmakers, and were comparatively expensive matters of large decision. Cassandra appears even to have bought a gown second-hand from an acquaintance, with Jane's encouragement. Even after making due allowance for the fun and irony which thread her letters to Cassandra, Jane Austen's correspondence certainly suggests that both women found it hard to make ends meet for their wardrobe. In her first surviving letter, Jane hoped that a commission to her youngest brother had not been fulfilled. 'You say nothing of the silk stockings; I flatter myself, therefore, that Charles has not purchased any, as I cannot very well afford to pay for them; all my money is spent in buying white gloves and pink persian.'[10] Her brother however proved all too prompt. 'What a good-for-nothing fellow Charles is to bespeak the stockings', Jane wrote a week later; 'I hope he will be too hot all the rest of his life for it.'[11]

Among several passages of dress gossip and information sent to Cassandra by Jane during her brief visit to Bath in May and June 1799, these two occur: 'If you do not think it [a lace border] wide enough, I can give $\frac{d}{3}$ a yard more for yours, & not go beyond the two guineas, for my Cloak altogether does not cost quite two pounds';[12] and

> Now I will give you the history of Mary's [her sister-in-law's] veil, in the purchase of which I have so considerably involved you that it is my duty to economise for you in the flowers [for hat trimming]. I had no difficulty in getting a muslin veil for half a guinea, and not much more in discovering afterwards that the muslin was thick, dirty, and ragged, and therefore would by no means do for a united gift. I changed it consequently as soon as I could, and, considering what a state my imprudence had reduced me to, I thought myself lucky in getting a black lace one for sixteen shillings. I hope the half of that sum will not greatly exceed what you had intended to offer upon the altar of sister-in-law affection.[13]

When another sister-in-law, Edward's wife Elizabeth, died after childbirth nine years later, Jane wrote to Cassandra, who was staying with her bereaved brother,

> I shall send you such of your mourning as I think most likely to be useful, reserving for myself your stockings and half the velvet, in which selfish arrangement I know I am doing what you wish.
>
> *I* am to be in bombazeen and crape, according to what we are told is universal *here....* My mourning, however, will not impoverish me, for by having my velvet pelisse fresh lined and made up, I am sure I shall have no occasion *this winter* for anything new of that sort. I take my cloak for the lining, and shall send yours on the chance of its doing something of the same for you, though I believe your pelisse is in better repair than mine.[14]

All this suggests that Jane and Cassandra Austen lived close to the margin when it came to clothes, their leading item of expenditure. It may also help to explain why their niece, Fanny Knight, in later years recalled them as countrified, perhaps even dowdy, in style.

> Both the Aunts (Cassandra & Jane) were brought up in the most complete ignorance of the World and its ways (I mean as to fashion

etc) & if it had not been for Papa's [Edward's] marriage which
brought them into Kent, & the kindness of Mrs Knight, who used
often to have one or the other of the sisters staying with her, they
would have been, tho' not less clever and agreeable in themselves,
very much below par as to good Society & its ways.[15]

The signs were those of genteel poverty, even while Mr Austen remained rector of Steventon. There was still less to divide after he
passed the living over to James in the spring of 1801 and retired to
Bath. It was hoped that he would have 'very nearly' £600 a year
(£550 net, for he was to allow James £50 per annum for a curate), but
this depended on his being able to increase the level of tithes and we
do not know if he succeeded. Some of the Austens' possessions were
auctioned, others sold to James for a valuation – not very profitably,
one would gather, from Jane's acidulous comments. Later she wrote,
apropos the valuation, 'The whole World is in a conspiracy to enrich
one part of our family at the expence of another'.[16] Jane's own sale-
able belongings were few. 'Eight [guineas] for my Pianoforte, is
about what I really expected to get; I am more anxious to know the
amount of my books, especially as they are said to have sold well.'[17]
When Mr Austen died on 21 January 1805 the family income was
reduced to some £210 per annum, including Cassandra's £50. But
James arranged that he and his brothers should between them contribute £250 a year. He himself had succeeded fully to his father's
livings, and undertook, Henry Austen wrote, to 'appropriate[d] fifty
pounds a year to our dear trio'. Henry agreed to do the same 'as long
as I am *an Agent*', and the generous Frank offered £100 per annum,
although Mrs Austen, aware of Frank's comparative poverty, would
accept only half this amount. Edward was 'put down' for £100, and
presumably this was allowed, and paid.[18] Given their circumstances,
the Austen sons had behaved well – and ungrudgingly, for they
spoke of their undertakings only in terms of elementary filial duty
and affection. Mrs Austen greeted their proposition in the same
spirit, – 'with the proudest exultations of maternal tenderness the
Excellent Parent has exclaimed that never were Children so good as
hers' – and James looked forward complacently to her future: 'It is a
just satisfaction to know that her Circumstances will be easy, & that
she will enjoy all those comforts which her declining years & precarious health call for'.[19]
James's easy optimism about the comfort of the reduced ménage
was scarcely justified. After a year and a half of long stays with rela-

tives and difficulties with new, less commodious lodgings in Bath, Mrs Austen decided to move to Southampton. This decision was precipitated by Frank's marriage in July 1806; he was for the time being without a ship to command, but wished to live close to Spithead. Whether or not at Frank's suggestion, it was arranged that he and his new wife should join forces with Mrs Austen and her daughters and another bereft female, James's sister-in-law, Martha Lloyd. The conjoined 'family' of six could afford to rent a whole dwelling instead of an apartment, and eventually a sufficiently roomy and attractive house was found in Castle Square, Southampton. This curious arrangement lasted, apparently in reasonable amity, for over two years, until Frank, for reasons of professional convenience and growing family, decided to move to Yarmouth on the Isle of Wight. Once again, Mrs Austen had to uproot herself; but this time Edward offered her a choice of two houses belonging to his Kent and Hampshire properties, respectively. She finally selected Chawton Cottage, which was close to her old home at Steventon. The 'cottage' approximated in scale and style to a fair-sized rectory. From mid-1809 until her death eight years later, Chawton was to be Jane Austen's home.

Edward gave his mother and sisters the house rent-free, and even helped them in minor ways, such as by gifts of game or fuel, so that life must have been a little less penurious for the female Austen (cum Lloyd) household after 1809. Mrs Austen had no rent to pay or repairs to make, and her capital appears meanwhile to have increased modestly. On 7 January 1807, Jane wrote that her mother 'began 1806 with 68 *l*., she begins 1807 with 99 *l*., and this after 32 *l*. purchase of stock'.[20] Thus the joint clear income of Mrs Austen and her daughters and daughter-in-law's sister, when they moved to Chawton, was probably some £500 per annum. In one important respect however Jane Austen differed from the others. She had no money whatever of her own, except for a windfall legacy of £50 from a Bath acquaintance in 1806. This enabled her to make 1807 a golden year, with an expenditure of some £44.[21] 'Single Women have a dreadful propensity for being poor', she once observed;[22] and of the four single women who made their home at Chawton Cottage in 1809, she was the poorest. Down to 1812 at least her sole ordinary income was her annual allowance from the meagre family pool; and even thereafter the increase in her 'spending' income was very small. In fact she may have had to contribute to the household expenses of Chawton after she began to earn royalties on her books, for from

1815 both Frank and Henry were unable to continue their annual allowances to Mrs Austen. At any rate, as late as the close of 1815, Jane Austen was still calculating, down to the nearest pence, the relative cost of sending her soiled garments home for washing (her second largest item of spending during her year of 'affluence') when she was away from Chawton. 'The Parcel [of laundered clothes]', she wrote to Cassandra from London on 26 November 1815,

> arrived safely, & I am much obliged to you for your trouble. It cost 2s 10 – but as there is a certain saving of 2s 4½ on the other side, I am sure it is well worth doing. – I send 4 p^r of silk stock^{gs} – but I do not want them washed at present. In the 3 neckhandfs. I include the one sent down before. – These things perhaps Edw. may be able to bring [thus saving postage]. . . .[23]

But Jane Austen also had an intimate knowledge of the lives of the very well-to-do. Some of the Hampshire friends with whom she stayed belonged to wealthy gentry families; and members of the neighbouring nobility commonly attended the Basingstoke and other balls which she frequented. Both her mother's brother, James Leigh Perrot, and her own brother, Edward, were rich men, with incomes which probably exceeded, and possibly much exceeded, £5,000 per annum. On her lengthy visits to Godmersham Park, Edward's grand 'place' in Kent, she was surrounded by moneyed comfort, and even modest splendour. 'In another week', she wrote from there on 30 June 1808,

> I shall be at home – & then, my having been at Godmersham will seem like a Dream, as my visit at Brompton [Henry's home] seems already. The Orange Wine will want our Care soon. – But in the meantime for Elegance & Ease & Luxury –; the Hattons & Milles' dine here today – & I shall eat Ice & drink French wine, & be above vulgar Economy.[24]

Moreover, Edward moved in high circles in east Kent. Through his wife as well as his benefactress Mrs Knight (who had made over all her property to him, reserving only £2,000 per annum for herself), he was connected to a fair portion of the local aristocracy and baronetage. Jane Austen came to know several of these families; with Mrs Knight, she was an especial favourite, even to being given small presents of money by her from time to time. Similarly, on visits to her brother Henry in London, Jane entered a prosperous upper-middle-class world of bankers and professional men. She was present at a soirée held by Eliza Austen in April 1811, which was attended by over sixty people, graced by professional singers and reported in the London press. Thus, her social and economic experience extended far beyond obscure village rectories and the Assembly Rooms at Basingstoke or even Bath. She also knew, *en famille*, the daily round of the superior orders.

Again, Jane was privy to both the low and high finances of her own family. She relayed information about agricultural prices and her father's and brothers' purchases and sales of stock and produce. She was told of James's increase in income and what Edward paid for carriage horses. She knew of all the losses and gains, and costs and charges, of her father's removal to Bath, as well as the everyday minutiae of domestic expenditure. Clearly, money was often, openly and comprehensively discussed within the Austen family. Moreover, Jane fully shared in the family's 'great expectations' from James Leigh Perrot's estate: 'a Legacy is our sovereign good', she wrote, half-playfully, in 1808.[25] Perrot appears to have helped Mr Austen financially during his early married years, but thereafter no Perrot money was forthcoming. For years, however, his anticipated bequests (he was childless) to Mrs Austen and her children had held out hope of financial relief to the hard-pressed among them. But when Perrot died in March 1817, his will (to quote *Sense and Sensibility*), 'like almost every other will, gave as much disappointment as pleasure'.[26] Mrs Austen received nothing and the Austen children (apart from James who was to get £24,000, much less than had been anticipated) only £1,000 apiece, and none of these legacies was payable until Perrot's widow died. 'I am ashamed to say', wrote Jane from her sick-bed to her brother Charles, 'that the shock of my Uncle's Will brought on a relapse.... I am the only one of the Legatees who has been so silly, but a weak Body must excuse weak Nerves. My Mother has borne the forgetfulness of *her* extremely well.'[27] There can be no doubt that Jane Austen was thoroughly grounded in the significance of all sums great and small.

II

It is still the fact however that, until she was a woman in her later thirties, Jane Austen had no money of her own, apart from the chance legacy and what was given to her by her relations and Mrs Knight. She alone was a *complete* dependant. There is no evidence to support the sequential proposition, which nowadays thrusts itself forward almost automatically, that she resented or was especially sensitive about her lot. To all outside appearances, the extraordinary family solidarity and mutual helpfulness of the Austens insulated her against the expected effects of so ignominious a status. Some might infer suppressed anger or revolt as the necessary result of being in others' power, or even read these feelings into her novels. But, right or wrong, such reasoning would have to be a priori. In her surviving letters, there is no hint that she smarted under her financial dependence on either her parents or her brothers.

None the less, even if unresented, dependence was an irksome condition. The undertone of Jane's letters home when she stayed with her sister-in-law, Eliza (Henry's wife), in London make it clear that she had to mind her p's and q's. 'Do not', she instructed Cassandra on 25 April 1811, 'have your col[oure]^d muslin unless you really want it, because I am afraid I c^d not send it to the Coach without giving trouble here.'[28] When in London again later on, she told her niece Anna,

> you mu[st be] aware that in another person's house one cannot command one's own time or actions, & though your Uncle Henry is so kind as to give us the use of a Carriage while we are with him, it may not be possible for us to turn that Carriage towards Hendon without actually mounting the Box ourselves. . . .[29]

As with Marianne Dashwood's endeavours to reach and return from London, travel was always a difficulty for Jane Austen, not merely because of the impropriety of her journeying alone on public transport, but also because she could not afford high fares or charges and was forced to rely on seats in others' carriages or post-chaises. 'Since breakfast', she wrote from Godmersham in June 1808,

> I have had a *tête-á-tête* with Edward in his room; he wanted to know James's plans and mine, and from what his own now are I think it already nearly certain that I shall return when they do, though not with them. Edward will be going about the same time to Alton, where he has business with Mr Trimmer, and where he means his son should join him; and I shall probably be his companion to that place, and get on afterwards somehow or other.
>
> I should have preferred a rather longer stay here certainly, but there is no prospect of any later conveyance for me, as he does not mean to accompany Edward [his son] on his return to Winchester, from a very natural unwillingness to leave Elizabeth [his wife,

who was pregnant] at that time. I shall at any rate be glad not to be obliged to be an incumbrance on those who have brought me here, for, as James has no horse, I must feel in their carriage that I am taking his place. We were rather crowded yesterday, though it does not become me to say so, as I and my boa were of the party. . . .[30]

Unhappy with the final arrangements for the return journey, she sadly noted, 'till I have a travelling purse of my own, I must submit to such things'.[31] Again, during her 1811 visit to London, she depended on being met by her brother James at Streatham, and conveyed home thence. This in turn depended on her staying with her friend, Catherine Hill (née Bigg), at Streatham, and it was with relief that she reported to Cassandra that Catherine had sent 'a most kind & satisfactory answer' to her proposal. 'I shall leave Sloane St. [Henry's house]', she continued, 'on the 1st or 2^{d} [May] & be ready for James on ye 9th; & if his plan alters, I can take care of myself. – I have explained my veiws here, & everything is smooth & pleasant; & Eliza talks kindly of conveying me to Streatham'.[32] All this may have been too everyday for conscious notice; but it is also possible that Jane Austen often envied those women who had homes and travel at their own command.

Certainly, it seems quite plausible to interpret her buying back the unpublished manuscript of *Sense and Sensibility* on the eve of her departure for Chawton in 1809 as marking a new determination to earn some money for herself, and win a measure of financial independence. (After all, her 'investment' in this venture, £10, represented a considerable sum for her.) Equally, her steady application to composition from that time on would seem to confirm this conjecture. So too would her later remark to Fanny Knight, 'People are more ready to borrow & praise, than to buy . . . but tho' I like praise as well as anybody, I like what Edward calls *Pewter* too',[33] as well as her first surviving comment on her sales, made to Frank in the course of a letter of 3 July 1813,

You will be glad to hear that every Copy of S. & S. is sold & that it has brought me £140 besides the Copyright, if that sh^{d} ever be of any value. – I have now therefore written myself into £250 – which only makes me long for more. – I have something in hand – which I hope on the credit of P. & P. will sell well, tho' not half so entertaining.[34]

It was presumably to obtain better terms that she changed from the house of Thomas Egerton to that of John Murray for the publication

of *Emma*. 'He [Murray] is a rogue of course', she told Cassandra on
17 October 1815, 'but a civil one. He offers £450 but wants to have
the copyright of M.P. & S. & S. included.'[35] The age–old author's
cry of pain on learning of the pitiful rewards offered for grinding
labour is to be heard again in the reply to Murray dictated by Henry
Austen but written (and possibly 'improved on' in the course of tran-
scription) by Jane.

> The Terms you offer are so very inferior to what we had expected,
> that I am apprehensive of having made some great Error in my
> Arithmetical Calculation. – On the subject of the expense & profit
> of publishing, you must be much better informed than I am; – but
> Documents in my possession appear to prove that the Sum offered
> by you for the Copyright of Sense & Sensibility, Mansfield Park &
> Emma, is not equal to the Money which my Sister has actually
> cleared by one very moderate Edition of Mansfield Park.[36]

Sense and Sensibility however, re–swelled her capital in later years,
and every little gain was pleasing. 'I have just rec[eive]^{d}', she wrote
on 14 March 1817, 'nearly twenty pounds myself on the 2^{d} Edit: of S
& S – which gives me this fine flow of Literary Ardour'.[37] Ironically,
within three days she was too ill to add any more to her draft of *Sanditon*; but at least by then she had 'written herself into' enough to
leave a net sum of £910 in her will. Her greatest source of pride may
well have been the £600 of 5 per cent Bank Annuities (Navy Stock) in
her name. Such securities were a sacred sign of independence in 1817.

III

The basic social grid on which *Sense and Sensibility* rests is that of the
country gentry. Norland Park, whose ownership is central to the
story, was a large estate in Sussex, well–timbered and with a rental of
£4,000 per annum, which better management might easily increase –
'capable', as Mr Henry Dashwood believed, 'of almost immediate
improvement'.[38] It had long been the property of the Dashwood
family: 'for many generations, they had lived in so respectable a
manner, as to engage the general good opinion of their surrounding
acquaintance' (p. 1). Barton Park in Devonshire was seemingly a
counterpart of Norland. The 'house was large and handsome', and
the proprietor 'dwelt in a style of equal hospitality and elegance' (p.
32). Certainly the owner, Sir John Middleton, spent money freely,

even lavishly, without, apparently, distressing himself in any way. Cleveland, in Somerset, may not have been as substantial as either of the Parks, but clearly it was opulent and splendidly maintained.

> Cleveland was a spacious, modern-built house, situated on a sloping lawn. It had no park, but the pleasure-grounds were tolerably extensive; and like every other place of the same degree of importance, it had its open shrubbery, and closer wood walk, a road of smooth gravel winding round a plantation, led to the front, the lawn was dotted over with timber, the house itself was under the guardianship of the fir, the mountain-ash, and the acacia, and a thick screen of them altogether, interspersed with tall Lombardy poplars, shut out the offices. (p. 302)

It had even a Grecian temple on a distant eminence, from which a wide stretch of the surrounding country might be viewed. Cleveland's owner, Mr Palmer – married, like Sir John, to a well-endowed Miss Jennings – was a comparatively rich young man. His considerable social standing and resources may be inferred from the fact that he intended to run for the county constituency at the next election; county elections were notoriously expensive. Whitwell, the domain of Colonel Brandon's brother-in-law, and 'a very fine place about twelve miles from Barton' with 'highly beautiful' grounds and 'a noble piece of water' (p. 62), may well also have belonged to the same category as Norland. But it appears only off-stage in *Sense and Sensibility*, for the excursion planned to view it was cancelled at the eleventh hour.

Colonel Brandon's own property, Delaford, belongs to the second level of gentry homes, although his house is twice spoken of as a 'mansion'. According to Mrs Jennings, whose curiosity and acumen should have made her a shrewd and accurate judge, the 'estate at Delaford was never reckoned more than two thousand a year, and his brother [from whom Colonel Brandon inherited] left every thing sadly involved' (p. 70). However, the Colonel was 'very prudent', and had doubtless restored Delaford to the £2,000 per annum level by the time that he met Marianne Dashwood. Elinor Dashwood, by no means prone to exaggerate values, speaks of it confidently as worth at least as much, before the book's end. One would guess that Allenham, the estate of Mrs Smith, John Willoughby's aunt, was more modest – perhaps worth about £1,300 per annum – but Marianne found it 'a charming house... On one side you look across the bowling green, behind the house, to a beautiful hanging wood' (p.

69). Willoughby's own place at Combe Magna in Somerset was more modest still, with an annual produce of only £600 to £700, according to Sir John Middleton's calculation. As always in the book, people seem both able and eager to 'price' others' incomes with precision.

Two widows stand at the head of those living mainly – we may assume – on investment income. Mrs Ferrars seems to have been the sole beneficiary of her husband, 'a man who had died very rich' (p. 15), and Mrs Jennings enjoyed 'an ample jointure' (p. 36), that is, a life interest in her husband's considerable estate. These financial indicators are not translated into specific sums; but before the conclusion of the novel Mrs Ferrars has parted with the equivalent of £40,000 to her children without any notable decline in her style of living; while, quite apart from their eventual inheritances, both the Misses Jennings married well-to-do squires whose minimum expectation would have been dowries of £10,000 apiece. They are described as 'respectably' settled – and 'respectable' acts as a code word throughout the novel to signify solid wealth.

Very different was the standing of Mrs Henry Dashwood after her husband died. From being mistress of a large country house on an income (we might estimate) of some £5,000 per annum, she falls to a rented cottage and an annual income of £500. Even the £500 was not wholly hers; £150 of it derived from the interest on her three daughters' legacies of £1,000 each from Henry Dashwood's uncle. This does not mean that the Dashwoods suddenly became 'new poor' on Henry's death; to some extent, they retained their upper-gentry status through their family networks. But clearly their mode of life was severely curtailed, and, unless fortune intervened, sooner or later they might well dwindle into poor relations. In fact, Mrs John Dashwood relegated them at once to a lower station. She persuaded her husband that when his father had made his death-bed plea for help for his wife and daughters, he had meant only such assistance as impoverished relatives might hope for *de haut en bas* – 'looking out for a comfortable small house for them, helping them move their things, and sending them presents of fish and game and so forth'. They would be 'excessively comfortable' if they accommodated themselves to their reduced circumstances.

Altogether, they will have five hundred a-year amongst them, and what on earth can four women want for more than that? – They will live so cheap! Their housekeeping will be nothing at all. They

will have no carriage, no horses, and hardly any servants; they will
keep no company, and can have no expences of any kind! Only
conceive how comfortable they will be!   (p. 12)

Primarily, this passage is of course a satire on meanness and self-
serving. But it is not impossibly distant from ordinary people's reaction to a catastrophic fall in somebody else's income. Indeed, is
there not something *generally* recognizable even in Mrs John Dashwood's 'the[ir] set of breakfast china is twice as handsome as what
belongs to this house. A great deal too handsome, in my opinion, for
any place *they* can ever afford to live in' (p. 13)?

This is all the more piquant because John Dashwood had gained
what Mrs Dashwood and her daughters lost. Not merely did he
secure a life interest in Norland Park (which he proceeded quickly to
improve on) but also he received the moiety of his mother's fortune
hitherto enjoyed by Henry Dashwood. The latter augmentation
meant that, in addition to his rental, his investment income was very
considerable. His wife's dowry brought in £500 annually, and his
mother's money (which was now his alone) must have earned still
more, for her fortune is described as 'large' and he had lived com-
fortably even before inheriting Norland Park and the second moiety.
We can safely assume that as a *rentier* alone – and quite apart from his
'improved-on' £4,000 per annum from the estate – John Dashwood
was at least three times as wealthy as his stepmother after she had
been widowed.

The young men of the novel, Edward and Robert Ferrars, were
still dependants on their tyrannical and capricious mother, with
whom they lived. Edward had a 'trifling' income of his own, £100
per annum, from an inheritance of £2,000; but his mother must have
supplied some additional allowance, as he kept horses and a manser-
vant, which £100 per annum would certainly not have supported.
Robert's allowance, whether regular or irregular, was probably
much larger, if his life among the smart set and his particularity in
choosing an ivory, gold and pearl toothpick case are any indication.
For most of the novel both are 'poor rich' young men. Contrariwise
the Steeles were truly poor, if would-be genteel, young women.
One of their friends observed that 'Lucy Steele . . . had nothing at all'
(p. 272). This may not have been absolutely true. The Steeles enjoyed enough pin-money to live creditably as visitors among the
affluent, and Mrs Jennings spoke of 'what little matter Mr Steele and
Mr Pratt [the Steeles' uncle]' could give Lucy as a dowry (p. 276).

But clearly they were next door to penniless.

One remarkable feature of *Sense and Sensibility* is the homogeneity of its internal society. The Steeles, who would scarcely have had £50 a year between them, were house guests of both the Middletons and the John Dashwoods, whose incomes might well have been a hundred times as large. The thin thread of an apparently distant relationship to Mrs Jennings was enough to draw them aboard the splendid vessels for a time. Conversely, however, each level of income is correlated exactly to a particular style of living. The rich families in the novel either own or rent homes for the season in the 'elegant' part of London, Conduit Street, Harley Street, Hanover Square and Berkeley Street, off Portman Square – all within a radius of half a mile of one another in the most fashionable quarter of the capital. The bachelors Brandon and Willoughby take rooms in the adjoining St. James's Street and Bond Street respectively. The Steeles, on the other hand, begin their London sojourn decidedly to the east; they stay with a cousin in an apartment block in Holborn, markedly lower in the social scale.

Jane Austen is quite precise in setting out what the £500 per annum of the widowed Dashwood family will buy in terms of a way of life. They were favoured by a rent so low that Jane Austen never deducts it in speaking generally of their income. On the other hand, their 'cottage' was no larger than a respectable modern villa, 2,500 to 3,000 square feet. Their two downstairs rooms were 'parlours', each about 16 feet wide by 16 feet long, separated by a narrow entrance hall and passage. The rest of the bottom storey consisted of kitchen, scullery and pantries. Up a dark cramped staircase, the next floor was divided into four bedrooms and a landing. There were two servants' rooms in the attic. This was a much more modest 'cottage' than the sort built as, or converted into, holiday houses for the rich. That of Robert Ferrars's friend, Lady Elliot, for instance, had four reception rooms on the ground floor: it would have been almost twice as large as Barton Cottage.

The quota of domestic help for a house the size of Barton Cottage, and £500 a year, was three servants, one of them a man. That this was nicely gauged is clear from Mrs Jennings's prescribed establishment for a similar cottage – 'or [one] a little bigger' – but with an annual income of £800. It was worth, according to her calculation, 'two maids and two men' (p. 262). When however it looked as if this might be reduced to a curate's dwelling and £250 per annum, she scaled things down drastically. 'Two maids and two men indeed! . . .

No, no, they must get a stout girl of all works. – Betty's sister [an experienced housemaid] would never do for them' (p. 277).

Perhaps the greatest single divide for middle-class families was whether or not they kept a carriage. Carriage horses and a carriage meant a heavy outlay of capital; and the concomitants – stables, fodder, coach-house and groom – could scarcely be maintained for less than £200 a year, and might well have cost a great deal more. Mrs Dashwood's social descent on her husband's death was marked straightaway by the sale of his horses, and then his carriage; Mrs John Dashwood – rightly – took it for granted that both would be beyond Mrs Dashwood's means in her new condition. Marianne forwent Willoughby's gift of a horse, even after she had persuaded herself that most of the cost of upkeep could be transferred to Sir John Middleton, once Elinor pointed out that their mother would have to bear some of the new expenses none the less. Conversely, it was a matter of course that someone with Mrs Jennings's income should maintain an elegant carriage or carriages, although she spent a considerable part of the year in her daughters' houses and the remainder in her own house in the heart of fashionable London. Horses loomed large in the expenditure of such young men as Willoughby.

> 'And yet two thousand a-year is a very moderate income,' said Marianne. 'A family cannot well be maintained on a smaller. I am sure I am not extravagant in my demands. A proper establishment of servants, a carriage, perhaps two, and hunters, cannot be supported on less.'
>
> Elinor smiled again, to hear her sister describing so accurately their [Willoughby's and Marianne's] future expenses at Combe Magna.
>
> 'Hunters!' repeated Edward – 'But why must you have hunters? Everybody does not hunt.'
>
> Marianne coloured as she replied, 'But most people do.'
>
> (pp. 91-2)

In fact, horses were, according to Mrs Jennings, responsible for Willoughby's being 'all to pieces', in such desperate straits financially as to clutch at Miss Grey's £50,000 dowry for salvation. 'No wonder! dashing about with his curricle and hunters!' (p. 194).

Although horses and carriages are not specifically costed in *Sense and Sensibility*, there was probably no need for Jane Austen to do more than point to their presence or absence. To apply her own joking phrase, she did not write for such dull elves as had not a sound grasp of the elements of the contemporary cost of living, as well as a good deal of ingenuity, themselves. Having told her readers earlier that Mrs Henry Dashwood had sold her horses and carriage, and lived, with her daughters, at her son-in-law's expense for six months, Jane Austen has no need to explain why and how the widow had, at the time of her removal to Barton Cottage, 'ready money enough to supply all that was wanted [of furniture] of greater elegance to the apartments' (p. 29). Much else is however precisely costed in the book. John Dashwood was careful to calculate the income of an estate not gross but 'clear of land-tax' (p. 266). In arriving at the capital value of the Delaford living, he did the necessary sum, as we have seen, upon the standard actuarial basis of seven years' purchase. The same indefatigable estimator put a pretty close valuation on what her 'nervous complaint' would cost Marianne. 'At her time of life, any thing of an illness destroys the bloom for ever! Her's has been a very short one!... I question whether Marianne *now*, will marry a man worth more than five or six hundred a-year, at the utmost' (p. 227). This was no isolated satirical shaft, for elsewhere Jane Austen's characters often cast marriage prospects in money terms, as with Miss Maria Ward's uncle who 'allowed' her dowry of £7,000 'to be at least three thousand short of any equitable claim' on the hand of Sir Thomas Bertram of Mansfield Park, whom none the less she married.[39] In *Sense and Sensibility*, the relative meagreness of the Hon. Miss Morton's marriage portion, £30,000, *vis-à-vis* the matching estate of 'a thousand a-year' which Mrs Ferrars was willing to make over in return for her wedding to Edward (p. 224), is explicable by the fact that peers' daughters could expect a sort of discount for their noble blood and aristocratical connections.

Even where no sum of money is specified, Jane Austen so particularizes as to leave a clear impression of the actual financial implications. When Mrs Henry Dashwood adumbrates an extension to Barton Cottage, it is in exact form (a new wing, comprising a drawing-room on the first floor, a bedroom on the second and a garret overhead, together with a wider central passage), so that we can appreciate all the better the absurdity of such improvements being 'made from the savings of an income of five hundred a-year by a woman who had never saved in her life' (p. 29). Similarly, the irony of the passage in which John Dashwood describes the closeness of his escape from financial embarrassment, has a much sharper edge because of the extraordinary particularity with which the expenditure is set out.

'The inclosure of Norland Common, now carrying on, is a most serious drain. And then I have had made a little purchase within this half year; East Kingham Farm, you must remember the place, where old Gibson used to live. The land was so very desirable for me in every respect, so immediately adjoining my own property, that I felt it my duty to buy it. I could not have answered it to my conscience to let it fall into any other hands. A man must pay for his convenience; and it *has* cost me a vast deal of money.'

'More than you think it really and intrinsically worth.'

'Why, I hope not that. I might have sold it again the next day, for more than I gave; but with regard to the purchase-money, I might have been very unfortunate indeed; for the stocks were at that time so low, that if I had not happened to have the necessary sum in my banker's hands, I must have sold out to very great loss.'

Elinor could only smile.

'Other great and inevitable expenses too we have had on first coming to Norland. Our respected father, as you well know, bequeathed all the Stanhill [Henry Dashwood's original residence] effects that remained at Norland (and very valuable they were) to your mother. Far be it from me to repine at his doing so; he had an undoubted right to dispose of his own property as he chose. But, in consequence of it, we have been obliged to make large purchases of linen, china, &c. to supply the place of what was taken away. You may guess, after all these expenses, how very far we must be from being rich, and how acceptable Mrs Ferrars' kindness [a gift of £200] is.' (pp. 225-6)

Sense and Sensibility is remarkable, even among Jane Austen's novels, for the solidity of its background. To borrow Hawthorne's praise of Trollope's fiction, we seem to see the people re-animated in their daily rounds and ordinary existences as if we were watching them under glass.[40] This specificity is largely attributable to the plenitude and exactness of the material detail. The frame of income and outgoings in which everyone is placed is built so sturdily that we implicitly accept its power to shape character and influence action. While a Marxist might not allow *Sense and Sensibility* as a novel within the canon, he or she would have no difficulty in fitting large parts of it into their patterns. Money constitutes a sort of underlying beat below the narrative. Even the central antithesis of the book can be expressed – though this is far from saying that it was meant primarily or deliberately to be expressed – in economic terms. In a key exchange, Marianne asks her elder sister what either wealth or grandeur has to do with happiness.

'Grandeur has but little,' said Elinor, 'but wealth has much to do with it.'

'Elinor, for shame!' said Marianne; 'money can only give happiness where there is nothing else to give it. Beyond a competence, it can afford no real satisfaction, as far as mere self is concerned.'

'Perhaps,' said Elinor, smiling, 'we may come to the same point. *Your* competence and *my* wealth are very much alike, I dare say; and without them, as the world goes now, we shall both agree that every kind of external comfort must be wanting. Your ideas are only more noble than mine. Come, what is your competence?'

'About eighteen hundred or two thousand a-year; not more than *that*.'

Elinor laughed. '*Two* thousand a-year! *One* is my wealth! I guessed how it would end.'   (p. 91)

It is no coincidence perhaps that this is how it in fact ended. Elinor Dashwood did not quite attain her 'wealth' of £1,000 per annum, but her eventual £850 per annum with the chance of raising the level of the parish tithes materially and a renovated house to live in may have amounted to much the same. Marianne was to enjoy her 'competence' of 'two thousand a-year', when 'she found herself at nineteen, submitting to new attachments, entering on new duties, placed in a new home, a wife, the mistress of a family, and the patroness of a village' (p. 379). Is there perhaps a satisfying aptness in 'Sense' settling for cautious comfort, but 'Sensibility' needing a much larger canvas and more generous range of colour to express itself? Whatever about this conceit – and it is I dare say arguable that 'Sense' would be better represented by the mansion house than by the parsonage at Delaford – character and financial fate are often linked in *Sense and Sensibility*. Edward and Elinor seem natural £1,000-a-year persons; Lucy Steele and Robert Ferrars, more; Willoughby, still more; John and Mrs John Dashwood, most of all. People are rewarded financially according to their expectations or avarice rather than their merits. The good need competences but the wicked may prosper more.

The whole of Lucy's behaviour in the affair, and the prosperity which crowned it . . . may be held forth as a most encouraging instance of what an earnest, an unceasing attention to self-interest, however its progress may be apparently obstructed, will do in

securing every advantage of fortune, with no other sacrifice than
that of time and conscience. (p. 376)

The ultimate words imply, however, that there is a price to be paid
for everything, even – or perhaps particularly – riches.

IV

When we match Jane Austen's economic circumstances and encounters with those of the novel, we cannot doubt that it was based
on closely observed reality in all matters of income, property and
possessions. There is even evidence of a positive striving after exactitude. 'The *Incomes* remain as they were', Jane Austen wrote in the
course of proof-reading, 'but I will get them altered if I can'.[41] R. W.
Chapman suggests that she referred to the change of 'division of the
estate' to 'charge on the estate' made in the second edition of the
book.[42] But this would seem a matter of legal rather than monetary
substance; and a more likely candidate appears to be Mr John Dashwood's error in calculating Edward's income had he married the
Hon. Miss Morton at £2,500 instead of £2,600 per annum (p. 268).
Jane Austen may also – or alternatively – have had in mind her slip in
setting Elinor's dowry at 'no more than three [thousand pounds]' (p.
373); immediately it would have been £1,000 with *over* £2,000 to
come on Mrs Dashwood's death. Such particularity is warranted in a
book remarkable for and even resting on material accuracy.

This is not to claim that Jane Austen transposed her own experiences simply to the novel. There is, it is true, a most striking correspondence between the widowed Mrs Dashwood's situation as an
almost rent-free tenant of Barton Cottage with three daughters, two
maidservants and a man, and a joint income of £500 a year, and the
widowed Mrs Austen's as the rent-free tenant of Chawton with two
daughters and one quasi-daughter, two maidservants and a man, and
a joint income of £500 a year. The patronage of Sir John Middleton at
Barton Park and of Edward, when he was in residence, at Chawton
Manor constitute a further resemblance. Yet it would be quite mis-
taken to regard the Chawton Cottage ménage as a model for that of
Barton Cottage. Unless there were wholesale changes in the text of
Sense and Sensibility after 1809, which is most unlikely, the fiction
pre-dated the fact by several years. Barton Cottage came first, by a
considerable margin.

How then is the close similarity to be explained? First, although life at Steventon, where the book was originally written, did not provide the perfect pattern for its arrangements, the system of prices, values and economic conduct prevailing in the real village was so solid and assured as to furnish safe building materials for an imaginary social segment which would be faithful to everyday behaviour. Secondly, the relationship between income and life-style in early-nineteenth-century England was more or less uniform. Hence, it is no surprise that, given the same basic resources to go on, art should anticipate nature – or more precisely that the artifice of the Dashwoods in *Sense and Sensibility* should anticipate that actuality of the Austens in Chawton Cottage. For that matter, the middle-class widow and her daughters living in 'reduced circumstances' was all too common a phenomenon of the day. Growing up, Jane Austen knew just such a family very well – Mrs Lloyd and her three girls, who rented Deane rectory from her father up to 1792.

But it is as needless as it would be tedious to set about matching the economic particulars of *Sense and Sensibility* and Jane Austen's own life. It is enough to say that a secure but straitened girlhood in Steventon; stays at Godmersham and Manydown, the Biggs' country house, and other homes of the wealthy gentry; the constant family interchange on spending, values and receipts; businesslike and business-loving brothers (Edward and Henry in particular); and domestic management and the casting of her own minuscule accounts, provided all the data bank she needed. The question remains, why did she draw on it so extensively in *Sense and Sensibility*? An obvious answer is that a great deal in the novel hung on money. The sudden impoverishment of Mrs Henry Dashwood and her daughters is central to the action; it is this which brings all else into play. It is Marianne's lack of money which 'preserves' her from Willoughby, and it is Edward's lack of income which saves him initially from Lucy. It is Robert Ferrars's acquisition of an independence which in the end renders Edward available for Elinor. For all their strength of character, Elinor and Marianne are cast in essentially passive roles. Their fates depend on others' gains and losses; they wait on the roulette wheel which determines others' fortunes. No more than Cassandra and Jane Austen do they contemplate becoming governesses or schoolmistresses, the only conceivable occupations for girls of their class unless, by some extraordinary chance, they had both the talent to earn their living by their pen and the luck to find an outlet for their writings.[43]

Doubtless it was instinct rather than design which led Jane Austen

to embody a profusion of material detail, to render economics omni-
present, and even to use John Dashwood and Mrs Jennings, as a sort
of ironic chorus, to price everything. But if so the instinct was sure.
It may well be argued that *Sense and Sensibility* was the first English
realistic novel, and that getting and spending is the ground floor, if
not the very foundation of realism. Moreover, in a book which set
out to face the material facts of contemporary marriage, it was most
effective as well as artistically right to be economically specific. Jane
Austen did not mean to set money high in the scale of things –
although she might have said, like Belloc, 'God preserve me from
riches – I mean, of course, very great riches'. Yet money mattered
vitally, although also most variously, in life. *Sense and Sensibility* is,
among other things, a protracted exegesis of this text.

CHAPTER 4

GIRLHOOD:
Catharine, or The Bower, Northanger Abbey and Pride and Prejudice

I

WE HAVE ONLY a little evidence of what Jane Austen did as a young girl, and still less of what she was like. Her severe elder cousin Philadelphia Walter, meeting her for the first time in 1788, described her as 'not at all pretty & very prim, unlike a girl of twelve: but it is a hasty judgement... the more I see of Cassandra the more I admire [her] – Jane is whimsical & affected'.[1] Four years later, however, another cousin, the much more flighty Eliza de Feuillide, reported Jane to be, like Cassandra, 'greatly improved as well in manners as in person... sensible... to a degree seldom met with' and fully sharing the 'uncommon abilities, which indeed seem to have been bestowed, tho' in a different way upon each member of this family'. Eliza preferred her to Cassandra; Jane's 'partiality to me, indeed requires a return of the same nature'.[2] For the rest, we must infer as best we can Jane's character when young from her own later writing, and the undoubted fact that the reserved, disciplined, intelligent Cassandra served her as a role model from early childhood onwards.[3]

Jane Austen's first extant letters date from her twenty-first year. There is an air of girlishness, and even a breath of *naïveté*, about these which are not apparent in the next batch of surviving letters to Cassandra, written more than two years later. Jane's own extra-fictional 'principles' of girlhood are mainly to be found in correspondence with, or about, her nieces, and in particular the two eldest, Fanny (Edward Austen's first daughter) and Anna (James Austen's first daughter). Both were born early in 1793, when Jane was seventeen years old. Jane by no means regarded the two with equal affection or indulgence. When Anna had two small daughters of her own, Jane wrote, 'How soon, the difference of temper in Children appears! –

Jemima has a very irritable bad Temper... and Julia a very sweet one. ... I hope... that she [Anna] will give Jemima's disposition the early & steady attention it must require'.[4] So it had always been with Jane's (and Cassandra's) bearing towards Anna and Fanny. Anna was stigmatized as moody and unstable, Fanny lauded as loving and constant, with appropriate aunly treatment in either case.

Jane Austen's comments on Anna, even as a child, were generally adverse, and she replied to Cassandra's report on her when she was fifteen years old, 'Her manners must be very much worsted by your description of them'.[5] When, three years later, Mrs Austen and her friend Martha Lloyd wrote 'with great satisfaction of Anna's behaviour', Jane brushed aside their findings: 'She is quite an Anna with variations – but she cannot have reached her last, for that is always the most flourishing & shewey – she is at about her 3[d] or 4th which are generally simple & pretty'.[6] Jane was greatly irritated by Anna's search for friends and amusement when she visited Chawton from 1811 on. On one such visit, when Anna was eighteen, she was absent when her uncle Henry called at Chawton. Mrs Austen was much distressed, 'a distress', wrote Jane, 'I could not share. – She [Anna] does not return from Faringdon [where she stayed with her friend, Harriet Benn] till this even[g], – & I doubt not, has had plenty of the miscellaneous, unsettled sort of happiness which seems to suit her best'.[7] A later comment of 1813, made when Cassandra and Jane were both away from Chawton and Anna was on a visit to her much more complaisant grandmother, points to an earlier domestic storm over Anna's waywardness. 'An Anna sent away & an Anna fetched are different things. – This will be an excellent time for Ben [Lefroy, Anna's fiancé] to pay his visit – now that we [Cassandra and Jane], the formidables, are absent.'[8] Even Anna's mode of purchasing a pelisse earned Jane's disapproval. 'Her purple Pelisse rather surprised me', Jane wrote to Fanny on 30 November 1814,

> I thought we had known all Paraphernalia of that sort. I do not mean to blame her, it looked very well & I daresay she wanted it. I suspect nothing worse than it's being got in secret, & not owned to anybody. – She is capable of that you know.[9]

There is no substantial evidence either to confirm or modify Jane Austen's estimate of Anna. Certainly, Jane appears to have allowed nothing for Anna's being unhappy at home under an unsympathetic stepmother. Moreover, although she responded fully and courteously to Anna's drafts of a novel sent to her for criticism – much to

the later benefit of students of Jane Austen's system of composition –
she did not enter as lightly into the easy traffic of book gossip with
Anna as with the less gifted Fanny. There is a certain pathos in
Anna's repeated endeavours to win her aunt's favour between her
marriage in 1814 and Jane's death in 1817. She was always met
politely, sometimes approvingly, but never with much warmth.
Anna herself was evidently unaware of her aunt's disapproval – or
else memory played her kindly false. In later years, she wrote:

> The two years before my marriage and the three afterwards,
> during which we lived near Chawton, were the years in which my
> great intimacy with her [Jane Austen] was formed; when the
> original seventeen years between us seemed reduced to seven, or
> none at all. It was my amusement during part of a summer visit to
> the cottage to procure novels from the circulating library at Alton,
> and after running them over to narrate and turn into ridicule their
> stories to Aunt Jane, much to her amusement, as she sat over some
> needlework which was nearly always for the poor. We both en-
> joyed the fun, as did Aunt Cassandra in her quiet way.... [10]

It is true that Jane softened a little towards Anna in the end. On 20
February 1817, she told Fanny that she had seen Anna recently, looking 'so young & so blooming & so innocent, as if she had never had a
wicked Thought in her Life – which yet one has some reason to suppose she must have had . . . if we remember the events of her girlish
days'.[11] But Anna never really secured her aunt's confidence or
favour.

By contrast, Jane Austen was indulgent towards her eldest niece,
Fanny, from the start. In 1808, when Fanny was fifteen years old,
Jane reported to Cassandra that she 'looks very well, and seems as to
conduct and manner just what she was and what one could wish her
to continue'.[12] Later in the same year, when Cassandra sent Jane an
equally favourable judgment on Fanny, Jane replied,

> I am greatly pleased with your account of Fanny; I found her in the
> summer just what you describe, almost another Sister, – & could
> not have supposed that a niece would ever have been so much to
> me. She is quite after one's own heart; give her my best Love, &
> tell her that I always think of her with pleasure.[13]

Fanny had already been admitted to the intimacy of sharing books,
in-jokes and in-language, and she was soon to advance to the special
privilege of being permitted to read one of Jane Austen's as yet un-

published novels (probably *Sense and Sensibility*). Jane pretended to fear that 'the knowledge of my being exposed to her discerning Criticism, may...hurt my stile, by inducing too great a solicitude'.[14] In 1813, when Fanny was twenty, she and Jane stayed together at her brother Henry's house in London; this, like similar visits later, seems to have cemented their 'sisterhood', as well as rendering Jane the confidante – with secrets kept even from Cassandra – in Fanny's love affairs.

The stage of courtship was the culmination of girlhood, and Jane Austen was too clear-sighted to suppose that this was always or altogether a passive experience, or one initiated only by a man. *Northanger Abbey* is an almost book-long exposition of this truth, with a delicate delineation of the outermost limits which female pride and propriety might touch in pursuit of the objective. Both Fanny and Anna were always bent on marriage, and it is from their 'affairs', and in particular Fanny's, that we can best understand Jane Austen's precepts on girlhood in its ultimate form.

Even before the spring of 1814, when Jane Austen and Fanny again stayed together with Henry Austen in London, Fanny confided in Jane that she was in love with John Plumtre, the young heir to a substantial neighbouring Kent property. Although Jane did not then consider her 'so *much* in love as you thought yourself', she none the less believed Fanny to be 'quite sufficiently [attached] for happiness, as I had no doubt it would increase with opportunity'. After their London visit, however, she concluded that Fanny was 'really very much in love'. Some six months later Jane heard suddenly, and in the greatest secrecy, from Fanny that her feelings had changed. This was in part because (in Jane's paraphrase) 'being secure of him...made you Indifferent', and in part because Plumtre had come to seem rather, heavy, lumpish and solemn in Fanny's eyes. Jane diagnosed the 'mistake' as 'one that thousands of women fall into. He was the *first* young Man who attached himself to you. That was the charm, & most powerful it is'. None the less she was most surprised. Fanny had encouraged Plumtre 'to such a point as to make him feel almost secure of you – [and] you have no inclination for any other person'.[15]

Plumtre was able (he had taken a good university degree), uncommonly amiable, with 'strict principles, just notions, good habits' and even Evangelical inclinations. Jane Austen urged Fanny not to dismiss frivolously his learning, rectitude and piety. 'Oh! my dear Fanny, the more I write about him, ... the more strongly I feel the sterling worth of such a young Man & the desirability of your grow-

ing in love with him again.' Yet in the end feelings must decide. If
Fanny now felt that Plumtre really jarred on her, even if only in his
manners or bearing, she should give him up. Anything was better
than marriage to a man who was not congenial in nature. But an immediate decision must be made. Either the tacit engagement should
be confirmed or Fanny should now 'behave with a coldness which
may convince him that he has been deceiving himself'. Doubtless he
would suffer in rejection, 'but it is no creed of mine, as you must be
well aware, that such sort of Disappointments kill anybody'.[16]

Fanny was reluctant to let Plumtre go, and apparently appealed to
Jane for at least a stay of execution. But Jane was adamant that the
issue should be determined, and determined by 'Your own feelings
& none but your own'. Fanny might never again attract a man of
equal worth, 'but if that other Man has the power of attaching you
more, he will be in your eyes the most perfect'. Could Plumtre and
Fanny marry immediately, 'your present feelings... would be sufficient for his happiness' and 'with all his worth, you would soon love
him enough for the happiness of both'. But the prospect was for a
long engagement, and 'You like him well enough to marry, but not
well enough to wait'.[17]

To sum up Jane Austen's complex judgment, PlumPtre passed
with ease the initial tests of identity of class, style of life and neighbourhood; and, ultimately at least, he would enjoy a fine position
and fair prospects in the world. He also passed the individual tests of
rectitude, seriousness, good temper, intelligence and a sound religious disposition. Quite as important perhaps, he was both handsome and enamoured. Now came a still more important question.
Which predominated in Fanny's heart, personal sympathy or anti-
pathy? Or, rather, were Plumtre's irritating or disharmonious qualities such as to offset her affection for him? Even if they were at present, this was not necessarily fatal to a happy marriage. Jane Austen
placed great weight on the power of marital habit and contiguity,
and the common interests of home and family. Were Fanny and
Plumtre free to marry at once, all would be well. But they were not
so free; they might have to wait for years to marry. This was the
critical consideration for Jane Austen. Fanny's love was too sickly a
plant to endure a long engagement.

Anna's affairs, which she did *not* discuss with her aunt, received no
such sympathetic analysis. Anna (according to a much later account
by one of her daughters), 'being dull when her brother went to
school got engaged to Michael Terry, a good looking neighbour – to

the displeasure of... her parents. Later she broke it off – also to their displeasure'.[18] The initial disapproval may have been occasioned by Terry's age; he was seventeen years older than Anna. It could scarcely have been to his position for he was rector of Dummer, a nearby parish, where his family were the principal proprietors. Jane Austen's attitude may be gauged from her satisfaction when on 27 May 1811 Anna missed a dinner engagement at which she would have met the Terrys; 'I think it always safest to keep her away from the family lest she should be doing too little or too much'.[19] Jane was no better pleased with Anna's second engagement, to Benjamin Lefroy, although he was a son of the woman she had most admired.

> Anna's engagement to Ben Lefroy... came upon us without much preparation; – at the same time, there was *that* about her which kept us in a constant preparation for something. – We are anxious to have it go on well, there being quite as much in his favour as the Chances are likely to give her in any matrimonial connection. I beleive he is sensible, certainly very religious, well connected & with some Independance. – There is an unfortunate dissimularity of Taste between them in one respect which gives us some apprehensions, he hates company & she is very fond of it; – this, with some queerness of Temper on his side & much unsteadiness on hers, is untoward.[20]

Though Lefroy came of a well-to-do clerical family, he had little money himself, and his best prospect lay in taking orders and securing eventually a Lefroy or some other living. But this ran athwart his religious scruples; he was apparently an Evangelical. Jane Austen's comment of 26 October 1813 suggests impatience with high-wrought conscientiousness:

> I have had a late account from Steventon, and a baddish one, as far as Ben is concerned. He has declined a curacy (apparently highly eligible), which he might have secured against his taking orders; and, upon its being made rather a serious question, says he has not made up his mind as to taking orders so early, and that, if her father makes a point of it, he must give Anna up rather than do what he does not approve. He must be maddish. They are going on again at present as before – but it cannot last.[21]

Anna persisted with the match, and was married on 8 November 1814, albeit without éclat or the presence of either of her aunts, 'the formidables'.[22] Jane Austen did, however, approve Anna's absence of triumph or show in her new condition. 'Her Letters have been very sensible & satisfactory, with no *parade* of happiness, which I liked them the better for,' she told Fanny soon after the wedding; '– I have often known young married Women write in a way I did not like, in that respect'.[23]

II

From all this, we can develop and refine certain of the conclusions of Chapters Two and Three, 'The Female Economy' and 'Receiving and Spending'; we can deduce a good deal more of Jane Austen's complex system of evaluation in girls' chief concern, potential husbands and marriage. There were many initial considerations: sufficiency of money, parity of rank, the sort of family to be joined, the location of the new home, and seriousness of principle and religion. Beyond these, of course, personal attraction mattered. A girl's worst fate was a loveless marriage, which might well lead on to future misery or even vice. But love was by no means the automatic reward of merit; ultimately, it was a subjective thing, not easily explicable. Reason and prudence should be counsellors, not kings. Yet Jane Austen was painfully alive to girls' difficulties when called on for a decision. The heart did not always – perhaps did not often – speak imperatively. How were the degrees of inclination and disinclination to be balanced against each other, and how was the answer to be measured against unknown future possibilities? How far to submit to parental encouragement or disapproval? How much was one's fortune 'worth', if one possessed one? How rapidly did one have to calculate the sum of factors, with precipitance or delay presenting perhaps equal dangers?

Perhaps the most striking feature of Jane Austen's 'system' was her concept of the marital relationship as dynamic. Apparently, a moderate measure of affection was enough for a girl to launch herself safely into marriage, provided the man was worthwhile and attached. Marianne Dashwood's 'extraordinary fate' duly reflected her creator's belief.

> With such a confederacy against her – with a knowledge so intimate of his goodness – with a conviction of his fond attachment to herself... what could she do?... that Marianne found her own happiness in forming his, was equally the persuasion and delight of each observing friend. Marianne could never love by halves; and

her whole heart became, in time, as much devoted to her husband, as it had once been to Willoughby.[24]

Correspondingly, with some assistance from various disclosures of perfidy and magnanimity, Elizabeth Bennet 'grew' out of her initial enchantment with Wickham and into a respectful affection for Darcy, which would (we may safely assume) deepen as married love. It is true however that Jane Austen's heroines were, in general, totally committed in heart before being engaged by hand. The novel's conventions and her plots did not allow too close a reflection of reality.

They certainly did not allow too close a consideration of the dark aspect of contemporary matrimony. But in fact Jane Austen was acutely sensitive to the unpleasant side of one natural consequence of marriage, child-bearing. When James's second wife, Mary, was expecting her second child, she wrote, 'Mrs Coulthard and Anne, late of Manydown, are both dead, and both died in childbed. We have not regaled Mary with this news'; and after the baby was born, 'Mary does not manage matters in such a way as to make me want to lay in myself... things are not in that comfort and style about her which are necessary to make such a situation an enviable one'.[25] Two other of her sisters-in-law were to die later as a consequence of repeated child-bearing;[26] and once, hearing of another pregnancy in an already large family, she drily noted, ''I w^d recommend to her [Mrs Deedes] & Mr D. the simple regimen of separate rooms'.[27] Shortly before her death she wrote to Fanny, 'Mrs Clement too is in that way again. I am quite tired of so many Children'.[28] Jane Austen was no friend of early marriages. When Fanny was already twenty-four years old, she told her, 'by not beginning the business of Mothering quite so early in life, you will be young in Constitution, spirits, figure & countenance, while Mrs Wm Hammond [a friend of Fanny, younger than herself] is growing old by confinements & nursing'.[29] When she believed that her other elder niece, Anna Lefroy, was expecting her third child within three years of marriage, she wrote, 'Anna has not a chance of escape.... Poor Animal, she will be worn out before she is thirty'.[30]

It would be quite misleading however to suppose that Jane Austen was inimical to marriage or maternity. Whatever we make of it, she repeatedly used the metaphor of child-bearing for her own novel-writing, as in her well-known reply to Cassandra's query, 'No indeed, I am never too busy to think of S & S. I can no more forget it, than a mother can forget her sucking child',[31] or her note to Anna after her first baby was born, 'As I wish very much to see *your* Jemima, I am sure you will like to see *my* Emma'.[32] Even in middle age she was as eager as a girl in canvassing her favourite Fanny's marriage prospects. She believed her to be *'very* capable... of being really in love'; she told her, 'I do wish you to marry very much, because I know you will never be happy till you are'; and having written of spinsters' poverty as 'one very strong argument in favour of Matrimony', she continued, 'but I need not dwell on such arguments with *you*, pretty Dear, you do not want inclination'.[33] With what complacent and happy irony did she describe Fanny's flirtation with a young London surgeon, C. T. Haden:

> then came the dinner & Mr Haden who brought good Manners & clever conversation; – from 7 to 8 the Harp; at 8 Mrs L. & Miss E. arrived – & for the rest of the even^g the Draw^g-room was thus arranged, on the Sopha-side the two Ladies Henry & myself making the best of it, on the opposite side Fanny & Mr Haden in two chairs (I *believe* at least they had *two* chairs) talking together uninterruptedly. – Fancy the scene! And what is to be fancied next? – Why that Mr H. dines here again tomorrow.[34]

With what feigned alarm but underlying satisfaction did she greet the report that another east Kent heir, James Wildman, wished to fix his interest on Fanny:

> Oh! what a loss it will be when you are married. You are too agreable in your single state, too agreable as a Neice. I shall hate you when your delicious play of Mind is all settled down into conjugal & maternal affections.
>
> Mr J. W. frightens me. – He will have you. – I see you at the Altar. – I have *some* faith in Mrs C. Cage's observation, & still more in Lizzy's; & besides, I know it *must* be so. He must be wishing to attach you. It would be too stupid & too shameful in him, to be otherwise; & all the Family are seeking your acquaintance. – Do not imagine that I have any real objection, I have rather taken a fancy to him than not, & I like Chilham Castle for you; – I only do not like you sh^d marry anybody.[35]

Jane Austen did not try to be much wiser than the world at large. For her, as for almost all the rest, marriage and children were still a girl's natural and best aspiration. Everyday experience told her that matrimony cut short many girls' lives, and aged many girls pre-

maturely and that sometimes, it might even end in utter wretchedness: 'nothing can compare to the misery of being bound *without*
Love, bound to one, & preferring another'.[36] All this may have made
her an advocate of sincere attachment and circumspect delay, as well
as material prudence, in the marking down or acceptance of a marriage partner. But if these conditions were met, there should be no
hesitation in marrying. Whatever the risks, it was the accepted – and
for nine-tenths of people, the only – mode of self-fulfilment for a
woman.

III

'Poor woman, I shall support her as long as I can, because she *is* a
Woman, & because I hate her Husband', Jane Austen wrote of Prin-
cess Caroline on 16 February 1813.[37] It was one of her very rare expressions of female solidarity. Generally she spoke of her own sex,
relative to men, in deprecatory terms. This is reflected quite commonly in her novels. In *Northanger Abbey* Mrs Allen is introduced as
one 'of that numerous class of females, whose society can raise no
other emotion than surprise at there being any men in the world who
could like them well enough to marry them'.[38] Mrs Bennet (of *Pride
and Prejudice*) and Mrs Palmer (of *Sense and Sensibility*) are also members of 'that numerous class', though in these particular cases the surprise might be tempered by their having once been lovely girls. Mr
Bennet,

> captivated by youth and beauty, and that appearance of good
> humour, which youth and beauty generally give, had married a
> woman whose weak understanding and illiberal mind, had very
> early in their marriage put an end to all real affection for her. Re-
> spect, esteem and confidence, had vanished for ever; and all his
> views of domestic happiness were overthrown.[39]

Mr Palmer had made the same mistake. 'His temper might perhaps
be a little soured by finding, like many others of his sex, that through
some unaccountable bias in favour of beauty, he was the husband of
a very silly woman, – but she [Elinor] knew that this kind of blunder
was too common for any sensible man to be lastingly hurt by it'.[40]
There are, it is true, some male counterparts in the novels, most
notably perhaps Sir Walter Elliot in *Persuasion*, whose 'good looks
and rank' had won him 'a wife of very superior character to any

thing deserved by his own'. Lady Elliot paid as dearly as Mr Bennet or Mr Palmer for her 'youthful infatuation'. But a distinction must be made. Whereas Bennet and Palmer could take some general revenge on the world at large for their early folly, Lady Elliot perforce 'humoured, or softened, or concealed his [Sir Walter's] failings, and promoted his real respectability for seventeen years', until her death.[41] Silliness, like so much else, was not an equal matter between the sexes.

Whether because of girls' conditioning, or because of self-disparagement, or her own dependent status, or the masking of her real opinion, Jane Austen placed a low value on female capacities where they trenched on men's 'fields'. With perhaps a little, but not very much, tongue in cheek, she told the Revd J. S. Clarke that a clergyman such as he had proposed to her for a character

> must at times [converse] on the subjects of science and philosophy, of which I know nothing; or at least be occasionally abundant in quotations and allusions which a woman who, like me, knows only her own mother tongue, and has read very little in that, would be totally without the power of giving. . . . I think I may boast myself to be, with all possible vanity, the most unlearned and uninformed female who ever dared to be an authoress.[42]

She seemed almost determined to argue against intellectuality or erudition in or for girls. Her own formal school years were few. Before she was eight years old she was sent to Mrs Cawley's school at Oxford (and later Southampton), probably so that she would not be separated from her beloved Cassandra. When 'putrid fever' struck the school disastrously, the little girls were transferred to another in Reading. This, the Abbey School, was a pleasant, easygoing and haphazard establishment, where the pupils were not hard pressed by instruction. After nearly two years there however the young Austens were withdrawn (probably for economy, possibly to pick up a better education from even the casual ministrations of their father and brothers at home, perhaps because the rectory at Steventon was now less crowded than before), so that Jane's schooling proper ended when she was eleven years of age. None the less, she read and listened herself into a wide knowledge of English literature, considerable information on history and religion, and a miscellaneous but impressive general culture.

Yet either she did not realize or she concealed the extent of her own attainments; and this was emblematic of her attitude to girls' education. It was with complacency rather than contempt that she declared that the mind of the heroine of *Northanger Abbey* was 'as ignorant and uninformed as the female mind at seventeen usually is'.[43] She did not expect a great deal from girls' schools. When the headmistress of a school in Bath consulted her about an applicant for a position, she reported: 'having a very reasonable Lady to deal with, one who only required a *tolerable* temper, my office was not difficult. – Were I going to send a girl to school I would send her to this person; to be rational in anything is great praise, especially in the ignorant class of school mistresses'.[44] In *Emma* she clearly endorsed Mrs Goddard's modest venture, with forty pupils, at Highbury.

> Mrs Goddard was the mistress of a School – not of a seminary, or an establishment, or any thing which professed, in long sentences of refined nonsense, to combine liberal acquirements with elegant morality upon new principles and new systems – and where young ladies for enormous pay might be screwed out of health and into vanity – but a real, honest, old-fashioned Boarding-school, where a reasonable quantity of accomplishments were sold at a reasonable price, and where girls might be sent to be out of the way and scramble themselves into a little education, without any danger of coming back prodigies.[45]

Mrs Goddard (probably based on the warm-hearted but decidedly unintellectual proprietress of the Abbey School, Mrs La Tournelle) was prized for her motherliness, health care and lavish provision of 'wholesome food' rather than her academic values.

With this particular type of education, Jane Austen contrasted – altogether to its disadvantage – that which stressed refinements, accomplishments and ladyship. Her best-known satire on the second form is probably Miss Bingley's encomium of it in *Pride and Prejudice*:

> 'no one can be really esteemed accomplished, who does not greatly surpass what is usually met with. A woman must have a thorough knowledge of music, singing, drawing, dancing, and the modern languages, to deserve the word; and besides all this, she must possess a certain something in her air and manner of walking, the tone of her voice, her address and expressions, or the word will be but half deserved.'[46]

Jane Austen's most direct and downright criticism was delivered, however, when she was only sixteen years old. Camilla Stanley, a rich girl of eighteen and the anti-heroine of her very early fragment, *Catharine, or The Bower,*

> had been attended by the most capital Masters from the time of her being six years old to the last Spring; which, comprehending a period of twelve Years, had been dedicated to the acquirement of Accomplishments which were now to be displayed and in a few Years entirely neglected.
>
> She was not...naturally...deficient in Abilities; but those Years which ought to have been spent in the attainment of useful knowledge and Mental Improvement, had been all bestowed in learning Drawing, Italian, and Music, more especially the latter, and she now united to these Accomplishments, an Understanding unimproved by reading and a Mind totally devoid either of Taste or judgement.... All her ideas were towards the elegance of her appearance, the fashion of her dress, and the Admiration she wished them to excite. She professed a love of Books without Reading, was Lively without Wit, and generally good humoured without Merit.[47]

But *Catharine, or The Bower* also expounds Jane Austen's more positive conceptions of feminine education – all the more effectively because, in this respect at least, Kitty (Catharine) was patently Jane's *alter ego*. Kitty was 'a great...tho' perhaps not a very deep' reader, well versed in modern history as well as literature 'of a lighter kind'. She begins the sounding out of Camilla by discussing particular novels. Whereas Kitty is a sharp and indefatigable critic, Camilla's opinion of the books can go no further than 'the sweetest things in the world', though overlong. Kitty presses her on particular passages and episodes, only to find that Camilla has 'missed them all, because I was in such a hurry to know the end of it' (pp. 198-9). Later, when the ground shifts to English history, Kitty refuses to allow any intrinsic merit to Queen Elizabeth's extraordinary cleverness and length of reign:

> 'they are very far from making me wish her return, for if she were to come again with the same Abilities and the same good Constitution She might do as much Mischief and last as long as she did before – Then turning to Camilla, who had been sitting very silent for some time, she added, What do *you* think of Elizabeth, Miss Stanley? I hope you will not defend her.'
>
> 'Oh! dear, said Miss Stanley, I know nothing of Politics, and cannot bear to hear them mentioned.' Kitty started at this repulse,

but made no answer; that Miss Stanley must be ignorant of what she could not distinguish from Politics she felt perfectly convinced.   (p. 201)

The essential point of these contrasts is to explain, at least partially, the differences in moral development between the girls. Camilla is not vicious by nature, but vain, vapid and materialistic by education. Kitty falls into errors from inexperience and impulsiveness, but has acquired the fundamentals of judgment and self-control by serious reading and application. Camilla's 'temper was by nature good, but unassisted by reflection, she had neither patience under Disappointment, nor could sacrifice her own inclinations to promote the happiness of others'(p. 198). But Kitty, when cruelly prevented by illness from dancing at a ball to which she had most eagerly looked forward,

> was not so totally void of philosophy as many Girls of her age, might have been in her situation. She considered that there were Misfortunes of a much greater magnitude than the loss of a Ball, experienced every day by some part of Mortality, and that the time might come when She would herself look back with wonder and perhaps with Envy on her having known no greater vexation.
> (p. 208)

The values with which they have been respectively imbued are manifested in an early exchange between them on sending a fortuneless girl out to India to find a husband. 'I cannot conceive the hardship of going out in a very agreeable Manner with two or three sweet Girls for Companions', declared Camilla,

> 'having a delightful voyage to Bengal or Barbadoes or wherever it is, and being married soon after one's arrival to a very charming Man immensely rich –. I see no hardship in all that.'
> 'Your representation of the Affair, said Kitty laughing, certainly gives a very different idea of it from Mine. But supposing all this to be true, still, as it was by no means certain that she would be so fortunate either in her voyage, her Companions, or her husband; in being obliged to run the risk of their proving very different, she undoubtedly experienced a great hardship –. Besides, to a Girl of any Delicacy, the voyage in itself, since the object of it is so universally known, is a punishment that needs no other to make it very severe.'
> 'I do not see that at all. She is not the first Girl who has gone to

the East Indies for a Husband, and I declare I should think it very
good fun if I were as poor.'   (p. 205)

The bringing up of girls is an underlying theme of *Catharine*.
There is no suggestion that their education should emulate or even
equal boys'. Obedient to the principle of the day (doubtless reinforced by the unquestioned assumptions of her father and
brothers), Jane Austen took classics to be the bedrock of advanced
education, and this was almost universally denied to females. Yet she
evidently regarded her own sort of education – in part guided reading, in part participation in the endless family 'seminar' of the dining
table and sitting-room, in part autodidactic – as the feminine
counterpart to the sort of intellectual gymnasium which the classics
were meant to afford boys. The mind was not only accumulatively
furnished, it was also exercised into strength and power. It is perhaps
not too much to see in a debate between Kitty and Camilla's brother
on the character of Richard III (like Queen Elizabeth, one of Jane
Austen's own *bêtes noires*) a symbol of the differences which nature
and the forms of education produced in girls and boys. Kitty, to
whom the king was abhorrent, believed

> that both in Natural Abilities, & acquired information, Edward
> Stanley was infinitely superior to his Sister. Her desire of knowing
> that he was so, had induced her to take every opportunity of turn-
> ing the Conversation on history and they were very soon engaged
> in an historical dispute, for which no one was more calculated than
> Stanley who was so far from being really of any party that he had
> scarcely a fixed opinion on the Subject. He could therefore always
> take either side, & always argue with temper. In his indifference on
> all such topics he was very unlike his Companion, whose judge-
> ment being guided by her feelings which were eager & warm, was
> easily decided and though it was not always infallible, she
> defended it with a Spirit & Enthusiasm which marked her own re-
> liance on it.   (pp. 230-1)

Although Kitty remained infatuated with him, Edward Stanley
proved something of a self-willed puppy, certainly not the ideal pro-
duct of any system of education. None the less, even in what she
wrote as a sixteen-year-old, Jane Austen's educational philosophy
stands firm. As with courtship and marriage decisions, she made
temperate and realistic judgments under the conditions of the day.
Girls should be brought up – or so directed as to bring themselves up
– as rational, considerate, well-judging beings of taste, integrity and

discrimination. To reach such a height, their best climbing frame was history and literature in their own language and the general culture to be acquired from serious conversation and interchange. This was the closest approximation to the classical proving ground available to the female young. At all costs was mere 'ladyism' to be eschewed. Its fruits were affectation, vanity, pretension, ignorance and selfishness. True to her mentor Dr Johnson, and even as a girl herself, Jane Austen believed that the final ends of all didacticism should be sound morality and the capacity to comport oneself sensibly and judiciously in the world.

IV

Although we know even less about Jane Austen's early girlhood than Catherine Morland's, we know enough at least to make it clear that Catherine in *Northanger Abbey* was no portrait of the artist when young. The description of Catherine at ten, a 'thin awkward figure ... dark lank hair, and strong features',[48] might have fitted Jane – but for the hair; and there is a ring of actual author's experience about

> 'Catherine grows quite a good-looking girl, – she is almost pretty today,' were words which caught her ears now and then; and how welcome were the sounds! To look *almost* pretty, is an acquisition of higher delight to a girl who has been looking plain the first fifteen years of her life, than a beauty from her cradle can ever receive.   (p. 15)

But there is no evidence that Jane Austen was at any stage 'fond of all boys' plays' (p. 13). She was dextrous manually. For all we know, she might, like Catherine, have 'loved nothing so well in the world as rolling down the green slope at the back of the house' (p. 14); Steventon rectory no less than Fullerton Parsonage offered the necessary amenity.[49] But nothing hints at tomboyishness in Jane, and, unlike Catherine, she had an elder sister, a feminine pattern to follow, in Cassandra. Jane Austen did not abandon music, as Catherine did, at the first chance, but played the piano regularly in the early mornings all her life, whenever an instrument was available. She belonged moreover to a decidedly bookish and even scholarly family, whereas the Morlands' reading matter may have extended no further than the conventional collections of Shakespeare and poetry, and the *Mirror* among 'the books upstairs' (p. 241). We may be sure that Catherine did not follow her creator in becoming steeped in, let alone admiring, Dr Johnson, Richardson, Pope or Cowper. Catherine had no literary-minded elder brothers to help form her taste, no plays to watch or perform in the parlour or farmyard barn, no home industry of skit- and pastiche-making for family entertainment from which to learn. At seventeen, she was ill-read and naïve enough to take trashy novels seriously; by the same age, Jane had already spent several years in gibbeting them savagely.

Yet Catherine embodied Jane Austen's values. She did so by nature rather than philosophy. We are told at the outset – it is a sort of governing text – 'what her character is meant to be. . . . her heart was affectionate, her disposition cheerful and open, without conceit or affectation of any kind' (p. 18). Catherine stands for various qualities which Jane Austen, in principle at any rate, prized most in a girl: candour, artlessness, sincerity, directness and simplicity. In all this, Isabella Thorpe is the complete foil. She epitomizes everything that is censurable in a girl. She is incapable of true affection, neither cheerful nor open, steeped in pretence and artifice, a false friend and conscienceless pursuer of self-interest.

Both Catherine's troubles and her later joys arise from her ingenuousness and humility. It is these qualities which attract Henry Tilney – even if only, at first, in providing him with a theatre to display his social talents. It is also these which expose her to Isabella's exploitation. To Isabella, Catherine constitutes merely another means of securing James Morland for her husband; and with Isabella's vastly superior knowledge of the critical subjects of 'dress, balls, flirtations and quizzes', Catherine is almost effortlessly overcome at their first meeting.

> Their increasing attachment was not to be satisfied with half a dozen turns in the Pump-room, but required, when they all quitted it together, that Miss Thorpe should accompany Miss Morland to the very door of Mr Allen's house; and that they should there part with a most affectionate and lengthened shake of hands, after learning, to their mutual relief, that they should see each other across the theatre at night, and say their prayers in the same chapel the next morning. Catherine then ran directly up stairs, and watched Miss Thorpe's progress down the street from the drawing-room window; admired the graceful spirit of her walk, the fashionable air of her figure and dress, and felt grateful, as well she might, for the chance which had procured her such a friend.   (p. 34)

The intimacy ripens with such tropical exuberance that Catherine is soon led, though innocently, into joining Isabella's enterprise of hunting down two unknown young men in order to deny them the satisfaction of thinking that they were pursued.

Catherine is almost equally taken in by John Thorpe initially. To conquer her instinctive repugnance, it was enough that he should engage her at once to dance at the Upper Rooms and (according to Isabella) declare her to be delightful. 'Had she been older or vainer, such attacks might have done little; but, where youth and diffidence are united, it requires uncommon steadiness of reason to resist the attraction of being called the most charming girl in the world, and of being so very early engaged as a partner' (p. 50). In this particular instance, however, Catherine's social 'education' began almost immediately. John Thorpe failed to present himself to her when the dancing started, and she suffered all the shame of seeming to be an unchosen girl while in reality she had been bespoken for more than half a day. Worse still, her engagement with Thorpe forced her, most unwillingly, to decline Henry Tilney's invitation to partner him. Her first ill-impression of Thorpe bounded back as 'one mortification succeeded another, and from the whole she deduced this useful lesson, that to go previously engaged to a ball, does not necessarily increase either the dignity or enjoyment of a young lady' (p. 55). Next day, in relief at her own unexpected physical safety in his curricle, Catherine was happy enough to echo John Thorpe's high estimate of his own horse and carriage. But when he turned his laudations on himself, even she timidly revolted.

> Little as Catherine was in the habit of judging for her self, and unfixed as were her general notions of what men ought to be, she could not entirely repress a doubt, while she bore with the effusions of his endless conceit, of his being altogether completely agreeable. It was a bold surmise, for he was Isabella's brother; and she had been assured by James, that his manners would recommend him to all her sex; but in spite of this, the extreme weariness of his company, which crept over her before they had been out an hour, and which continued unceasingly to increase till they stopped in Pulteney-street again, induced her, in some small degree, to resist such high authority, and to distrust his powers of giving universal pleasure.   (pp. 66–7)

From this on, Thorpe's odious interventions tended to come between her and meeting Henry Tilney. Nothing could have sharpened

her judgment more. After her second drive with Thorpe, at the in-
voluntary cost of an afternoon's walk with Henry and his sister, it
was clear to Catherine – all 'expert' opinion notwithstanding – that
'John Thorpe himself was quite disagreeable' (p. 69). John's sister
however continued to impose upon the simple Catherine. The
glamour of her engagement to James, combined with her continued
cataracts of professed affection, kept Catherine enthralled. The
female confidante was much more difficult to see through than the
boorish suitor. So it was that, despite several premonitory indications of Isabella's double-dealing, the ardent 'friendship' was still intact when Catherine set out for Northanger Abbey. 'The embraces,
tears, and promises of the parting fair ones may be fancied' (p.153).

V

Henry Tilney 'educated' Catherine differently. At first meeting, even
she was momentarily offended at being fooled by his mock praise of
ladies' letter-writing, and 'feared, as she listened to their [Mrs Allen's
and his] discourse [on muslins], that he indulged himself a little too
much with the foibles of others'. A short time before, she had been
on the point of calling him 'strange' to his face (pp. 28-9).

This was however the beginning and end of Catherine's interior
criticism of Henry. From then on, his dazzling attraction blinded her
to any fault, and she and he fell into a type of pupil-master interchange. She was a pupil who longed to please as well as learn. On the
walk around Beecham Cliff, Catherine's ignorance of drawing
served her well.

> Where people wish to attach, they should always be ignorant. To
> come with a well-informed mind, is to come with an inability of
> administering to the vanity of others, which a sensible person
> would always wish to avoid. A woman especially, if she have the
> misfortune of knowing any thing, should conceal it as well as she
> can. . . . Catherine did not know her own advantages – did not
> know that a good-looking girl, with an affectionate heart and a
> very ignorant mind, cannot fail of attracting a clever young man,
> unless circumstances are particularly untoward. In the present in-
> stance, she confessed and lamented her want of knowledge;
> declared that she would give any thing in the world to be able to
> draw; and a lecture on the picturesque immediately followed, in
> which his instructions were so clear that she soon began to see

1 Jane Austen, a portrait by Cassandra Austen, *c*. 1810.

2 Portrait of Revd George Austen, Jane's father.

3 Portrait of Revd James Austen, Jane's eldest brother.

4 Portrait of Revd Henry Austen,
Jane's fourth brother.

5 Portrait of Anna Austen, Jane's
niece.

beauty in every thing admired by him, and her attention was so earnest, that he became perfectly satisfied of her having a great deal of natural taste. (pp. 110–11)

Yet Catherine herself has something to teach the Tilneys. From time to time, her utter candour cuts more deeply than the stock opinion of the sophisticated. Given the nature of the books used in the contemporary schoolroom, her appraisal of history as the 'quarrels of popes and kings, with wars or pestilences, in every page; the men all so good for nothing, and hardly any women at all', and her distaste for historians' 'inventions' (the imaginary speeches put in the mouths of their characters), seem much more apropos than Miss Tilney's anodyne commendations (p. 108). And how close to the reality of the thing seems her simple account of child education, in the course of the same exchange:

'You think me foolish to call instruction a torment, but if you had been as much used as myself to hear poor little children first learning their letters and then learning to spell, if you had ever seen how stupid they can be for a whole morning together, and how tired my poor mother is at the end of it, as I am in the habit of seeing almost every day of my life at home, you would allow that to *torment* and to *instruct* might sometimes be used as synonimous words.' (p. 110)

Earlier the same limpid simplicity had turned the tables on Henry Tilney, when at the theatre Catherine pleaded her innocence in missing their earlier engagement for the walk.

'But, Mr Tilney, why were *you* less generous than your sister? If she felt such confidence in my good intentions, and could suppose it to be only a mistake, why should you be so ready to take offence?'
'Me! – I take offence!'
'Nay, I am sure by your look, when you came into the box, you were angry.'
'I angry! I could have no right.'
'Well, nobody would have thought you had no right who saw your face.' He replied by asking her to make room for him, and talking of the play. (pp. 94–5)

Up to a point, the history of Catherine's romance is contained in the single phrase, 'in finding him irresistible, becoming so herself' (p. 131). But this describes only the physics and chemistry of love. Moral

worth and depth have also to be established. Miss Tilney's intervention is critical in clearing Henry of possible coxcombry or mild
cruelty disguised as teasing.

> 'We shall get nothing more serious from him now, Miss Morland.
> He is not in a sober mood. But I do assure you that he must be en-
> tirely misunderstood, if he can ever appear to say an unjust thing
> of any woman at all, or an unkind one of me.'
>
> It was no effort to Catherine to believe that Henry Tilney could
> never be wrong. His manner might sometimes surprize, but his
> meaning must always be just: – and what she did not understand,
> she was almost as ready to admire, as what she did.   (p. 114)

Catherine's faith was wonderfully justified by Henry's delicate concern for her, and chivalry, when he uncovered her grotesque suspicion (bred by Gothick fantasies) that his father had murdered Mrs
Tilney. He drew the truth from her gradually and gently, and when
he next met her 'the only difference in his behaviour to her, was that
he paid her rather more attention than usual' (p. 199). Thereafter, his
'astonishing generosity and nobleness of conduct, in never alluding
in the slightest way to what had passed', restored her self-esteem,
and in time 'her spirits became... capable, as heretofore, of continual
improvement by any thing he said' (p. 201).

Catherine's education had advanced decisively. She could no
longer comprehend her own gullibility, and inability to distinguish
the real and the imagined, of even a few days before. The schoolgirl
had been sloughed off. When Isabella, having meanwhile jilted James
Morland, attempted to regain her footing with him by pretending
that he had misunderstood her, Catherine now saw through her
'shallow artifice.... She was ashamed of Isabella, and ashamed of
having ever loved her. Her professions of attachment were now as
disgusting as her excuses were empty, and her demands impudent'.
Henry richly rewarded Catherine's new-found penetration by telling
her, when she sought to palliate Isabella's treachery by blaming Fred-
erick Tilney also, that her mind was 'warped by an innate principle
of general integrity' (pp. 218-19). In growing up, Catherine had
grown out of the illusions of inexperience, but had not changed
essentially. Henry Tilney was extraordinarily percipient, and had he
not discerned almost at once her moral excellence, her irresistibility
in finding him irresistible would never have become operative. As
early as their fifth meeting, he made clear the pre-condition which,
satisfied, had allowed her undisguisable admiration for him to do its

work. 'How very little trouble it can give you', Henry said to her,

'to understand the motive of other people's actions.'

'Why? – What do you mean?'

'With you, it is not, How is such a one likely to be influenced? What is the inducement most likely to act upon such a person's feelings, age, situation, and probable habits of life considered? – but, how should *I* be influenced, what would be *my* inducement in acting so and so?'

'I do not understand you.'

'Then we are on very unequal terms, for I understand you perfectly well.'

'Me? – yes; I cannot speak well enough to be unintelligible.'

'Bravo! – an excellent satire on modern language.'

'But pray tell me what you mean.'

'Shall I indeed? – Do you really desire it? – But you are not aware of the consequences; it will involve you in a very cruel embarrassment, and certainly bring on a disagreement between us.'

'No, no; it shall not do either; I am not afraid.'

'Well then, I only meant that your attributing my brother's wish of dancing with Miss Thorpe to good-nature alone, convinced me of your being superior in good-nature yourself to all the rest of the world.' (pp. 132-3)

As the story advances and Catherine matures, Henry's rather patronizing playfulness and superior mien towards her drop away; and she in turn justifies being taken seriously by the dignity, yet justness, with which she meets the blow of her sudden expulsion from Northanger Abbey. When Miss Tilney begged to learn of her safe arrival at her home, but (to escape the General's wrath) under cover of a letter addressed to the maidservant, Catherine at first refused, in resentful indignation; but a further appeal 'with the look of sorrow accompanying it, was enough to melt Catherine's pride in a moment, and she instantly said, "Oh, Eleanor, I *will* write to you indeed"' (p. 229). On her *via dolorosa* to Fullerton, it was one of her chief dreads that the innocent Henry and Eleanor would be blamed equally with the General by her outraged family: 'should a dislike be taken against them, . . . on their father's account, it would cut her to the heart' (p. 232). Her trust in Henry never wavered. Had he (she told herself) revealed her odious suspicion to the General, it must have been by some wretched accident or inadvertence.

It is effective to have the last scenes in the book played out in Catherine's home, for this deepens our comprehension of her fair-mindedness, freedom from affectation, and basic good sense by showing us the seed-bed from which these had sprung. The Morlands proved that they 'were far from being an irritable race; far from any quickness in catching, or bitterness in resenting affronts'. Mr and Mrs Morland could not but regard the General's conduct as not only inexplicable but also ungentlemanly and irresponsible. But 'it did not oppress them . . . and, after a due course of useless conjecture, that, "it was a strange business, and that he must be a very strange man," grew enough for all their indignation and wonder' (pp. 233–4). Henry Tilney discovered their equability and magnanimity for himself when he made his embarrassed way to the Parsonage. When he apologized to Catherine's mother, he

> did not address himself to an uncandid judge or a resentful heart. Far from comprehending him or his sister in their father's misconduct, Mrs Morland had been always kindly disposed towards each, and instantly, pleased by his appearance, received him with the simple professions of unaffected benevolence; thanking him for such an attention to her daughter, assuring him that the friends of her children were always welcome there, and intreating him to say not another word of the past.   (p. 242)

After being surprised by Henry's application for Catherine's hand (though only temporarily, for 'nothing, after all, could be more natural than Catherine's being beloved'), Mrs Morland provided what may serve as a sort of retrospective motto for *Northanger Abbey*: '"Catherine would make a sad heedless young house-keeper to be sure" . . . but quick was the consolation of there being nothing like practice' (p. 249). Catherine had gone to Bath a sad heedless young girl, having grown up in country isolation. But a little practice in society at large had soon dispersed the silliness and credulity which went with her inexperience and youth. The solidity of her worth and merit of her character then stood clear. In speaking satirically of Isabella, and unintentionally of Catherine herself, Henry Tilney had given shape to Jane Austen's idea of what a girl emerging in the world should be: '"Open, candid, artless, guileless, with affections strong but simple, forming no pretensions, and knowing no disguise"' (p. 206).

VI

In every sense, girls are the problem in *Pride and Prejudice*. The Bennets' superfluity of daughters and lack of a male heir form the book's
central difficulty. The Lucases share the first part of this difficulty, in
a lesser form. Miss Darcy has been (and to some extent still is) a
problem for her brother. Miss Bingley's problem is to dispose of
herself as she desires. The heiresses, great and small, Anne de
Bourgh and Mary King, are problems for their mothers to dispose
of. At least eight girls in the novel (stretching the term 'girl' to cover
at least a twelve-year span in age) are fully, or fairly fully, delineated.
Their characters and prospects vary widely. But all pose essentially
the same question to themselves or others – how were they to be
settled in the world?

The Bennet girls form the book's core group. Each has the identical disadvantage of a negligible dowry (£1,000 at most after their
parents' deaths) and the prospect of a calamitous decline in social significance after their middle-aged father dies and the family estate
passes into other hands. Elizabeth and Lydia Bennet are the counterparts of Catherine Morland and Isabella Thorpe, standing respectively for what is commendatory and condemnatory in girls. The
first pair are much the more finely and intricately drawn as characters, but the respective roles are substantially the same. Elizabeth is
three years older than Catherine, far more sophisticated, far cleverer,
wittier and (despite her disclaimer that she is '*not* a great reader' and –
to Darcy – 'Books – Oh! no. – I am sure we never read the same'[50])
probably much the better read. Yet she undergoes a similar change to
Catherine. Albeit at greater depth at each particular stage, she grows
from girlhood to young womanhood during the novel's span.

For all her confidence in her own judgment, Elizabeth was for
long too callow to value either Darcy or Wickham at his true worth.
Perhaps the usual attribution of qualities should be here reversed.
Pride, and its cousin vanity, were *her* particular blinkers in this case,
just as the prejudices of class and conventionality were Darcy's.
(Characteristically, he observes early in the piece that the Bennet
girls' 'low connections' would '"very materially lessen their chance
of marrying men of any consideration in the world"' [pp. 36-7]).
Elizabeth was piqued that Darcy, at first meeting, thought her only
'tolerable' in looks and probably a bore to dance with (p. 12). Then
mortification was heaped upon mortification at the Bingleys' ball
when one member after another of her family exposed their vulgar-

ity, folly or indecorum to his disdain. Her humiliation fed her en-
mity towards him for a time. Conversely, she was flattered, and her
judgment accordingly warped, by Wickham's initial attentions. He
was, after all, 'the happy man towards whom almost every female
eye was turned' when he entered the Philips' drawing-room, 'and
Elizabeth was the happy woman by whom he finally seated himself'
(p. 76). Later, she was so infatuated by his continued preference for
her as to tell her aunt that

> 'he is, beyond all comparison, the most agreeable man I ever saw –
> and if he becomes really attached to me – I believe it will be better
> that he should not. I see the imprudence of it... [but] how can I
> promise to be wiser than so many of my fellow creatures if I am
> tempted, or how am I even to know that it would be wisdom to
> resist?'
> (pp. 144-5)

Elizabeth was however essentially just-minded, and the exculpa-
tory letter that she received from Darcy at Rosings opened her eyes
to her misjudgments.

> 'How despicably have I acted!' she cried. – 'I, who have prided
> myself on my discernment! – I, who have valued myself on my
> abilities!... Had I been in love, I could not have been more
> wretchedly blind. But vanity, not love, has been my folly. –
> Pleased with the preference of one, and offended by the neglect of
> the other, on the very beginning of our acquaintance, I have
> courted prepossession and ignorance, and driven reason away,
> where either were concerned. Till this moment, I never knew
> myself.'
> (p. 208)

Even Darcy's strictures on her family now struck her as no less than
'merited reproach'. Correspondingly, she at last saw Wickham for
what he truly was. As she recollected her first meeting with him in
the Philips' drawing-room, everything seemed to fall out in the
opposite pattern, as when the angle of vision is changed on the tumb-
ling cubes. Now his 'communications' to a stranger appeared gross
impropriety, 'his professions with his conduct' inconsistent, and his
self-assertion extraordinarily indelicate. She recalled that he had
assailed Darcy's character to no one but herself until Darcy and the
Bingley party had quit the neighbourhood.

> How differently did every thing now appear in which he was con-
> cerned! His attentions to Miss King were now the consequence of
> views solely and hatefully mercenary; and the mediocrity of her

fortune proved no longer the moderation of his wishes, but his eagerness to grasp at any thing. His behaviour to herself could now have had no tolerable motive; he had either been deceived with regard to her fortune, or had been gratifying his vanity by encouraging the preference which she believed she had most incautiously shewn.   (pp. 207, 209)

In her newly-found maturity, Elizabeth builds on fresh foundations, eschewing the apparently 'impulsive' choice that often masked self-regard. After her last meeting with Darcy at Lambton, 'gratitude and esteem' softened her feelings towards him. She had tried instant partiality with Wickham, and its 'ill-success might perhaps authorise her to seek the other less interesting mode of attachment' (p. 279). By the time that Lydia's marriage had been arranged, Elizabeth had become 'convinced that she could have been happy with him [Darcy]... the proposals which she had proudly spurned only four months ago, would now have been gladly and gratefully received!' Her change of heart sprang in part from her growing appreciation of all she would have gained from 'his judgment, information, and knowledge of the world' (pp. 311-12). The final revelation of Darcy's goodness, his decisive intervention in the odious Wickham's affairs, completed the conversion. 'For herself she was humbled; but she was proud of him. Proud that in a cause of compassion and honour, he had been able to get the better of himself' (p. 327). Morally, emotionally and intellectually, we have now a superior Elizabeth.

By contrast, Lydia's was a deteriorating course. She is introduced as a handsome, 'stout, well-grown girl of fifteen, with... high animal spirits, and a sort of natural self-consequence', but also silly, reckless and wild (p. 45). These traits have been thoroughly displayed, in speech and conduct, by the time that Elizabeth, after absorbing Darcy's condemnation of the majority of the family, elaborates it (and Kitty's subordinate character) in a dispirited reverie.

Her father, contented with laughing at them, would never exert himself to restrain the wild giddiness of his youngest daughters; and her mother, with manners so far from right herself, was entirely insensible of the evil... while they were supported by their mother's indulgence, what chance could there be of improvement? Catherine, weak-spirited, irritable, and completely under Lydia's guidance, had been always affronted by their advice; and Lydia, self-willed and careless, would scarcely give them a hearing. They were ignorant, idle, and vain.   (p. 213)

None the less, Elizabeth makes a last vicarious attempt at Lydia's reform. At home, she appeals to her father to intervene while there yet was time.

> 'If you, my dear father, will not take the trouble of checking her exuberant spirits, and of teaching her that her present pursuits are not to be the business of her life, she will soon be beyond the reach of amendment. Her character will be fixed, and she will, at sixteen, be the most determined flirt that ever made herself and her family ridiculous... from the ignorance and emptiness of her mind, wholly unable to ward off any portion of that universal contempt which her rage for admiration will excite. In this danger Kitty is also comprehended. She will follow wherever Lydia leads. Vain, ignorant, idle, and absolutely uncontrouled!'   (p. 231)

But, as ever, Mr Bennet laughed his way out of his family obligations, and Lydia more than realized Elizabeth's fears by eloping and then living 'in sin' with Wickham. Lydia was irredeemable. She returned to Longbourn, quite without consciousness of her wrongdoing, in fact glorying in her near-shotgun wedding. 'Lydia was Lydia still; untamed, unabashed, wild, noisy, and fearless' (p. 315). Her character was fixed: she retained, in later years, 'all the claims to reputation which her marriage had given her' (p. 387).

How did two girls in the same family come to differ so widely as Elizabeth and Lydia in development and fate? As we have seen, this would not in itself have presented Jane Austen with much perplexity: she took the sharp contrast which she noted in the personalities of her infant Lefroy grand-nieces in her stride, merely looking to severe discipline to bring the delinquent one closer in conduct to the meritorious. None the less, some answers to the question may be suggested.

First, the effects of heredity seem marked in both the girls. In her critical intelligence, readiness to face truth, wit, and ironic temper, Elizabeth is certainly Mr Bennet's child. As she is but a twenty-year-old girl, these qualities are softened and feminized in her case. Besides, 'there was a mixture of sweetness and archness in her manner which made it difficult for her to affront anyone' (p. 52). She is still – and because of other elements in her character and situation which are likely to remain – unsoiled, uncynical and unembittered. Even if '"Follies and nonsense, whims and inconsistencies *do* divert me... and I laugh at them whenever I can"' (p. 57), it was not too much for her to claim – or at least to 'hope' – that she never ridiculed what was wise or good. None the less, if we could blot out our knowledge of who is speaking, there are times when we might take a sally of Mr Bennet for Elizabeth's, and a sally of Elizabeth for Mr Bennet's, so close are their styles and temperaments to one another. Correspondingly, Lydia Bennet would seem to be drawn as a bolder, stronger version of her mother. Where Mrs Bennet is petulant, weak-minded and self-pitying, Lydia is wilful, giddy and wild. But the general lineaments of the two are much the same; and Mrs Bennet empathizes instinctively with Lydia's every move, whether it be chasing officers in scarlet coats, setting off for Brighton in high glee or glorying in the wedding ring itself, however disreputably acquired. Possibly Mrs Bennet was born less brazen than her youngest daughter; possibly her own mother had been less foolishly indulgent than herself, or her father a less negligent and destructive parent than Mr Bennet. No matter how we account for the differences, however, they are differences of degree, or shade, rather than differences of kind.

What of models as a contributory explanation of the divergence between the sisters? Despite her vigour and independent spirit, Elizabeth seriously respected, and even acknowledged the moral superiority of her elder sister Jane, who was close to her in age and interest. Are we meant to infer that Jane exerted a moderating influence on Elizabeth, perhaps even acted as her second conscience? Bitterly did she reproach herself, after Darcy had opened her eyes to the truth about Wickham and his family, that she had so '"often disdained the generous candour of my sister, and gratified my vanity, in useless or blameable distrust"' (p. 208). It may even be that Mr Bennet too helped to instil probity in the young Elizabeth. Presumably it took some time to complete even *his* disillusionment with his married state and he might still have exercised some positive force upon her while a child. Lydia however was not a girl for models, and Mrs Bennet's example could have done little more than license and accentuate her headlong self-indulgence. Contrariwise, Lydia dominated Kitty, the sister next to her in age, affording a deplorable but powerful model of one particular form of ill-reared girl.

The principal differentiating factor for Jane Austen was, however, education – including of course self-education. She makes it clear that this was sufficiently available to the Bennet girls, in what the Victorians would have termed a 'permissive but not compulsory' form. '"Do you play and sing?"', Lady Catherine demanded of Elizabeth,

'A little.'

'Oh! then – some time or other we shall be happy to hear you. Our instrument is a capital one, probably superior to – You shall try it some day. – Do your sisters play and sing?'

'One of them does.'

'Why did not you all learn? – You ought all to have learned. The Miss Webbs all play, and their father has not so good an income as your's. – Do you draw?'

'No, not at all.'

'What, none of you?'

'Not one.'

'That is very strange. But I suppose you had no opportunity. Your mother should have taken you to town every spring for the benefit of masters.'

'My mother would have had no objection, but my father hates London.'

'Has your governess left you?'

'We never had any governess.'

'No governess! How was that possible? Five daughters brought up at home without a governess! – I never heard of such a thing. Your mother must have been quite a slave to your education.'

Elizabeth could hardly help smiling, as she assured her that had not been the case.

'Then, who taught you? who attended to you? Without a governess you must have been neglected.'

'Compared with some families, I believe we were; but such of us as wished to learn, never wanted the means. We were always encouraged to read, and had all the masters that were necessary. Those who chose to be idle, certainly might.'   (pp. 164–5)

Elizabeth had certainly acquired an education for herself. Though she might depreciate her reading in order to score off Miss Bingley, her delight in Colonel Fitzwilliam's easy discussion of 'new books and music' (p. 172), as well as her common discourse, tell another story. Lydia, however, was chief among those who had chosen to be idle. Both Elizabeth and Mr Bennet call her 'ignorant' repeatedly; and her speech is occasionally ungrammatical as well as vulgar. Three times in succession she says 'Kitty and me' for 'Kitty and I' in describing their adventures when meeting Jane from the London coach: it is significant that the two other Austen characters guilty of this solecism are Mrs Elton and Lucy Steele. Evidently, then, the familiar climbing frame for girls' education was available to the Bennets – the fresh moral being that those who would not make the effort to train themselves must be both disciplined and set good example if they were not to end as frivolous and ill-formed as Lydia.

The 'accomplishments' type of girls' upbringing is dealt with as scathingly as the dark side of the *laissez-faire* 'system'. Its prime exemplars in *Pride and Prejudice* are Mrs Hurst and Miss Bingley. They 'had been educated in one of the first private seminaries in town', whence they emerged not only 'very fine ladies; not deficient in . . . the power of being agreeable where they chose it' but also 'proud and conceited', and devotees of frippery, and tawdry cultural adornment, as the hallmarks of the lady (p. 15). Mary Bennet is another professor of the creed of feminine accomplishments, an autodidact in the field. But in her case talentless 'playing and singing' and banal 'philosophy' represent only the desperate attempt of a plain girl to make some standing room for herself in the midst of a family of pretty sisters. Once the competitive pressure is relaxed, so too is Mary's devotion to her superficial acquirements. When she was at last the only girl regularly at home, she was 'necessarily drawn from the pursuit of accomplishments by Mrs Bennet's being quite unable to sit alone . . . and as she was no longer mortified by comparisons between her sisters' beauty and her own, it was suspected by her father that she submitted to the change without much reluctance' (p. 386).

Mary was not the only girl in the novel to be improved by a change in her circumstances in her later years, although in the cases of Georgiana Darcy and Kitty Bennet the change was essentially an improvement in their social training. After her brother's marriage, Georgiana left her chaperon-governess in London to live at Pemberley. She 'had the highest opinion in the world of Elizabeth' (p. 387) from whom she learned a new sort of tact and discrimination. Kitty also spent much of her time with Elizabeth and most of the remainder with Jane, now Mrs Bingley. Living with such sisters worked 'to her very material advantage. . . . In society so superior to what she had generally known, her improvement was great . . . removed from the influence of Lydia's example, she became, by proper attention and management, less irritable, less ignorant, and less insipid' (p. 385). Even at seventeen or eighteen years of age, a girl such as Kitty might still be saved.

Dissimilar in every other way, Charlotte Lucas resembles Lydia in pursuing her chosen course unwaveringly to the end. As we have seen, her first private words to Elizabeth laid out her credo, that,

with or without affection, it was the business of girls to scheme
themselves into marriage, the outcome being, in terms of happiness,
altogether a question of luck. As we have also seen, Jane Austen
allows Charlotte to elaborate fairly her own defence. Better still, she
later finds her a most generous advocate in Jane Bennet, when Elizabeth denounces Charlotte's marriage as '"in every view...unac-
countable"' (p. 135). But Jane Austen could not wholly suppress her
partiality for Elizabeth and her standpoint. 'I must confess', she
wrote, not altogether in play, when *Pride and Prejudice* was published,
'that I think her as delightful a creature as ever appeared in print, and
how I shall be able to tolerate those who do not like *her* at least I do
not know'.[51] Elizabeth must be given the last word. '"You shall not
defend her, though it is Charlotte Lucas"', she answered her elder
sister. '"You shall not, for the sake of one individual, change the
meaning of principle and integrity, nor endeavour to persuade yourself or me, that selfishness is prudence, and insensibility of danger,
security for happiness"'.[52] Charlotte must be condemned for her
betrayal of the very first principle of girlhood, the integrity of the
heart. Was a female education which ended in cold rationality any
better after all than those ending in heedless self-gratification or tin-
kling vanities? It is surely not by chance that Jane Austen anticipates
the day when Charlotte's household delights at Hunsford will lose
their charm, or that she leaves Charlotte pregnant – by Mr Collins –
in the end.

CHAPTER 5

FAMILIES:
Persuasion

RICHARD SIMPSON, ONE of Jane Austen's most penetrating as well as earliest critics, wrote of her fiction, 'Platonist as she was in her feelings, she could rise to contemplate the soul as a family, but not as a republic'.[1] This might serve as a manifesto for any of the novels, but for *Persuasion* perhaps most of all.

In Christian if not Platonic imagery, however, souls may be troubled or even damned, and even the most blessed have to struggle for their harmony. *Persuasion* is deeply concerned with both the crushing and sustaining forces, the attractive and repulsive powers, the narrowing and expansive tendencies implicit in family relations. Of course, Jane Austen placed close boundaries about this subject. Not only does neither state activity nor regional heterogeneity impinge much on her domestic units but also these units themselves are heavily governed by conventional restraints. As Henry Tilney said, when scouting Catherine Morland's fears that the conduct of the households of Gothick literature manifested itself also at Northanger Abbey,

> 'Remember the country and the age in which we live. Remember that we are English, that we are Christians. Consult your own understanding, your own sense of the probable, your own observation of what is passing around you – Does our education prepare us for such atrocities? Do our laws connive at them? Could they be perpetrated without being known, in a country like this, where social and literary intercourse is on such a footing; where every man is surrounded by a neighbourhood of voluntary spies, and where roads and newspapers lay everything open?'[2]

Jane Austen certainly remembered the country and age in which she lived. The blackest domestic villainy in *Persuasion* is gross callousness; its worst vices are hypocrisy and pride. But within the limits of her selected range, she runs the gamut of family felicity and un-happiness, and, still more to the point, reveals the complexity with which these are intertwined.

I

The Elliots in *Persuasion* are essentially, but cannot be classed crudely as an unhappy family. Sir Walter and his eldest daughter have their times of discontent, but Sir Walter's are mostly moments of injured vanity, while Elizabeth Elliot's are suspended once a husband worthy of herself appears to have risen on the horizon. Moreover, both are deeply gratified by their manifest superiority in looks and station. They glory in the standing of their family, and their hand-some persons perfectly become their social roles. The youngest Elliot daughter, Mary, is inclined to querulousness. 'While well, and happy, and properly attended to, she had great good humour and ex-cellent spirits; but any indisposition sunk her completely; she had no resources for solitude; and inheriting a considerable share of the Elliot self-importance, was very prone to add to every other distress that of fancying herself neglected and ill-used.'[3] As Mrs Charles Musgrove, she now belonged primarily to another family; but having been born an Elliot remained her unfailing consolation – as well as a provocation to her new relations. '"Mary is good-natured enough in many respects,"' observed her sister-in-law, Louisa, to Captain Wentworth, '"but she does sometimes provoke me exces-sively, by her nonsense and her pride; the Elliot pride. She has a great deal too much of the Elliot pride"' (p. 88). None the less, even a little listening, sympathy or notice soon coaxed her out of her baseless dis-satisfactions.

In so far as Anne Elliot was unhappy (or melancholy or sad, as one may choose), her family was principally the cause. She was unvalued and carelessly degraded by both her father and elder sister. Elizabeth preferred even the scheming widow Mrs Clay as her initial com-panion when she and Sir Walter removed to Bath: '"nobody will want her [Anne] in Bath"' (p. 33), Elizabeth told Mary and Anne herself, with characteristic indifference to Anne's feelings. The family friend, Lady Russell, was grieved at 'the affront it contained to Anne, in Mrs Clay's being of so much use, while Anne could be of none' (p. 34). Yet it was Lady Russell who had been primarily re-sponsible for Anne's chief reason for unhappiness, the abandonment of her engagement to Captain Wentworth seven years before. In this intervention (in which she was at least passively supported by Sir Walter and Elizabeth), Lady Russell had acted as virtually a member of the Elliot family. She was 'as solicitous for the credit of the family, as aristocratic in her ideas of what was due to them' as any Elliot; 'she had prejudices on the side of ancestry' (p. 11). Such prejudices played a considerable part in her opposition to Anne's being 'snatched off by a stranger without alliance or fortune. . . . It must not be, if by any fair interference of friendship, any representations from one who had almost a mother's love, and mother's rights, it would be prevented' (p. 27). It was prevented. Anne, at nineteen years of age, could withstand her father's disapproval but not the pressure of her acting mother. The engagement was broken off, and Anne had sorrowed for it ever since.

In the pathology of families, vanity was the sovereign Elliot ailment. For Sir Walter even 'the blessing of beauty' was inferior 'to the blessing of a baronetcy' (p. 4). This had one benign effect, or sideeffect. He would alienate no whit of his inheritance; he 'would never condescend to sell' an acre in Elliot possession (p. 10). Yet even such a resolution had its ill consequences. Since his pride of station also forbade him to live at less than his accustomed level, and he was too incompetent to save on even what was inessential to a baronet's dignity, he had to rent his home to others and abandon – apparently for years if not for ever – the duties as well as the local glories of his rank. Elizabeth was also a casualty of vanity. She was still angry at her tacit rejection, a decade or so before, by her cousin, William Elliot, who was also Sir Walter's heir presumptive. Her 'strong family pride could see only in *him*, a proper match for Sir Walter Elliot's eldest daughter. There was not a baronet from A to Z, whom her feelings would have so willingly acknowledged as an equal' (p. 8). Now, twenty-nine years old, she would have given much 'to be certain of being properly solicited by baronet-blood within the next twelvemonth or two' (p. 7). If, as a prospective spinster who could not stoop to the level of attainable marriages, Elizabeth was the victim of family vainglory, she also doled out the same arrogance to the world at large – with the exception, characteristically, of her social betters. Anne Elliot was shamed by the servility of Elizabeth and Sir Walter before their titled relatives, the Dalrymples. She 'had never seen her father and sister before in contact with nobility, and she must acknowledge herself disappointed. She had hoped better things from their high ideas of their own situation in life, and was reduced to

form a wish which she had never foreseen – a wish that they had
more pride' (p. 148).

The seeds of the family disease were present in William Elliot from
the beginning. His initial defiance of Elliot grandeur sprang from his
need of immediate money. But it also expressed the resentment of
the heir presumptive who might not succeed for years or even ever.
Sir Walter was at that time a widower in his early forties who might
yet produce a lawful son; and even at best the prospect of future rank
and landed wealth which was perhaps a quarter of a century or more
away was cruelly tantalizing. By the time the novel opens, however,
all this is in the past, and William is as ready an Elliot aggrandizer and
as unbending an upholder of Elliot privilege and pretension as Elizabeth herself. Even when tactfully softening his words for hostile
ears, he none the less makes his new-found hauteur quite clear to
Anne:

> 'Good company requires only birth, education and manners, and
> with regard to education is not very nice.... My cousin, Anne,
> shakes her head. She is not satisfied. She is fastidious. My dear
> cousin, (sitting down by her) you have a better right to be fastidious
> than almost any other woman I know; but will it answer? Will it
> make you happy? Will it not be wiser to accept the society of these
> good ladies in Laura-place [the Dalrymples], and enjoy all the
> advantages of the connexion as far as possible? You may depend
> upon it, that they will move in the first set in Bath this winter, and as
> rank is rank, your being known to be related to them will have its
> use in fixing your family (our family let me say) in that degree of
> consideration which we must all wish for.'   (p. 150)

However discreetly phrased, William Elliot's avowal of family
aggression signals both his own unscrupulosity and the natural consequences of Elliot conceit.

The Elliots constitute a disharmonious and (in its dominant members) selfish and unfeeling group. Their polar opposites in the novel
are the Crofts, including Mrs Croft's brother, Captain Wentworth.
The Crofts are deeply affectionate towards each other, inter-suppor-
tive, quite above artifice or pretence, kind, modest and truth-loving.
When Anne reflected on the perfect sympathy that had once flowed
between Wentworth and herself, she thought that no couple had ever
been so united, 'With the exception, perhaps, of Admiral and Mrs
Croft, who seemed particularly attached and happy' (p. 63). The
Admiral's manners moreover 'delighted Anne. His goodness of heart

and simplicity of character were irresistible' (p. 127). She was equally pleased with Mrs Croft. 'Her manners were open, easy, and decided, like one who had no distrust of herself, and no doubts of what to do; without any approach to coarseness, however, or any want of good humour.' In fact, Anne was much struck by the delicacy of her tact and her 'great consideration towards herself' when they met after Kellynch (the Elliot home) had been let (p. 48). Mrs Croft made no disguise of her affection for her husband. In fifteen years, she had accompanied him four times on his voyages to North America and once to India, as well as on shorter journeys to Gibraltar and Portuguese and Irish stations. 'I can safely say', she told Mrs Musgrove,

> 'that the happiest part of my life has been spent on board a ship. While we were together, you know, there was nothing to be feared.... The only time that I ever really suffered in body or mind, the only time that I ever fancied myself unwell, or had any ideas of danger – was the winter that I passed by myself at Deal, when the Admiral (*Captain* Croft then) was in the North Seas. I lived in perpetual fright at that time, and had all manner of imaginary complaints from not knowing what to do with myself, or when I should hear from him next; but as long as we could be together, nothing ever ailed me, and I never met with the smallest inconvenience.'   (pp. 70-1)

The family resemblance, as well as rapport, between Captain Wentworth and his sister was very marked. He too was unostentatiously considerate, as when he noticed Anne's weariness on a walk and swiftly and quietly arranged that she be taken home by carriage, or when he silently removed a troublesome child clinging to her back. He too found it difficult to dissimulate even in the cause of charity, but his good feeling would eventually triumph. This is brought home to us when, after a moment of amused contempt as Mrs Musgrove lauded her worthless, now dead, son, he conquered himself 'and entered into conversation with her, in a low voice... doing it with so much sympathy and natural grace, as shewed the kindest consideration for all that was real and unabsurd in the parent's feelings' (pp. 67-8).

In the Crofts together we have a portrait of delightful union. When, on the journey back to Uppercross, Mrs Croft more than once saved the Admiral from mishap by giving the reins a tug this way or that, Anne reflected 'with some amusement... [that] their style of driving... [was] no bad representation of the general guidance of their affairs' (p. 92). Through Captain Wentworth we are given a portrait of a happy 'family' in the larger, looser sense as well. Unlike *Mansfield Park, Persuasion* presents the Navy – a 'shabby fellow' or two such as Admiral Brand excepted (p. 170) – as 'that profession which is, if possible, more distinguished in its domestic virtues than in its national importance' (p. 252); and the little naval colony in Lyme Regis is the epitome of quasi-familial, fraternal association. 'There was so much attachment to Captain Wentworth' in the welcome that he received from the Harvilles and Captain Benwick,

> and such a bewitching charm in a degree of hospitality so uncommon, so unlike the usual style of give-and-take invitations, and dinners of formality and display, that Anne felt her spirits not likely to be benefited by an increasing acquaintance among his brother-officers. 'These would have been all my friends,' was her thought; and she had to struggle against a great tendency to lowness.

In themselves, the Harvilles equal the Crofts in naval virtue, household and general alike. Captain Harville 'was a perfect gentleman, unaffected, warm, and obliging. Mrs Harville, a degree less polished than her husband, seemed however to have the same good feelings ... they seemed almost hurt that Captain Wentworth should have brought any such party to Lyme, without considering it as a thing of course that they should dine with them' (pp. 97-8).

The Harvilles were to demonstrate over and over again their simplicity and goodness of heart, which embraced everyone associated with their outward naval 'family'. Anne was especially thanked at her second meeting with them because she had befriended their afflicted friend, Captain Benwick; and the rest of the Uppercross party were as struck as she by their boundless generosity of feeling. Even before she benefited directly from it, by their hospitality and nursing, Louisa Musgrove 'burst forth into raptures of admiration' at the conduct of the Harvilles and the fellow officers, 'their friendliness, their brotherliness, their openness, their uprightness' (p. 99). The contrast with the older Elliots could not have been more absolute at every point.

II

The Musgroves hold an intermediate position between the Elliots and the naval families, though on the whole they fall on the right side of benignity. Mr Musgrove was (after Sir Walter) the largest land-owner in the area and his wife 'had money'. Old-established and well-to-do, they moved 'in the first class of society in the country [neighbourhood]' (p. 74). Their extended family of Uppercross was more or less congenial to Anne, and she was happy enough to move for a time into their orbit despite, or perhaps because of, the fact that Elliot affairs were of so small an interest there as would have astonished Elizabeth or her father. 'She acknowledged it to be very fitting, that every little social commonwealth should dictate its own matters of discourse; and hoped, ere long, to become a not unworthy member of the one she was now transplanted into' (p. 43).

At the Great House, Mr and Mrs Musgrove presided in the 'old English style' of squirearchy (p. 40). They were deficient in educa-tion and refinement. Neither could appreciate Anne's playing of the pianoforte; Mr Musgrove's chief interest was apparently his sport; and, 'fair or not fair', his wife is ridiculed for her bulk and bathos with the deadly phrase, 'her large fat sighings over the destiny of a son, whom alive nobody had cared for' (p. 68). But overall the Mus-groves were kindly, genial, honest and affectionate. Their elder chil-dren were trying hard to supply the missing 'refinement'. Henrietta and Louisa had brought 'the usual stock of accomplishments' back from school, and 'were gradually giving the proper air of confusion' to the old-fashioned parlour at the Great House by installing a piano, harp, flower stands and 'little tables placed in every direction' (p. 40). Charles Musgrove's contribution to modernity was to 'elevate' a farmhouse into Uppercross Cottage by the addition of a 'viranda, French windows, and other prettinesses' (p. 36). But in *Persuasion* (unlike *Sanditon*) Jane Austen's satire on 'improvement' is mild and sunny. This is a gentle contest of generations. There are no rifts in the family unity of the Musgroves. Even when Louisa and Henrietta enter into rivalry for Captain Wentworth's attentions, their affection for one another remains intact. Although Anne Elliot, 'saved as we all are by some comfortable feeling of superiority from wishing for the possibility of exchange', would not have given up her own elegance and cultivation of mind for all their busy happiness and high spirits, she did envy them their 'perfect good understanding and agreement together, that good-humoured mutual affection, of which she had known so little herself with either of her sisters' (p. 41).

It was the Elliot immigrant, Mary, who was principally responsible for such discord as agitated the Musgrove commonwealth. In
part, this may have been no more than the common consequence of
a daughter-in-law and sister-in-law living cheek by jowl with
numerous female relatives by marriage. But the friction was certainly intensified by the Elliot petulance and self-importance that
were part of Mary's incoming baggage. Mrs Musgrove complained
that Mary so mismanaged her children that she could not invite them
as often to the Great House as she would have wished, even though
this gave some offence to 'Mrs Charles'. Conversely, Mary complained that her mother-in-law invited them *too* often, '"for she
humours and indulges them to such a degree, and gives them so
much trash and sweet things, that they are sure to come back sick
and cross for the rest of the day."'. Each complained that the other's
servants were liable to lead their own astray. Mrs Musgrove's were
(according to Mary) ' "gadding about the village, all day long"', and
Mary's nursery maid was (according to Mrs Musgrove) '"always
upon the gad . . . [and] such a fine dressing lady, that she is enough to
ruin any servants she comes near"' (pp. 44-5). Again, it was Mary's
complaint that Mrs Musgrove did not allow her the precedence due
to a baronet's daughter in the making up of the dinner procession,
while one of the Musgrove girls (Jane Austen does not specify
which) was aggrieved at her

> 'always putting herself forward to take place of mamma. Nobody
> doubts her right to have precedence of mamma, but it would be
> more becoming in her not to be always insisting on it. It is not that
> mamma cares about it the least in the world, but I know it is taken
> notice of by many persons.'   (p. 46)

Charles complained of both his wife's hypochondria and her over-
indulgence of their children; Mary complained of her husband's in-
sensitivity towards herself and *his* over-indulgence of their children.
They agreed in wishing that Mr Musgrove would augment their income by a handsome present, but whereas Mary blamed her father-
in-law for his omission, Charles defended him as having many other
calls upon his money. Mary strove to break the Musgroves' links
with their neighbouring poor relations, the Hayters, as 'giving bad
connections to those who have not been used to them [the Elliots]'
(p. 76). But Charles refused to throw the Hayters (and in particular
his old friend, Charles Hayter) over; and there was 'only such a con-

sciousness of superiority in the Miss Musgroves, as made them pleased to improve their cousins' (p. 74).

All these fissures in the family wall were small, scarcely more than hair-line breaks across the surface. Women's rivalries over household things and beings, marital disagreements springing from different self-perceptions, and refusal or reluctance to transfer allegiance from one's old family to one's new, are common form and ordinarily evanescent. The ordinariness is however just what counts. In reviewing *Emma* when it was first published, Sir Walter Scott wrote of Jane Austen's work as revolutionary; no longer would novel-writers deal in idealized figures of romance, but instead practise 'the art of copying from nature as she really exists in the common walks of life, and presenting to the reader, instead of splendid scenes of an imaginary world, a correct and striking representation of that which is daily taking place around him'.[4]

The little antagonisms and irritations and confidential denigrations of even such a 'model' family as the Musgroves were precisely what were taking place daily around the reader – instantly recognizable yet striking once painted in. They were not nearly enough to cause the family to be relegated from the 'happy' to the 'unhappy' category. Jane Austen leaves us in no doubt of the inner warmth and comfort of the Musgrove domain. 'On one side', runs the description of the parlour at Uppercross after the Harville children had arrived,

> was a table, occupied by some chattering girls, cutting up silk and gold paper; and on the other were tressels and trays, bending under the weight of brawn and cold pies, where riotous boys were holding high revel; the whole completed by a roaring Christmas fire, which seemed determined to be heard, in spite of all the noise of the others. Charles and Mary also came in, of course, during their visit, and Mr Musgrove made a point of paying his respects to Lady Russell, and sat down close to her for ten minutes, talking with a very raised voice, but, from the clamour of the children on his knees, generally in vain. It was a fine family-piece.   (p. 134)

A certain degree of friction might even have been pleasurable. To fuss and gossip, indulge in indignation, suppose oneself to be in the right and feel the glow of another's failings, might well break the tedium of idle country life and set loose a little essentially harmless excitement. Mary was probably worst off. Normally she had no confidante, and a confidante was an essential ingredient of this rather ignoble form of domestic gratification.

Anne Elliot's arrival at Uppercross was a godsend for its established 'citizens'. 'One of the least agreeable circumstances of her residence there, was her being treated with too much confidence by all parties, and being too much in the secret of the complaints of each house' (p. 44). Not only had Mary now a safe audience for the recital of her grievances, but also Charles, Mrs Musgrove and the Musgrove girls could press Anne to use her influence with Mary to induce her to moderate or improve her conduct. The Musgrove complainers may have had the added satisfaction of striking obliquely – through Anne – at the entire Elliot connection. Anne had to endure these attempts to use her for small family ends without much hope of doing good to anyone. 'She could do little more than listen patiently, soften every grievance, and excuse each to the other; give them all hints of the forbearance necessary between such near neighbours, and make those hints broadest which were meant for her sister's benefit' (p. 46). But meanwhile she contributed, unwittingly, to the confidential shuttling and weaving between the parties which added so much interest to Uppercross daily life.

Such a degree of domestic disturbance could be borne safely and easily because of the immense strength of the family framework. This is wonderfully illustrated by the passage describing the preliminaries to the fateful walk, in the course of which Anne was to learn (as she thought) how Captain Wentworth evaluated her character.

It was a very fine November day, and the Miss Musgroves came through the little grounds, and stopped for no other purpose than to say, that they were going to take a *long* walk, and, therefore, concluded Mary could not like to go with them; and when Mary immediately replied, with some jealousy, at not being supposed a good walker, 'Oh, yes, I should like to join you very much, I am very fond of a long walk,' Anne felt persuaded, by the looks of the two girls, that it was precisely what they did not wish, and admired again the sort of necessity which the family habits seemed to produce, of every thing being to be communicated, and every thing being to be done together, however undesired and inconvenient. She tried to dissuade Mary from going, but in vain; and that being the case, thought it best to accept the Miss Musgroves' much more cordial invitation to herself to go likewise, as she might be useful in turning back with her sister, and lessening the interference in any plan of their own.

'I cannot imagine why they should suppose I should not like a long walk!' said Mary, as she went upstairs. 'Everybody is always supposing that I am not a good walker! And yet they would not have been pleased, if we had refused to join them. When people come in this manner on purpose to ask us, how can one say no?'

(p. 83)

Family confinement limited the range of action but also enlarged the range of participation.

The family confinement of *Persuasion* does not include the common, near-universal contemporary form of the overcrowded dwelling. Even in the Harvilles' cramped lodgings at Lyme, 'all the ingenious contrivances and nice arrangements of Captain Harville' had turned 'the actual space to the best possible account' (p. 98); and although Uppercross Cottage was apparently without a hall, and entered directly from the veranda, there is nothing to suggest that the living quarters were particularly close. None the less, the Musgrove ménages (with the Hayter satellite) constituted a more or less self-contained entity whose governing 'idea' was the family. Writing in the mid-twentieth century, T. S. Eliot observed:

Now [in 1948] the family is an institution of which nearly everybody speaks well: but it is advisable to remember that this is a term that may vary in extension. . . . What is held up for admiration is not devotion to a family, but personal affection between the members of it. . . . [5]

By contrast, in 1815-16, devotion to a family generally overrode – without of course excluding or displacing – personal affection between its members. Such devotion, in a deep-rooted and wide-branched 'happy' family like the Musgroves, implied a wide and remarkably detailed knowledge of what everybody else was doing; a great deal done in common; and the holding back of preferences of companionship, and still more of the very mention, let alone explanation, of such preferences – all in the interest of the group at large.

Often the discourse had to be at odds with the actuality. In planning their excursion on the 'very fine November day', that was to produce a fateful revelation, the Musgrove girls were unable to see Anne alone or propose that she alone accompany them. They were driven in consequence to suggest that the walk would be too long for Mary. But this merely led Mary to feel slighted and, instead, to insist on going. At the same time she satisfied her own *amour propre* by telling Anne that she went because the *Musgroves* would have felt slighted had the 'invitation' been turned down. Meanwhile, Anne, understanding the true state of things, set out to appease Louisa and Henrietta, first, by trying to dissuade Mary from joining them, and, then, by joining them herself in order to draw Mary off the sooner from the party. It was a typical family comedy of the unsaid, of misdirection, and of unintended, and even unwanted, results. Anne's own humble hope for the morning was merely 'not to be in the way of any body' (p. 84).

Yet the constraints had their compensations. First, to repeat, the consequent domestic manœuvring added a spice to intercourse and helped to fill empty hours. Secondly, a high degree of civility was maintained and wrangling practically avoided. But a third, and much more important, blessing of the sovereignty of family was the sense of safety and ultimate comfort in mutuality that it engendered. One might have to yield up measures of privacy, liberty and the exercise of predilections. But in return all upheld all within the system.

III

'I *have* lost a treasure, such a Sister, such a friend as never can have been surpassed', Cassandra Austen wrote to Fanny Knight on 20 July 1817, two days after Jane had died:

> she was the sun of my life, the gilder of every pleasure, the soother of every sorrow, I had not a thought concealed from her, & it is as if I had lost a part of myself. I loved her only too well, not better than she deserved, but I am conscious that my affection for her made me sometimes unjust to & negligent of others, & I can acknowledge, more than as a general principle, the justice of the hand which has struck this blow.[6]

Although we may allow some set-off for the high emotion running at the time, there can be no doubt that Cassandra and Jane Austen were extraordinarily closely bonded. It was the central relationship in Jane's life. In this particular case, personal affection between two of its members may even have matched in significance allegiance to the family as an entirety.

Cassandra was remarkably strong in character – authoritative, incisive and reserved. That she was well aware that she had such a reputation – and took pride in it – is evident from her next observation in the letter to Fanny Knight. 'You know me too well to be at all afraid that I should suffer materially from my feelings, I am perfectly conscious of the extent of my irreparable loss, but I am not at all overpowered & very little indisposed, nothing but what a short time, with rest & change of air will remove.'[7] She had borne stoically, all her life, the loss of her fiancé, and with it the hope of marriage and a home governed by herself. In silent endurance at least, she seems to have resembled Anne Elliot; and it would have been fitting if in fact Jane Austen used her as a part model for any of her heroines, for Cassandra had stood before her as the pattern since early childhood. So it continued. 'Something of this feeling [of deference] always remained', according to their nephew, Edward Austen; 'and even in the maturity of her powers, and in the enjoyment of increasing success, she [Jane] would still speak of Cassandra as of one wiser and better than herself.' Jane would insist on having her own head cut off, Mrs Austen said, if Cassandra had been doomed to such a fate.[8]

In the controlled and individually repressive setting of the late-eighteenth- and early-nineteenth-century family, it was important to have some person with whom one could be as open as was compatible with the interior privacies that everybody must maintain. Jane Austen had just such a benefit ready-made in Cassandra. The correspondence between the two contains some expressions of deep affection; but these are comparatively rare. Emotional display was not in the Austen style. Moreover, no letters from Cassandra to Jane survive, and again we may presume that the letters from Jane to her which Cassandra destroyed were precisely those that dealt with their most intimate concerns. None the less, even the extant material reveals something of Jane's release from everyday constraints when she was in communion with her sister. In part, this manifested itself in faint, occasional, internal criticism of her family, especially in ironic comment on her mother's doings or ideas: this irony is usually so delicate that the third party – as in irony proper – might well fail to catch the hint of mockery should the letter happen to fall into her hands. In part, Jane Austen's 'freedom' took the form of indulging in mild malice, or 'pleased contempt', to use the phrase which she herself coined in *Persuasion*.[9] Often she loosed her pleased contempt on other young women, as with 'Miss Langley is like any other short girl with a broad nose & wide mouth, fashionable dress, & exposed bosom',[10] or 'I looked at his [Sir Thomas Champneys's] daughter & thought her a queer animal with a white neck'.[11] Sometimes she wantonly, almost joyously, trampled the accepted decencies, as when she wrote of Mrs Holder's death, 'she has done the only thing in the World she could possibly do, to make one cease to abuse her',[12] or of Mrs Hall of Sherborne being 'brought to bed ... of a dead child, some weeks before she expected, owing to a fright. I suppose she happened unawares to look at her husband'.[13]

During the last three years of her life, Jane Austen began to use her niece Fanny as a sort of second vent for her occasional irritation or asperity. After Jane died, Cassandra told Fanny that Jane was, 'I believe ... better known to you than to any human being besides myself. ... There are certainly many points of strong resemblance in your characters; in your intimate acquaintance with each other, and your mutual strong affection, you were counterparts'.[14] None the less, Jane Austen's letters to Fanny do not give off the same air of spontaneity and untrammelled traffic as those written to Cassandra. Only to Cassandra did she truly 'express on paper', as she said herself, 'exactly what one would say to the same person by word of mouth'; significantly, she added, 'I have been talking to you almost as fast as I could the whole of this letter'.[15] Cassandra was the pivot on which her world turned, her other self, at once the epitome of and refuge from an extraordinary family propinquity. By contrast, Anne Elliot's situation in *Persuasion* is peculiarly poignant. She has no Cassandra. Although perpetually surrounded by her family, and chafed by one or other of its members, she has no one to whom she can open her thoughts or feelings, no one from whom she can seek or to whom she can proffer sympathy.

IV

The internal relationships in the Austen family were very different from those governing the Elliots. Jane invariably wrote of her father in respectfully affectionate terms. Occasionally she was playful, as when, on 18 September 1796, in the midst of difficulty in finding a travel escort, she told him, through Cassandra, 'My Father will be so good as to fetch home his prodigal Daughter from Town, I hope, unless he wishes me to walk the Hospitals, Enter at the Temple, or mount Guard at St James. It will hardly be in Frank's power to take me home; nay, it certainly will not'.[16] In turn, Mr Austen, whose scholarship and literary judgment she respected, encouraged and supported Jane in her writing. In November 1797, he sought to launch her on the world by offering, on her behalf, the manuscript of

First Impressions (the early version of *Pride and Prejudice*) to the well-known publisher, Thomas Cadell. So anxious was he that Jane should have her chance that he even proposed – though without result – to pay the cost of its publication, if need be.[17] 'He had started all his sons off on their respective careers and would do no less for his talented younger daughter.'[18]

It is true that, in one important instance, his treatment of Jane may appear harsh. At first sight, his failure to forewarn her of his decision in late 1800 to retire, and remove to Bath, may seem inconsiderate, or even cruel: certainly, the effect on her of a sudden discovery was shattering. It might be expected that the matter would have been well canvassed and discussed within the vestigial family of parents and unmarried girls, even if the final word belonged altogether to the elders. Clearly, James Austen must have been taken into council, as he was to succeed his father and share the spoils, and James was not the man to hold back any secret from his wife. But we do not know enough of the internal workings of the household, or of the contemporary conventions of authority in such cases, to pronounce an outright condemnation of Mr Austen's action. It may even be that he considered a lightning fiat the most merciful way of apprising Jane of her fate; and it would surely have been unreasonable to expect him to work on after his seventieth year or to spend the remainder of his life in country isolation. At any rate, it was aberrant offence, if any. There is nothing to suggest that any other cloud lay over Jane's relationship with her father.

On the day he died, Jane Austen told her brother Frank, 'Our dear Father has closed his virtuous & happy life, in a death almost as free from suffering as his Children could have wished. . . . Next to that [the 'comfort'] of the consciousness of his worth & constant preparation for another World, is the remembrance of his having suffered, comparatively speaking, nothing'.[19] On the next day, she continued, 'We have lost an Excellent Father. . . [but] he was mercifully spared from knowing that he was about to quit the Objects so beloved, so fondly cherished as his wife & Children ever were. – His tenderness as a Father, who can do justice to?'[20] In all this, there was very little, perhaps nothing, of pious exaggeration. After his funeral, his son Henry wrote of him (again to Frank) as 'the best of fathers, and men'.[21] George Austen's steady benevolence and care for his children's interests were generally attested. He provided Jane, and the rest, with secure surrounds within which to develop; he set the tone for the Austen temperateness, loyalty to one another, and judicious sacrifice to the corporate cause.

Mrs Austen was the stronger and more trenchant character, fit mother for her elder daughter. Since she outlived her younger, we have no equivalent to the sort of lapidary inscription that Jane's letters provided for her father. Had there been, it is doubtful whether she would have written with equal warmth or employed such a term as 'tenderness'. Her relations with Mrs Austen appear to have been proper and dutiful rather than affectionate. Jane's first surviving letter calls her 'Mamma'; thereafter she invariably wrote, even to Cassandra, not of 'Mamma' or 'Mother', but 'my Mother'. Moreover, if her references to Mrs Austen do have a flavour, it is generally tart. Occasionally, tedium is suggested. 'I suppose my mother will like to have me write to her', she told Cassandra on 21 October 1813 while visiting Godmersham. 'I shall try at least.'[22] Jane also believed Mrs Austen to be hypochondriacally inclined. When she was complaining off and on of an 'oppression in *her head*' and her daughter-in-law, James's wife, said something about Ben Lefroy which exacerbated her nervous state, Jane wrote,

> How can Mrs J. Austen be so provokingly ill-judging? – I should have expected something better from her professed if not her real regard for my Mother. Now my Mother will be unwell again. Every fault in Ben's blood does harm to hers, & every dinner-invitation he refuses will her give an indigestion.[23]

Again, Mrs Austen did not share all Cassandra's and Jane's (*they* seem to have thought as one) personal antipathies to particular friends or family members such as Mary Austen and her step-daughter, Anna. This contributed further small elements of disharmony.

But it would not do to suppose that the rubs and jars of coexistence weakened the family bond for either Mrs Austen or her younger daughter. The roughnesses in their relationship were, in part at least, circumstantial. Mrs Austen was thirty-six years old when Jane was born. She was elderly already, by contemporary standards, by the time that Jane's surviving letters first throw light on her attitude towards her mother. Soon Jane was to become, like Cassandra, a doomed spinster daughter, in standing contrast to five handsome, thriving and (not least important) generally absent sons. Conversely, Mrs Austen by then needed – or at any rate exacted – constant attendance, so that only rarely, when Martha Lloyd stood sentry, could Jane and Cassandra be away together. Moreover, in nature Jane would seem to have been much more her father's than her mother's child; she and Mrs Austen were temperamentally uncongenial. Yet, particularly from 1801 onwards, they lived habitually atop of one another, in comparatively cramped apartments or houses.

All this magnified discordance, but even so it was a trifling matter in the scales of family communality as a whole. It was the business of mothers to furnish a home for unmarried daughters; it was the business of unmarried daughters to care, respectfully, for parents, especially as they aged. These were the simple social laws. There were of course many transgressors on either side in early-nineteenth-century England; but such people as the Austens were not among them. Far from it: the formal 'honouring' of parents was an unquestioned rule of conduct in such homes as theirs, or for that matter, those imagined by Jane Austen. Anne Elliot would never have spoken to her proto-mother, Lady Russell, a single word of her interior disagreement or the dissonances between them. Even Elizabeth Bennet inwardly consumed her mortifications and revulsion at her mother's folly and ill conduct – and the level-headed, well-bred, educated and sharp-witted Mrs Austen, who wrote remarkably elegant light verse, was a very far cry from Mrs Bennet. Even Elizabeth 'loved' her mother according to the conventional assumption of the day; filial love then consisted essentially in bearing and forbearing, and only additionally or supererogatorily in personal affection. We can surely impute at least this much to Jane Austen's relationship to her mother.

V

Jane's brothers and their families formed a further and ever more dense context for her life. Prima facie, the eldest, James, should have been a favourite with his younger sister. He was the most cultivated and intellectual of his generation of Austens; he wrote copiously – at least when young – and always had a literary inclination; he taught Jane much and gave her early kindness; he was an upright clergyman and an assiduous, perhaps even uxorious, husband. None the less, he was the only member of her immediate family of whom (so far as we are aware) Jane Austen was directly critical. Even while he was still a young widower, she mocked him softly as he sought another wife. 'We were so terrible good as to take James in our carriage [to a ball]

...', she wrote on 9 January 1796, 'indeed he deserves encouragement for the very great improvement which has lately taken place in his dancing';[24] and a week later, when listing James as one of the party bound next night for the Lefroys, she added that now 'a ball is nothing without *him*'.[25]

Conventional wisdom has it that it was his second marriage, to Mary Lloyd, which narrowed James and accentuated his less agreeable traits. This wisdom may well be wise. Mrs Austen welcomed her new daughter-in-law as a prize. 'Had the Election been mine, you, my dear Mary, are the person I should have chosen for *James's Wife, Anna's Mother* and *my Daughter*; being as certain, as I can be of anything in this uncertain world, that you will greatly increase and promote the happiness of each of the three.'[26] But she neither increased nor promoted the happiness of the Austens as a whole. For a clergyman's daughter with some high connections, she had been reared in relative poverty and ignorance: 'the other Mary, I believe', Jane Austen once wrote of her, 'has little pleasure from that [a particular novel] or any other book'.[27] She was also disfigured by small-pox which had 'scarred and seamed her face dreadfully'.[28] Perhaps such disadvantages and early blows set her on edge against the fortune-blessed Austens. At any rate, she turned out to be close-fisted, envious and insensitive. 'These were faults', Maggie Lane argues, 'quite foreign to the Austen nature. Contentment with one's lot, forbearance, mildness, unselfishness, pleasant manners and attention to the comfort of all those with whom one's life overlapped – these were the qualities the Austens valued and upon which they built their remarkable family unity.'[29] At the same time, it must be remembered that much of the evidence for a harsh characterization of Mary Austen comes from Jane, a hostile witness. Even shortly before she died, Jane wrote, 'Now that[lending the family carriage for the final journey to Winchester]'s a sort of thing which Mrs J. Austen does in the kindest manner! – But still she is in the main *not* a liberal-minded Woman, & as to this reversionary Property[a prospective fortune for James]'s amending that part of her Character, expect it not...; – too late, too late in the day'.[30]

The tenor of several of Jane Austen's observations while the move from Steventon to Bath was in train is that James and Mary Austen were grasping. James took both Mr Austen's horses well before the actual departure. Evidently, he had his own put down; its 'death', Jane satirically observed on 8 January 1801, 'tho' undesired was not wholly unexpected, being purposely effected'; and this 'made the im-

mediate possession of the Mare very convenient'. She added, 'everything else I suppose will be seized by degrees in the same manner'.[31]
Soon afterwards she devised a scheme for the sale of the family
library in which James was cast as purchaser – 'My father has got
above 500 volumes to dispose of, – I want James to take them at a
venture at half a guinea a volume'[32] – but he was apparently unwilling to buy the books. When it looked as if a young Mr Rice, engaged to Lucy Lefroy, might succeed James as Mr Austen's curate at
Deane, Jane wrote sardonically, 'I rather wish they may have the
Curacy. It will be an amusement to Mary to superintend their
Household management, & abuse them for expense, especially as
Mrs L[efroy] means to advise them to put their washing out'.[33]

Jane Austen's gibes at James's and Mary's parsimony continued
even after the retirement to Bath had come and gone. On 7 January
1807, for instance, she wrote from Southampton that their little girl's

> new pelisse depended upon her mother's being able or not to come
> so far in the chair; how the guinea that will be saved by the same
> means of return is to be spent I know not. Mrs J.A. does not talk
> much of poverty now, though she has no hope of my brother's
> being able to buy another horse *next* summer.[34]

When, late in the following year, James's Aunt Perrot undertook to
provide him with an additional £100 per annum, as a reward for his
conscientious rejection of the living of Hampstead Marshall, Jane
commented ironically on his proposed new expenditure and economies; on Mary's turning their luck to still better account by calling
on her brother-in-law to fulfil an old undertaking; and on Mrs Austen's intense interest in money and vicarious pleasure in her son's
having more of it than before.

> James means to keep three horses on this increase of income; at
> present he has but one. Mary wishes the other two to be fit to
> carry women, and in the purchase of one Edward [James's
> brother] will probably be called upon to fulfil his promise to his
> godson [James's son]. We have now pretty well ascertained
> James's income to be eleven hundred pounds, curate paid, which
> makes us very happy – the ascertainment as well as the income.
>
> Mary does not talk of the garden; it may well be a disagreeable
> subject to her, but her husband is persuaded that nothing is want-
> ing to make the first new one good but trenching, which is to be
> done by his own servants and John Bond [James's steward], by de-
> grees, not at the expense which trenching the other amounted to.[35]

Meanwhile, Jane found James's visits to Southampton irksome. His mannerisms had become irritating, as Mary's influence drove a wedge between him and his sisters. 'I am sorry & angry that his Visits should not give one more pleasure,' Jane had written to Cassandra on 8 February 1807:

> the company of so good & so clever a Man ought to be gratifying in itself; – but his Chat seems all forced, his Opinions on many points too much copied from his Wife's, & his time here is spent I think in walking about the House & banging the doors, or ringing the bell for a glass of water.[36]

In general, the temptation to find prototypes for characters or relationships in Jane Austen's novels in actual people or pairings that she knew should be fought off. Since she dealt largely in universals, it is all too easy to match elements in the real and imagined individuals. But perhaps there is a case for exempting James and Mary Austen and Mr and Mrs John Dashwood from such self-denial. Of course, the imaginary Dashwoods are a monstrous exaggeration of the real Austens, and the scales of living of the respective sets very different. There is moreover no evidence that Jane Austen was conscious of any likeness, let alone used it in her planning; and neither James nor any other member of the family appears ever to have noticed even the most general of resemblances. None the less, in the special matters of self-regarding economy and husband-and-wife relations, James and Mary Austen do seem to have provided the germ for the odious Dashwoods. Just as the caricaturist seizes on a facet or two of personality or line of conduct, and balloons them into governing passions, Jane Austen's starting-point for Mr and Mrs John may well have been the Revd and Mrs James.

Yet, as we have seen, Jane Austen also testified that there were things which 'Mrs J. Austen does in the Kindest manner',[37] and among these was sharing with Cassandra, Jane's nursing during the harrowing final stages of her illness. Cassandra wrote, of the day that Jane died, 'fatigue made me then resign my place to Mrs J.A. for two hours & a half when I took it again & in about one hour more she [Jane] breathed her last'.[38] Correspondingly, James seems to have been tirelessly punctilious in performing his duties to his sisters, in particular, in providing them with an escort for considerable parts of their journeys, whenever they required and he could manage it. 'James has offered to meet you anywhere, . . . [but] that would be to give him trouble without any counterpoise of convenience', Jane

7 Portrait of Fanny Knight, Jane's niece.

8 Portrait of Francis William Austen, Jane's fifth brother.

9 Portrait of Charles Austen (Jane's youngest brother) as a Commander by Field *c*. 1807.

10 (*above left*) Silhouette of James Leigh–Perrot, Jane's uncle.

11 (*above right*) Silhouette of Jane Leigh–Perrot, Jane's aunt by marriage.

12 (*left*) Silhouette of Mrs Cassandra Austen, Jane's mother.

13 Modern view of Chawton Cottage, Jane's home, 1811–17.

wrote to Cassandra in London on 11 February 1801, proposing an alternative arrangement.[39] He even came, at considerable inconvenience, to Jane's rescue on the Sabbath on which she needed to escape to Bath after the Manydown débâcle and the embarrassment which followed her throwing over of Harris Bigg Wither.

Henry, Jane Austen's fourth brother, and also her favourite, had much charm, especially for women. His siege of his capricious, independence-loving widowed cousin, Eliza de Feuillide, 'at length induced in me', Eliza wrote in 1797, 'an acquiescence which I have withheld for two years'.[40] He had persuaded her in the end that she would be handled tactfully in marriage. 'I shall probably meet with many unpleasant and untoward circumstances', she told another cousin,

> but all the comfort which can result from the tender affection and society of a being who is possessed of an excellent heart, understanding and temper, I have at least ensured – to say nothing of the pleasure of having my own way in everything, for Henry well knows that I have not been much accustomed to control and should probably behave rather awkwardly under it, and therefore like a wise man he has no will but mine, which to be sure some people would call spoiling me, but I know it is the best way of managing me.[41]

Jane repeatedly testified to Henry's gift of pleasing. 'He was as agreable as ever during his visit'; 'His [letter] to me was most affectionate & kind, as well as entertaining; – there is no merit to him in *that*, he cannot help being amusing';[42] he and Charles 'are each of them so agreable in their different way, & harmonize so well, that their visit is thorough enjoyment'.[43]

Henry was her man of affairs with publishers, and only *in extremis* (as when on 3 November 1815 'My Brother's severe Illness has prevented his replying to Yours [John Murray's] of Oct. 15, on the subject of the MS of *Emma*'[44]) did she deal with them directly. She also respected Henry's judgment of her writing. Over several anxious days, she reported to Cassandra his successive reactions while reading the manuscript of *Mansfield Park*.

> Henry's approbation hitherto is even equal to my wishes. He says it is very different from the other two, but does not appear to think it at all inferior. He has only married Mrs R. I am afraid he has gone through the most entertaining part. He took to Lady B. and Mrs N. most kindly, and gives great praise to the drawing of the

characters. He understands them all, likes Fanny, and, I think, foresees how it will all be.... He admires H. Crawford: I mean properly, as a clever, pleasant man.... Henry has this moment said that he likes my M.P. better & better; he is in the 3^{d} volume. I beleive *now* he has changed his mind as to foreseeing the end ... he defied anybody to say whether H.C. would be reformed, or would forget Fanny in a fortnight.[45]

He was however carelessly indifferent to her command to keep her authorship a secret, and in the autumn of 1813 revealed it to casual acquaintances in Scotland 'with as much satisfaction as if it were my wish'.[46] He compounded the offence by telling, not Jane, but Fanny Knight of his breach of confidence. As always, Jane judged Henry kindly. She reported to Frank:

Henry heard P. & P. warmly praised in Scotland, by Lady Robt Kerr & another Lady; – & what does he do in the warmth of his Brotherly vanity & Love, but immediately tell them who wrote it! A Thing once set going in that way – one knows how it spreads! – and he, dear Creature, has set it going so much more than once. I know it is all done from affection & partiality – but at the same time let me here again express to you & Mary [Frank's wife] my sense of the *superior* kindness which you have shewn on the occasion, in doing what I wished – I am trying to harden myself. After all, what a trifle it is in all its Bearings, to the really important points of one's existence even in this World![47]

Jane tried in future to minimize the operation of Henry's boastful indiscretion. On 23 March 1817 she told her niece Fanny that he had pressed her about 'having another ready for publication. I could not say No when he asked me [*Persuasion* was complete], but he knows nothing more of it'.[48]

Jane was quite alive to Henry's imperfections. Delicately she defended, in a letter to Frank, his rapid recovery of spirits after the death of his first wife, Eliza, whom he had pursued so ardently before their marriage.

If I may so express myself, his Mind is not a Mind for affliction. He is too Busy, too active, too sanguine. – Sincerely as he was attached to poor Eliza moreover, & excellently as he behaved to her, he was always so used to be away from her at times, that her Loss is not felt as that of many a beloved wife might be, especially when all the circumstances of her long and dreadful Illness are taken into the account.[49]

This was a generous gloss. The ardent, hopeful, resilient Henry does seem to have been more coarse-grained and insensitive than the remainder of the Austens. His comment on his mother's income after his father's death, for instance, sounds uncannily as well as unpleasantly close to Mr John Dashwood's on the equivalent occasion:

> she [Mrs Austen] will be in receipt of a clear 450 pounds per Ann. – She will be very comfortable, & as a small establishment will be as agreeable to them, as it cannot but be feasible, I really think that My Mother & sisters will be to the full as rich as ever. They will not only suffer no personal deprivation, but will be able to pay occasional visits of health and pleasure to their friends.[50]

Given Mrs Austen's delight in the arrangements made for her, and Henry's congenital zest for silver linings, it would be unfair to look on this as either presaging or echoing the cold-hearted calculation in *Sense and Sensibility*. But perhaps it is not too much to find in Henry's words (in a letter to Frank which Jane would almost certainly have read or heard of) the inspiration for the celebrated interchange between Mr and Mrs John in Chapter 1 of that novel, in which they discover that the widowed mother's new-found poverty will be practically to her advantage.[51]

There are further occasional indications of Henry's want of consideration for others in his making and changing of plans. Again, when his bank failed on 16 March 1816, and most of his family lost more or less considerable sums through his bankruptcy, he shrugged off their disasters and his own with, to all appearances, complete insouciance. Caroline Austen wrote that two weeks later he visited Steventon in, so far as his outward bearing went, 'unbroken spirits. I believe he had even then decided on taking Orders'. Perhaps Caroline best epitomized his characteristics when she described in her *Reminiscences* the mode of his succeeding her recently dead father, James, at Steventon rectory in 1820.

> We left Uncle Henry in possession. He seemed to have renewed his youth [he was then forty-nine years old], *if* indeed he could be said ever to have lost it, in the prospect before him. A fresh life was in view – he was eager for work – eager for pupils – was sure very good ones would offer – and to hear him discourse you would have supposed he knew of no employment so pleasant and honourable, as the care and tuition of troublesome young men. He was also looking forward secretly to his own [second] marriage

.... This we did not know of as certain, but his intention had been guessed in the family for some time. He was always very affectionate in manner to us, and paid my mother every due attention, but his own spirits he could *not* repress, and it is not pleasant to *witness* the elation of your successor in gaining what *you* have lost; and altogether tho' we left our home with sad hearts, we did not desire to linger in it any longer.[52]

People will weight such imperfections as Henry's in different scales; some might discern, and even value, an essential candour which made him incapable of concealing glee. At any rate, Jane Austen did not mark her brothers' characters by alphas and betas. Henry's ardency, joyousness and elasticity, his knowledge of the world and practical enthusiasms, made an irresistible appeal to a girl and woman living under various confinements. Henry signified dash and colour, as well as glow and kindness within his limits.

Her other brothers she treated with invariable amiability, and this appears to have been reciprocated. The youngest – 'our own particular little brother', as, imitating *Camilla*, she once spoke of him to Cassandra – was 'dearest Charles'.[53] Jane's references to him were always warm. When in 1803 he spent some of his £30 prize money in buying necklaces for Cassandra and her, she wrote (for Cassandra's eyes alone), 'of what avail is it to take prizes if he lays out the produce in presents to his sisters. He has been buying gold chains & Topaze crosses for us ... I shall write again by this post to thank & reproach him. – We shall be unbearably fine'.[54] She observed of a letter of his, 'How pleasantly & how naturally he writes! and how perfect a picture of his Disposition & feelings, his style conveys!';[55] and when, evidently, he told Cassandra that he would buy Jane's next book to spare her presentation copies, Jane responded, 'Poor dear Fellow! – not a present! – I have a great mind to send him all the Twelve Copies which were to have been dispersed among my near Connections'.[56]

Frank, 'Sweet amiable Frank',[57] was similarly appreciated, even to Jane's description of some 'Excellent Letters' as 'such thinking, clear, considerate Letters as Frank might have written'.[58] He emerges from Jane Austen's correspondence more distinctively and positively than Charles, or for that matter any other of her brothers, except perhaps Henry. As she implicitly delineates him, Frank combined Captain Harville-like simplicity, practicality and goodness with sense, intelligence and piety. Some of these virtues were extolled in the charming doggerel, refracting small childhood memories, with which she celebrated the birth of his first son, Francis.

Thy name possessing with thy Blood,
In him, in all his ways, may we
Another Francis William see! –
Thy infant days may he inherit,
Thy warmth, nay insolence of spirit; –
We would not with one fault dispense
To weaken the resemblance.

May he revive thy Nursery sin,
Peeping as daringly within,
His curley Locks but just descried,
With, 'Bet, my be not come to bide.' –

Fearless of danger, braving pain,
And threaten'd very oft in vain,
Still may one Terror daunt his soul,
One needful engine of Controul
Be found in this sublime array,
A neighbouring Donkey's aweful Bray.
So may his equal faults as Child,
Produce Maturity as mild!
His saucy words & fiery ways
In early Childhood's pettish days,
In Manhood, shew his Father's mind
Like him, considerate & kind;
All Gentleness to those around,
And eager only not to wound.

Then like his Father too, he must,
To his own former struggles just,
Feel his Deserts with honest Glow,
And all his self-improvement know. – [59]

The unity of the two years of cohabitation with him and his wife in Southampton testifies further to the good relations between Frank and Jane. From such small indications as survive, she seems also to have liked 'the other Mary', Mrs Francis. It was certainly praise to be prized when Jane Austen wrote, 'Mrs F.A., to whom it [*The Female Quixote*] is new, enjoys it as one could wish'.[60]

The only offset in Jane's dealings with Charles and Frank was her impatience with the conduct of their small children. Her criterion of proper behaviour in the young was evidently higher than that of parents who had to battle with them daily. She once declared after the visit of an assured little girl, 'What is become of all the Shyness in the world? – Moral as well as Natural Diseases disappear in the progress of time, & new ones take their place. – Shyness & the Sweating Sickness have given way to Confidence & Paralytic complaints'.[61] After another visit, from Anna Lefroy's little nephew, Charles, she told Anna, 'we thought him a very fine boy, but terribly in want of Discipline – I hope he gets a wholesome thump or two; whenever it is necessary'.[62] She seems to have found Cassy, Charles's eldest daughter, particularly trying – perhaps salving her conscience by placing the blame upon faulty rearing. 'The latter [Cassy] *ought* to be a very nice Child – Nature has done enough for her – but Method has been wanting.'[63] Anticipating the arrival at Chawton Cottage of Charles and his family in October 1813, she wrote to her sister Cassandra, 'I shall be most happy to see dear Charles, & he will be as happy as he can with a cross Child or some such care pressing on him at the time. – I should be very happy in the idea of seeing little Cassy again too, did I not fear she wd. disappoint me by some immediate disagreeableness'.[64]

Even Frank and Mary Austen, more orderly and 'methodical' parents than Charles and Frances, did not escape censure altogether. 'I spent two or three days with your Uncle & Aunt [Frank and Mary] lately', she told her niece Caroline on 23 January 1817, '& though the Children are sometimes very noisy & not under such order as they ought & easily might, I cannot help liking them & even loving them.'[65] One need not place great weight on this. Usually, Jane Austen's views of her nieces and nephews – and particularly her nephews – mellowed as they grew older. She eventually became much attached to James's son, Edward, whom she had apostrophized at the age of ten as 'a pompous Sermon-Writer, & a domineering brother';[66] and she later wrote about her brother Edward's sons, 'who', she had told Cassandra in 1813, 'are out with the Foxhounds [and] will come home & disgust me again by some habit of Luxury or some proof of sporting Mania',[67] in the warmest terms of praise. After all, she was an aunt twenty-four times over before she died; she had to spend much time, in close confines, with small children – not her own; and their noise and needs ate continually into the concentration she required for her writing. She once observed wonderingly of a fellow novelist, Mrs West, that her output 'with all her family cares is . . . a matter of astonishment. Composition seems to me Impossible, with a head full of Joints of Mutton & doses of Rhubarb'. She must have often needed 'exemption from the Thought & contrivances which any sort of company gives',[68] but especially that of infant and young charges.

Jane Austen's brother Edward, although burdened by many children and expectations, was rich, and, although rich, very generous and hospitable. He loved company, especially family company, excelling 'in doing the Honours to his visitors, & providing for their amusement'.[69] Despite his being, at least when young, either rather sickly or rather hypochondriacal (Jane often wrote of his minor illnesses and deplored the fact that among all his blessings health could not be counted one), he was a remarkably agreeable and good-humoured person. While there is no evidence that Jane was an especial favourite of his – he was the least scholarly of the brothers, if also the most diligent and capable in business – he behaved towards her (so far as we can judge, invariably) with all his usual kindness and sweet temper; and she responded with constant fondness. When his wife Elizabeth died, Jane greeted Cassandra's report on Edward with 'God be praised! that you can say what you do of him – that he has a religious Mind to bear him up, & a Disposition that will gradually lead him to comfort'.[70] Jane had always spoken of Elizabeth with mild approval,[71] and so it was too after her death. 'We need not enter into a Panegyric on the Departed –', she wrote to Cassandra in the same letter, 'but it is sweet to think of her great worth – of her solid principles, her true devotion, her excellence in every relation of Life. It is also consolatory to reflect on the shortness of the sufferings, which led her from this World to a better.'[72]

In 1798, 1802, 1803, 1805, 1808, 1809 and 1813, and possibly other years, Jane Austen spent lengthy periods at Godmersham, as well as two summer vacations at nearby Rowling. This effected a sort of renewed bonding with Edward. Together with counter-visits later to Chawton Manor by Edward and his children, it kept refreshing the relationship – just as living at times with or near Frank, Charles and Henry, and rarely far from James, kept her close to all of them. Jane was riven in her attitude towards Godmersham. She was – though she certainly was never treated as – a poor relation there; there, she received Mrs Knight's alms, however delicately and kindly given; there, she worried over tips for servants. Occasionally, she gently mocked herself, and perhaps her hosts. 'But I have no occasion', she wrote to Cassandra from Godmersham on 25 September

1813, 'to think of the price of Bread or of Meat where I am now; – let me shake off vulgar cares & conform to the happy Indifference of East Kent wealth.'[73] Whatever about riches, it was necessary for Jane Austen to conform to a society very different from that of her home, in numbers, movement and style, during her long stays at Godmersham. Perhaps it was in recollection of this that, in *Persuasion*, she put into Anne Elliot's mind the thought, 'With the prospect of spending at least two months at Uppercross, it was highly incumbent on her to clothe her imagination, her memory, and all her ideas in as much of Uppercross as possible'.[74] Moreover, despite her freedom from her usual domestic tasks at Godmersham, it must have been very difficult for Jane Austen to write there. 'In this House', she once observed, 'there is a constant succession of small events, somebody is always going or coming';[75] and there are continual references in her letters to visiting expeditions about the countryside in which she, like everyone else, appeared to join.

But Godmersham had its compensations. Contrasted with the household at Southampton, or even Chawton Cottage at the crossroads of Austen traffic, it stood for vivacity and variety. It furnished a family entire within a family, and eventually a second 'sister' in Fanny Knight. Its ease and grace of life cannot have been unenjoyable; however irksome its 'luxury' may have seemed at times, it cannot have been actually painful to endure. Moreover, there was the capital benefit that, at Godmersham, Jane Austen could observe a cross-section of higher society close at hand. As we have seen, the narrowness of Jane Austen's experience should not be overstressed. Just as her frequent stays with Henry after 1811 presented an unfamiliar range of London life and life-style for her to pore over, classify and ultimately put to use, so too her blocks of months at Godmersham revealed to her much more about the inner workings of the upper gentry than her occasional and often embarrassed intersections with them at Steventon or Bath could ever have provided. The family was not merely a restrictive institution; it also opened windows – if not doors – on to other worlds.

VI

Besides being complex intrinsically, Austen family relations constituted a complex in themselves. Jane and Cassandra, as the unmarried daughters and sisters, had more or less specific functions within this complex. Leonore Davidoff and Catherine Hall point out that middle-class men of the period 'who sought to be "someone" ... were, in fact, embedded in networks of familial and female support which underpinned their rise to public prominence';[76] and the same was true of the more modestly ambitious Austen males. In the sexual division of labour within the complex, either Jane or Cassandra (or occasionally, in later times, their quasi-sister, Martha Lloyd) always performed the duty of caring, and providing companionship, for Mrs Austen. They took turns in visiting their distressed brothers, Henry and Edward, after they had lost their wives, or during illness. The charge of various child nephews or nieces fell to them from time to time, as a sort of parent-relief during absences or other household disturbances. In one light, all these were services rendered to the family as a whole in return for wages in the form of indirect financial support and a guarantee of ultimate security.

The family was seen as a corporate enterprise. This was illustrated most dramatically at Henry's downfall. When he, who 'had been living for some years past at considerable expense, but not more than might become the head of a flourishing bank',[77] went bankrupt, his brother Edward and his uncle James Leigh Perrot forfeited £20,000 and £10,000, respectively, as his guarantors, and even his brothers James and Frank lost several hundreds each as sureties, as well as the sums deposited in their personal accounts. Jane herself was among the victims, although her loss, £13.7.0, was, absolutely speaking, very small. Yet, so far as we are aware, no Austen ever uttered a word of reproach or complaint to Henry. Only Aunt Perrot expressed a sense of outrage at his irresponsibility and impenitence, and she was merely an in-law – and ill-conditioned, into the bargain. Pressed hard, the Austens proper always formed a British square.

This was manifest again in 1817 during Jane Austen's long fatal illness. Not only Cassandra but also each of the five brothers committed themselves, in what ways they could, to her relief, and this, not just for the hour or day, but over months; even Mrs Austen seems to have shared in the attempted alleviation. In her last extant Chawton letter, dated 22 May 1817, Jane Austen told her friend Anne Sharp,

> How to do justice to the kindness of all my family during this illness, is quite beyond me! – Every dear Brother so affectionate & so anxious! – and as for my Sister! – Words must fail me in any attempt to describe what a Nurse she has been to me. Thank God!

she does not seem the worse for it *yet*. . . . I have not mentioned my
dear Mother; she suffered much for me when I was at the worst,
but is tolerably well. – Miss Lloyd too has been all kindness. In
short, if I live to be an old Woman, I must expect to wish I had
died now; blessed in the tenderness of such a Family, & before I
had survived either them or their affection.[78]

Shortly before her death she wrote from Winchester of her 'dearest
sister, my tender, watchful, indefatigable nurse. . . . As to what I owe
to her, and to the anxious affection of all my beloved family on this
occasion, I can only cry over it, and pray to God to bless them more
and more'.[79] About the same time, she wished her nephew Edward,
James's son, that 'the same Blessed alleviations of anxious, sim-
pathising friends be yours, & may you possess – as I dare say you will
– the greatest blessing of all, in the consciousness of not being unworthy of their Love. *I* could not feel this'.[80]

To present-day eyes, much of this may read almost cloyingly;
some may even read as if it were extracted from a pattern-book of
virtuous Victorian aspirations. But such impressions should not
carry us away. Perhaps some deduction should be made for the
extraordinary pathos of the circumstances, and the intensity and sin-
gularity of feeling which these engendered; and it might be argued
that, as she realized that she was dying, Jane Austen was unusually
uncritical, exalted or excited. There was however such a level-headedness and practicality in everyone's behaviour, and such undimi-
nished wit and playfulness in other parts of these very same letters
from Jane Austen, that any deduction made on account of the particular occasion should probably be very small. Moreover, the letters
themselves were written with no thought that they would ever be
seen except by the recipients. In fact, the family support, down to the
layer of elder nieces and nephews, was active, uninterrupted and
systematic. Even on the slow sad journey by carriage to Winchester
on 24 May 1817, 'it distressed me', Jane Austen wrote, 'to see uncle
Henry and [her nephew] Wm. K[night] – who kindly attended us on
horseback, riding in the rain almost all the way'.[81] Basically, the conduct of the Austens throughout the protracted crisis was but a con-
tinuation of their normal bearing towards, and treatment of, one
another. It is impossible to escape the conclusion that they fell little
short of the ideal of the contemporary family.

How was such a pitch of family love and mutuality reached, and
sustained? The essence of the answer must lie in the Austens' own

nature, their general equability, sound temper and forthrightness. But a small fraction – one can hardly rate it more – may be attributable to a sort of selective ruthlessness, in protection of the integrity of the group.

The Austens' mentally defective son, George, was totally excised from their ranks soon after birth. There is no mention of his existence, let alone of visits paid to him while he lived out his life with his paid guardians, in any of Jane Austen's surviving correspondence or other papers. He was simply non-personed. Although such a thing was common practice in Georgian England, it is a chilling index of the exclusive aspect of family solidarity. In mild form, Jane Austen herself occasionally showed a partiality for her own. When, for instance, the Knight estate was handed over to her brother Edward subject to the annuity to Mrs Knight, Jane commented defensively,

> Mrs Knight giving up the Godmersham estate to Edward was no such prodigious act of generosity after all, it seems, for she has reserved herself an income out of it still; this ought to be known, that her conduct may not be overrated. I rather think Edward shows the most magnanimity of the two, in accepting her resignation with such incumbrances.[82]

Again, she wrote of her niece Cassy, Charles's daughter, when she was four, 'Poor little Love – I wish she were not so very Palmery [Cassy's mother was a Palmer] – but it seems stronger than ever. – I never knew a wife's family-features have such undue influence'.[83]

But much the most important secondary cause of the Austen family solidarity was that, collectively, they willed that it be so. That one's first loyalty was to one's family was a form of faith, and like all faiths it implied the cultivation of particular attitudes, a behavioural code and the steady exercise of discipline. All this was epitomized in Jane Austen's note of 23 June 1814 to Cassandra – one of many such minute indications of self-subordination to the general interest –

> I certainly do not *wish* that Henry should think again of getting me to town. I would rather return straight from Bookham; but, if he really does propose it, I cannot say No to what will be so kindly intended. It could be but for a few days, however, as my mother would be quite disappointed by my exceeding the fortnight which I now talk of as the outside. . . .[84]

The diligent determination to live up to the inculcated idea of family performance was a crucial factor in the Austens' comparative success

as an enclosed community. It may have been only lightly that
Richard Simpson threw off the conceit of Jane Austen rising to contemplate the soul as a family. But, absurd though such high-flown
language might have seemed to Jane herself, it pretty well strikes the
mark.

Contrariwise, the Elliots of *Persuasion* stand for the negation of
faith in family – ironically, too, for the besetting sin of all its members, Anne excepted, is familial pride. But this pride is essentially selfish. Here 'family' is nothing more than the cloak for so many ego-
tisms; it knows nothing of sacrifice in the cause of others or the
collectivity. Its fruits are fragmentation, destruction and discontent.
Its principles are the precise opposites of the Austens'. Even the
'happy' families of *Persuasion* seem much inferior to their author's
own – the Musgroves commonplace, the Crofts commonsensical,
and the Harvilles depthless, for all their kindliness and goodwill to
the world at large. But in the ultimate union of Anne and Wentworth
we are perhaps meant to see the first moments in the creation of a
blessed new soul, of a new family as it was truly meant to be.

SOCIAL TRAFFIC:
Emma

I

THERE ARE AT least two interesting differences between *Emma* and the rest of Jane Austen's completed work. First, it operates with fewer active, or at any rate fewer speaking, characters than any of the other novels. Only sixteen of the ninety or so people who appear in the book[1] actually speak directly; and two of these, Mrs Ford, the proprietress of the draper's shop, and Mrs Bates, the vicar's widow, contribute no more than a humdrum sentence or two to provide continuity in a particular scene. In a third case, Mrs Cole's more lengthy passage, the object is merely to set up for discussion the mystery of Jane Fairfax's pianoforte. For all practical purposes, there are only thirteen speaking parts in what is a full-length 'play': three Knightleys, two Westons, two Woodhouses, two Eltons, Miss Bates, Jane Fairfax, Frank Churchill and Harriet Smith. The fewness of speakers is not immediately apparent. Instead one gets the impression of a crowded stage. I think the reason for this illusion is that Jane Austen uses reported speech especially extensively in *Emma*. At least thirty-five of the characters who do not actually say anything in the book have their observations reported by one or other of the dozen or so actual participants. The purpose – or at any rate the effect – is to engender a sense of social density and incessant social traffic without cluttering up the narrative or distracting attention from the selected patterns of interplay.

A second peculiarity of *Emma*, in contradistinction to any other of Jane Austen's writings, is that the entire action is practically confined to a single place. The horses may have to be taken out to convey Mr Woodhouse to Randalls, or Emma to the ball at the Crown Inn, and people walk ceaselessly to and fro, even a little beyond the extremities of the village proper. But it may all be fairly described as internal movement, at least within Greater Highbury. It is almost literally parochial: our attention is generally focused upon a single parish; the only excursions undertaken are to the neighbouring Donwell and Box Hill. As with the speech, much of the action is reported, and this includes all extra-Highbury activity, such as Jane Fairfax's *affaire* at Weymouth, Frank Churchill's efforts to extricate himself from Yorkshire and Richmond, and Mr Knightley's reawakened domestic appetite, and Harriet's and Robert Martin's reconciliation, in London. Half the active characters never leave Highbury at all during the twelve months covered by the story. The entrances and the exits of the rest are often abrupt, sometimes, as with Jane Fairfax's entry, quite undescribed. While they are absent from Highbury, nothing is known certainly or directly about their doings. Moreover, as Ronald Blythe observes (even if he does over-colour the matter somewhat),

> In spite of its [Highbury's] frequently being dull and boring, every other place is disparagingly compared with it, London most of all. 'In London it is always the sickly season', says Mr Woodhouse. Mr John Knightley has escaped from Highbury to Brunswick Square and his defection has been punished by a certain tough unpleasantness which has grown up round his outlook since he has been there. Emma longs to see the sea but she never thinks of going to London, although it is only sixteen miles away. And when Mr Knightley is upset he goes to London 'to learn to be indifferent'. Only Frank Churchill treats London non-morbidly. For Mr Elton, with Harriet's portrait under his arm, it is the destination of fools.[2]

Thus *Emma* realizes to a remarkable extent Jane Austen's famous recipe for the domestic novel, sent light-heartedly to her niece, Anna, on 9 September 1814, during the very period of composition: '3 or 4 Families in a Country Village is the very thing to work on'.[3]

The locality of *Emma* is a large village, almost a town – one would guess the population to be about one thousand persons – sixteen miles from London, at the northern extremity of Surrey. One sentence conveys its air and pace precisely:

> Much could not be hoped from the traffic of even the busiest part of Highbury; – Mr Perry walking hastily by, Mr William Cox letting himself in at the office door, Mr Cole's carriage horses returning from exercise, or a stray letter-boy on an obstinate mule, were the liveliest objects she could presume to expect; and when her eyes fell only on the butcher with his tray, a tidy old woman

travelling homewards from shop with her full basket, two curs
quarrelling over a dirty bone, and a string of dawdling children
round the baker's little bow-window eyeing the gingerbread, she
knew she had no reason to complain.... [4]

Highbury has its full social complement: a squire, a parson, a
lawyer, an apothecary, a draper, an innkeeper, a baker, a school proprietress and teachers, a snug tenant farmer, a smith-mechanic, a parish clerk, an ostler, a steward, three upper servants (Serle, the cook,
James, the coachman and Mrs Hodges, the housekeeper) and four
lower servants (Hannah, Harry, Patty and Tom). These are all
named and specified. It also possesses, although they are undifferentiated, the inevitable poor and labourers, towards whom Emma is
particularly 'compassionate... She understood their ways, could
allow for their ignorance and their temptations, had no romantic expectations of extraordinary virtue from those, for whom education
had done so little; entered into their troubles with ready sympathy,
and always gave her assistance with as much intelligence as goodwill' (p. 86).

What separates Highbury a little perhaps from the mass of large
villages and small towns in southern England is its *rentier* families –
first, the Woodhouses themselves, 'settled for several generations at
Hartfield, the younger branch of a very ancient family' (p. 136), but
in addition the Westons and the Coles. Both of these last had made
their money recently in trade in London, and Mr Weston at least still
kept some interest in metropolitan commerce, though not such as to
require him to leave Highbury more than once in an entire year. Possibly the proximity of Highbury to London has something to do
with the unusual number of *rentiers* it contains – but the exigencies of
the plot seem as likely an explanation. Certainly, we should be
wrong if we saw in Weston or Cole an early intimation of the outer-
suburbanite or the distant commuter. They had, as Jane Austen puts
it, come into the country for good; they were a humbler form of the
nabob who had bought a manor and a parish.

The social arrangement of the village is, of course, hierarchical.
The squire is predominant, although, despite their lack of acres, the
Woodhouses' capital and their generations of county status suffice to
place them on a practically equal level. In the second grade stand the
vicar and the former businessmen, Weston and Cole. These three,
together with Mr Knightley, constitute the magistracy of the place.
At least, this seems a fair inference from Mrs Elton's remark, '"Oh!

no, it is a meeting [of the magistrates] at the Crown, a regular meeting. Weston and Cole will be there too; but one is apt to speak only of those who lead. – I fancy Mr E. and Knightley have every thing their own way"'.[5]

Mr Elton takes his rank from his clerical office; he is only formally and superficially a gentleman, 'without any alliances but in trade, or any thing to recommend him to notice but his situation and his civility'.[6] Under his wife's example, he soon sinks back to his innate level of vulgarity. But this does not cost him his social place in the second grade any more than their acute poverty costs Mrs and Miss Bates, the widow and daughter of his predecessor, theirs. The Westons, natives of Highbury, have been steadily making their way forward in recent decades. But it is a fortune made in trade in London, after an early fling as a militia officer, which enables Mr Weston to establish himself firmly in the upper circles of Highbury. The Coles actually emerge from the chrysalis in the course of the narrative. Having enlarged their income as their business house in London prospers, they begin to entertain, in the full sense of dinner parties. The climax comes after an ironic moment of social agony for Emma when it seems that she and her father, alone in all Highbury, stand too high to be invited. But all ends well. Emma is asked, dines with the Coles and finds that the company consists largely of her own close friends and another 'proper unobjectionable country family' (p. 214).

The third rank is not so clearly delineated; the novel is not concerned with them. But it would certainly embrace the attorney and the apothecary (with the first superior, despite the fact that, in Emma's eyes, the Coxs are '"without exception, the most vulgar girls in Highbury"' [p. 233]). Mrs Goddard and her subordinate schoolmistresses and the farming Martins probably belong to the same social category. Below these would be set the shopkeeping class – incidentally, all those specified are women, Mrs Ford, Mrs Wallis, who keeps the pastry shop, and Mrs Stokes, the landlady of the Crown – and so on downwards through the artisans and servants until one reaches – presumably even Highbury has them – the undeserving poor. All these are suggested by the merest touch of the brush. They form an animated background barely sketched rather than elaborated. But this brush cannot so much as graze the canvas without adding something to the whole. Even the pastry-cook's wife comes to life when Miss Bates observes, '"I have heard some people say that Mrs Wallis can be uncivil and give a very rude answer, but we have never known any thing but the greatest attention"'.[7] An 'artist cannot do anything slovenly', as Jane Austen herself once mock-seriously told her sister.[8] It need hardly be added that the people of Highbury themselves recognized and were content to live within the hierarchical arrangement of society. This is too plain to require either comment or illustration.

Yet acceptance of the notions of rank and station was a very different thing from knowing precisely who fitted where, or from keeping within their boundaries in daily life, or from rejecting movement by individuals between the grades. Let me attempt to illustrate the discordance between the idea and the actuality of social organization in Highbury. Mr Knightley is a working farmer as well as a landowner; he sells his apples in the village; he is indiscriminate in his dining out; and Mrs Weston thought it likely that he would marry the penniless Jane – doomed otherwise to be a governess – while Emma once thought it 'far, very far, from impossible' (p. 413) that he should marry the pretty, silly Harriet, later to be revealed as the illegitimate daughter of a tradesman. Similarly Mr Woodhouse depends largely for his evening company on the schoolmistresses and old Mrs Bates. Harriet herself, with no certain status of her own, aspires to marry, first, a tenant farmer, next, the clergyman and, finally, Mr Knightley – and it is predicted that if all else fails she will sink in the end to snatching at the son of the writing master. Harriet might in fact stand as a symbol of volatility in social placement. The Coles were low-bred and 'only moderately genteel',[9] as well as tradespeople in origin; and they had waited ten years quietly in Highbury before their courage and fortune alike mounted sufficiently for them to attempt the entrée to the politest circles. Yet, in consequence of their accepted invitation, they must have ended up sitting about the new round dining-table at Hartfield, Emma's home, itself. At their own dinner-party, the male Coxs sat down to eat with Emma, Mr Knightley, the Westons and the 'proper unobjectionable country family'. But the 'less worthy' female Coxs were – like Miss Bates and Jane Fairfax – only admitted after dessert. It is clear that the Perrys have not reached the precarious eminence of the Coxs. Yet Mr Perry was on the brink of buying carriage horses and an equipage, which would have represented a significant advance.

Graham Hough, perhaps the most acute commentator on the difficult question of 'class' in Jane Austen's work, rejects both modern terminology and 'the massive abstractions of Marxism' as 'too general', and finds the most satisfactory categorization of the class with which she deals to be 'the gentry'. This he defines negatively, as the group below the aristocracy and above the commercial bourgeoisie.[10] Even this careful distinction seems insufficient, however, for all purposes. Certainly, nobility, gentry and merchants were distinguishable as orders and are indispensable as general categories. But so too were the professions, which in turn varied widely in the standing of the particular occupations and the social origins of the practitioners. Moreover, viewed in terms of actual persons, the members of all such categories formed a continuum rather than a series of sharply separated flocks. *Emma* itself, with Emma dining with the Coles, Robert Martin dining with the Knightleys and Mrs Goddard dining with Mr Woodhouse, is testimony to the uncertainties of the lower, no less than the upper social borderlands.

Similarly, it is impossible in Highbury to avoid anyone merely because one dislikes them personally. Emma is constrained to ask the repellent Mrs Elton to dine at Hartfield. 'They must not do less than others, or she should be exposed to odious suspicions, and imagined capable of pitiful resentment' (pp. 290-1). When Mrs Elton precipitates a strawberry-picking party at Donwell, the ill-assorted élite of Highbury has to be invited together. When this leads on to an excursion to Box Hill, the same jarring company has to be assembled. When the fatal excursion to Box Hill drove Jane to hide away, and she could not, in Miss Bates's words, '"bear to see anybody – anybody at all – Mrs Elton, indeed, could not be denied – and Mrs Cole had made such a point – and Mrs Perry had said so much"'(p. 390) that in the end she is constrained to receive all three. In short, in so compressed a society personal preference could not safely be indulged.

II

Let us now try to assemble the pieces strewn about like the letters of the child's alphabet for which Frank Churchill found new employment. Highbury forms a substantially independent and homogeneous society. Not only is it effectively isolated in geographic terms, but also its inhabitants exhibit important uniformities. It seems a fair inference that the village is exclusively Anglican and almost exclusively composed of native born. It also seems a fair assumption that all accept and work within the traditional social order and values of the small agricultural town; and this means, in turn, that Highbury classified itself internally in a precise though very complex fashion according to income, source of income, pre-scription, length of residence and function. On the other hand, this ideal arrangement is never matched exactly by the actual social order; or, more correctly, a fixed social order exists only as an abstract notion, or model, to be employed as a point of reference perhaps, but never realized. Moreover, even to the extent to which people are recognized and recognize themselves as belonging to particular ranks, they do not remain within them in their social intercourse.

Thus we find ourselves ending in a paradox. *Emma* presents a comparatively self-enclosed and static social organism, with clearly understood principles of stratification. Yet, within this society, social mobility, though circumscribed, is marked – not so much in the con-ventional sense of escalation and descent as in the more interesting Heraclitean sense of flux – while in practice social gathering is neither determined by personal choice nor hemmed in by rank. How is the dualism to be explained? The answer would appear to be – another paradox – stagnation and paucity of numbers.

Were the Woodhouses to limit themselves to their equals – and in Emma's estimation only Donwell (Mr Knightley's place) and Ran-dalls (the Westons' house) belonged to the 'regular and best families' (p. 207) – Emma would have been practically confined to Hartfield, in part for want of opportunity to go elsewhere and in part for want of evening company for her father, to procure her own release. For similar reasons, Jane Fairfax is forced to accept the patronage of Mrs Elton and the officious goodwill of Mrs Cole and Mrs Perry. In both cases, besides the absence of access to alternatives there is the further factor of the awkwardness that would be created, not only for them-selves but also for their families, by the unbridled exercise of in-dividual taste and liking in such a minute community.

In *Persuasion*, as we have seen, Anne Elliot reflects on the power of the family to determine the conduct of its members even against their individual desires.[11] The other side of this coin is of course that Anne acquiesces in such a subordination as a necessary and comparatively trivial price to pay for general harmony and support; and there can be little doubt that here she is expressing the judgment of her creator.

For Jane Austen a personality exists only interactively. Or if we examine 'individuality' from a sociological point of view, we notice that our 'identity crises' never occur in her fiction. The question 'who am I?' only arises when society does not com-fortably answer it before it can be asked. While the societies depicted in Jane Austen's novels are neither so static nor so idyllic as is sometimes suggested, it is true that she does not (as we tend to) conceive social relations to be inherently in crisis.[12]

It is the group which ultimately sustains each individual and provides him or her with his or her measure of harmony and order. But for Jane Austen this group was domestic, not national or regional or economic, in basis. Its primary form was of course the family in its ordinary sense. But beyond this was what we might name, for want of a better term, the 'vicinage' – the village or small-town equivalent of the 'county' or 'quality'. Without much stretching, Highbury may be classified as a species of extended household, and its upper classes – at any rate, the prescribed 'three or four families' and their associates – as just such a quasi-familial group. In such a community or sub-community, antagonism, no less than preference, rank and taste, had to be restrained if a tolerable level of harmony were to subsist. It follows, if this is true, that amongst the effects of economic stability and geographical isolation in *Emma* was a powerful tendency towards social convergence.

In an interesting passage in *Man's Place in Nature*, Teilhard de Chardin uses an analogy from the physical sciences, that of compression, to suggest the type of social change caused by density of people. When organisms are compressed, they adjust by developing, of their own 'volition', as it were, new patterns of behaviour; and quite new forms of interaction then take place.[13] De Chardin had in mind compression arising from multiplicity of, and growth in numbers, and the consequent organizational adjustments to reduce the new frictions. But paucity and stagnation might have a similar effect, in circumstances such as Highbury's. At any rate, whether the social restraint, communalism and abjuration of open conflict in Highbury derived from, or were prudentially nurtured in, the circumstances of the village, is a secondary consideration here. What matters is the existence of a contrived harmony, and the fact that its consequence was, paradoxically, a small degree of social turbulence, a little wake of undesigned vivacity.

It was of course Jane Austen's special skill to record such minutiae, structural and dynamic alike. Even before Scott pointed to the revolutionary character of her 'realism', another novel-reader was struck by Jane Austen's adherence to 'probability'. Annabella Milbanke, later Byron's wife, one of the very first to read *Pride and Prejudice*, reported to her mother, 'I have just finished a novel called "Pride and

Prejudice". It depends not on any of the common resources of Novel writings, no drownings, no conflagrations, nor runaway horses, nor lap-dogs and parrots, nor chambermaids and milliners, nor rencontres and disguises. I really think it is the most *probable* fiction I have ever read'.[14] Moreover, from the start there was unanimity among her critics about the delicacy and particularity of Jane Austen's art. It is as if she were born with microscopic vision; and, to repeat the clever metaphor employed by Archbishop Whately in reviewing her last work, 'to the eye of a skilful naturalist the insects on a leaf present as wide differences as exist between the elephant and the lion'.[15] To take one simple instance used before – the Coles' dinner-party and Emma's fears, first, that she may be subjected to the impertinence of an invitation, and then that she may be spared it; Mr Cox's presence at and Mr Perry's absence from the table; the choice of other guests; and the further choice of postprandial arrivals, place shade on shade on our picture of the social order in the counties. But who else then measured the hundredths of a millimetre, and left us the benefits of a precise recording?

III

The measurements and evaluations of *Emma* were also the measurements and evaluations of Jane Austen's own life. Having had four homes, in Steventon, Bath, Southampton and Chawton, during her forty-two years of life – not to add the protracted stays with her brothers in Kent and London, and with friends in Wiltshire – she was certainly less stationary than Emma. None the less, the constrictions and their consequences were similar. Let us take, in particular, her situation and surroundings at Chawton where she lived when *Emma* was being composed. Chawton, although smaller than Highbury, was more favourably placed for extramural social traffic. It lay at the junction of the main London-Winchester and London-Gosport roads, and was strategically placed for Austen family intercourse, all the more so as several Austen boys of the next generation were at school at Winchester. Still, the great isolating forces of difficult and very expensive travel and communication were, as we have seen, operative even for a woman in early middle age and easing financial circumstances. Journeys by public transport probably cost, in relative terms, twenty times what they would today – the London-Winchester fare, for instance, was half a guinea, roughly an agricul-

tural labourer's weekly wage[16] – and journeys by post-chaise were
perhaps four times as expensive as those by stage-coach. Moreover,
travelling more than, say, forty miles meant staying overnight at an
inn or with some friends or relatives; and this last usually involved
protracted and difficult correspondence to make the requisite
arrangements. Letters were also very costly, and the carriage of even
small parcels still more so: these two items alone accounted for one-
twelfth of Jane Austen's annual expenditure during 1807.[17] Fully half
of her published letters were sent by hand or franked or placed
within a parcel; and almost the same number concern themselves,
somewhere or other, with arranging for herself or for others to be
escorted or carried or accommodated on a journey.

Short periods of Jane Austen's life in Chawton can be recon-
structed to some degree, from letters written to Cassandra. One such
period, covered by four letters, ran from Sunday, 24 January to
Tuesday, 9 February 1813.[18] From the four letters, dealing with the
events of sixteen days, it is possible to recover fragments of the social
patterns of the village, to fit certain of them, archaeologist-like, together, and to learn something of Jane Austen's interpretation of her
own milieu. During all this time, a spell of incessant rain and cold,
mud and gales, Jane was busily engaged in the writing of *Mansfield
Park*, as we know from her seizing on the discovery that there was no
Government House at Gibraltar, and from the enquiries which she
launched among her family about both the procedures of ordination
to the Anglican priesthood and the character of the Northampton-
shire countryside.[19]

On 20 January Jane dined with Mr Papillon, the vicar of Chawton,
and his unmarried sister. It was a large party, worth enumerating as a
first step in establishing the social network. These were the other
guests: the Clements – Captain Clement was a half-pay naval officer,
now living in Chawton, and his wife the youngest daughter of the
squire of Chawton, William Prowting; the Digweeds – Harry Digweed was a gentleman farmer, who had long been a neighbour of the
Austens when they lived at Steventon some fifteen miles away, and
who now lived at Alton, two miles from Chawton; Mrs Digweed
was one of the Terrys, the landowning family at Dummer, which lay
on the road between Chawton and Steventon; Mary Terry – Mrs
Digweed's sister, then living with the Digweeds at Alton: their
brother was the Revd Michael Terry; Mr Twyford – a curate from the
adjoining parish, Great Worldham, and his friend from Cambridge,
Mr Wilkes; Mr White – vicar of another adjoining parish, Newton

Valence;[20] Mr Hinton – a neighbouring landowner; and Miss Benn, who lived at Chawton, and was the unmarried sister of yet another vicar, the Revd James Benn of Faringdon, one mile from Chawton.[21]

It is worth noting that all of these persons and families, with the exception perhaps of Mr Twyford and of course of Mr Wilkes, belonged to the Chawton Book Society. This was a powerful engine of social intercourse in Chawton, so much so that it seems strange that Jane Austen rarely used that great contemporary interlocker of genteel society, the book club, to bring the characters of her fiction into either communion or contention. Miss Benn is also worth noting. She was poor and pitied, and constituted an object of communal concern. At an earlier period she had been for a time without even a single servant, one of her nieces, Elizabeth Benn, coming from Faringdon to help her 'as housemaid and guest'. When her shawl became badly worn, Martha Lloyd, who was then of course living with the Austens at Chawton, provided her with another.[22] By 16 February 1813 Miss Benn was under notice to quit her cottage. 'Poor Creature', wrote Jane Austen to Martha, who happened to be away, '– you may imagine how full of cares she must be, & how anxious all Chawton will feel to get her decently settled somewhere. – She will have 3 months before her. – & if anything else can be met with, she will be glad enough to be driven from her present wretched abode; – it has been terrible for her during the late storms of wind & rain'.[23] After Jane Austen's sister-in-law, Mary (James's wife), expressed concern lest Miss Benn was being neglected, Jane reassured her on 24 January 1813 that not only had Miss Benn been a guest at the Papillons' on 20 January but also that she had dined with the Clements on the 21st, with the Austens on the 22nd, with the Digweeds on the 23rd and with the Papillons again on the 24th.[24]

On 23 January Jane Austen called at the Papillons' to pass on one of the Society books. She was on her way to make a charitable visit, and Miss Papillon 'invited herself very pleasantly' to accompany Jane upon her errand.[25] Later in the same day Miss Benn called on the Austens after her dinner with the Digweeds; and on the following day Miss Benn and Jane walked to Alton together. Then on the 27th an advance copy of Pride and Prejudice, sent from London by carrier, reached Chawton. Miss Benn was dining once again with the Austens, and she had one-half of the first volume read aloud to her, without knowing the identity of the author.[26] Two days later, when Mrs Digweed, Miss Terry and Miss Benn made a morning visit, Mrs Austen, much to Jane's chagrin, revealed the secret of her authorship.[27]

On 2 February Jane, it seems, attended another large dinner-party, this time at the Digweeds';[28] and on the following day, she walked to Alton by herself, having received a morning visit before she left, and avoided another four visitors during her absence. The four later visitors were Harriet Benn, another daughter of the vicar of Faringdon; Miss Woolls, the sister of a Chawton farmer; Miss Beckford, the youngest daughter of a Steventon squire, now living with her sister, Mrs Middleton; and Maria Middleton, who was Miss Beckford's niece. (At that time, the Middletons were renting Chawton Manor pro tem from Edward Austen.) Three days later, on 5 February 1813, Miss Benn dined again at the Austens', to be regaled later by further readings from *Pride and Prejudice*. Meanwhile – at least one would guess it was meanwhile – either Jane Austen had called again on Mrs Digweed to deposit, or Mrs Digweed had called again on Jane to receive, a Book Society volume.[29]

Even from these shreds of information we can form a clear idea of the close social shuttling and interweaving in the upper level of society in Chawton. The group was as compacted as that of *Emma*, and the resultant compression was in turn matched by a matching constraint. From Jane Austen's standpoint, several of the members of the group were discordant persons, perhaps even fools to be suffered – though silently; and doubtless the discordance was reciprocal. Few human beings are so stupid or insensitive as to fail to sense even kind contempt. 'The Clements', wrote Jane on 9 February, 'are at home, and are reduced to read. They have got Miss Edgeworth. I have disposed of M[rs] Grant['s *Letters from the Mountains*] for the 2nd fortnight to M[rs] Digweed – it can make no difference to *her*, which of the 26 fortnights in the year the 3 vols lay in her house.'[30] As to the later morning visitors of 3 February (the Misses Beckford, Benn, Middleton and Woolls), Jane observed that 'my Mother was glad to see, & I very glad to escape' all four.[31]

At the dinner on 20 January,

> Upon M[rs] Digweed's mentioning that she had sent the Rejected Addresses [by Horace and James Smith] to M[r] Hinton, I [Jane Austen] began talking to her a little about them, & expressed my hope of their having amused her. Her answer was 'Oh dear yes, very much, very droll indeed – the opening of the House, and the striking up of the Fiddles!' What she meant poor woman, who shall say? I sought no farther.[32]

This comment probably reveals more about Jane Austen's sense of discordance than Mrs Digweed's supposed stupidity, for it seems evident that Mrs Digweed had read the relevant lampoon in *Rejected Addresses* (a pastiche of the poet Crabbe, the third and fourth stanzas of which deal with 'the opening of the House' and the 'striking up of the Fiddles', respectively) and that Jane Austen had not.[33] Earlier in the same letter (of 24 January) Jane had written ironically of the polite muffling of feeling which was indispensable in this society, 'In consequence of a civil note that morning from Mrs Clement, I went with her & her husband in their Tax-cart – civility on both sides; *I* would rather have walked, & no doubt *they* must have wished I had'.[34]

There may also have been repressions so severe that they have left almost no trace, even in the intimate letters to Cassandra. Was Miss Benn's company endured from charity rather than enjoyed? She was a spinster, probably in her forties. Did Jane feel of her, as she wrote of another such, Miss Murden: 'at her age, perhaps, one may be as friendless oneself, and in similar circumstances quite as captious'?[35] Although Miss Benn is mentioned in no less than fourteen letters, Jane's comments on her are colourless from first to last. This is in itself extraordinary. The great majority of the hundreds of persons mentioned in the letters are characterized in some degree or other. Even the curate of Great Worldham, Mr Twyford, whose sole appearance in history is as a guest at Mr Papillon's dinner party, was transfixed in half a sentence, 'I don't know that Mr T. is anything except very dark-complexioned'.[36]

As ever, or almost ever, the strains of life with Mrs Austen – such as they were – show in only occasional and dulled gleams. After a reference to the unpleasantness arising from such a revelation, Cassandra is warned by Jane of Mrs Austen's disclosure of the existence and authorship of *Pride and Prejudice* in these oblique words, 'It was spoken of here one morning when Mrs D. called with Miss Benn [and Miss Terry]'. Perhaps irritation with her mother's style of reading aloud to Miss Benn was being indicated by, 'though she [Mrs Austen] perfectly understands the characters herself, she cannot speak as they ought'.[37] Certainly, Jane and her mother were quite out of sympathy about the second visitation of ladies of 3 February. What we should never guess at all from any of the four letters is that the Austen house at Chawton bordered a main street, at the very fork of the London-Winchester and London-Gosport highways, and that the room in which Jane Austen was writing *Mansfield Park* was entered almost directly from the footpath, so that each visitor meant an end of work, and the hasty concealment of the signs of composition.

IV

The sample of letters providing a vignette of the upper social life at Chawton was chosen at random, selected because they formed one of the few clusters grouped about a particular fortnight or so. But they are altogether typical of the whole. Let me take as another example the first three letters written by Jane Austen after she came to live permanently at Chawton. These yield the following information for the two weeks 25 May-6 June 1811. During the first week Miss Benn dined twice and had tea once with the Austens. Harriet Benn dined once with the Austens, had tea with them on another day and walked with Jane Austen for tea at Faringdon on a third. On yet another day Maria Middleton had tea with the Austens. The Austens dined once with the Digweeds and Mrs Digweed's family, the Terrys, who had come from Dummer. Anna Austen, then staying at Chawton Cottage, dined twice with the Benns of Faringdon and once with the Prowtings, who also belonged to the Chawton Book Society 'set'. During the second week, Miss Benn and Maria Middleton dined with the Austens. Anna Austen dined with the Middletons, stayed twice with the Benns at Faringdon, and went with Harriet Benn to the Whites of Selborne to attend a volunteer gala on Selborne Common – the Prowtings took Miss Benn to the same gala. Miss Papillon called on the Austens; Jane Austen called on the Webbs, another 'book club family' and link in the Chawton circle; Jane and Anna Austen and Harriet Benn walked together; and Henry, Jane's brother, stayed with the Austens overnight.[38]

I set out to establish a substantial correspondence between the social circumstances and behaviour described in *Emma* and Jane Austen's own; and it would appear that the correspondence between the imaginary and the actual societies *is* substantial. The basic units of Chawton (like those of Highbury) were familial, with the Austens, Benns, Digweeds and Middletons or Papillons constituting the regulation '3 or 4 Families in a Country Village'. Such families were often extended to include spinster relatives. Apart from Martha Lloyd, who had lived with the Austens since 1805, Miss Beckford and Miss Terry lived with their respective married sisters, and Miss Benn had moved to Chawton with her brother. Moreover, mar-

riages had produced a species of railway system in which most families intersected somewhere or other in the north-eastern Hampshire
network. Even in terms of the tiny company mentioned in the four
letters of early 1813, Jane Austen's niece, Anna, had, as we have seen,
become engaged to (though did not marry) Mrs Digweed's
brother,[39] and Jane Austen's brother Henry was destined to marry
Mr Papillon's niece, Eleanor Jackson, as his second wife.[40] But over
and above this, the upper level of society in Chawton formed a
quasi-family in itself, with almost daily meetings between many of
its members, with protracted morning and evening visits, with
walks together and frequent meals in common, and with such formal
mechanisms of intercourse as the book club and, doubtless, charities
and divine service. Isolation and compression impelled them so to
live, and living so, they could not afford to mark too closely such
differences as the possession or lack of carriages, or the size of house
or income, or the enjoyment of ten servants or three (the Austen
complement), or even none – they could not mark such differences
absolutely in their social dealings. Living so, they could not freely
choose their companions or give careless rein to their tongues or inclinations, perhaps not always to their thoughts.

In short, there were in Chawton the same inherent tendencies
towards social convergence and personal repression as in Highbury.
Nor is it to be supposed that, because I have not written of them
here, the subordinate social groups in Chawton were treated as a
mere base on which their betters rested. In even the handful of Austen letters examined here, there are shafts of comment on, or lightning individuation of many particular poor persons, servants and
working farmers. In all it seems fair to say that Chawton in the late
winter of 1812-13 provides an anticipatory verification of *Emma*.

V

Since this is a historian's book, it is fitting to consider somewhere
what Jane Austen's novels can offer history. A chapter on *Emma*
(which almost mirrors her own type of life in one significant respect)
is probably the best place of all. If it is true that Jane Austen repro-
duced in *Emma* essentially the social organization and habits which
she experienced in Chawton, of what value are her lances of insight
to the historian? First, they provide an implicit but coherent theory
of how society worked, at one of its levels, in the small towns and

large villages of south-eastern England during the Napoleonic wars.
They are evidence of an extraordinary kind – 'we are eavesdropping,
so to say, on an actual and unedited passage' of the vanished past[41] –
of how the leading members of such communities interacted with
one another and developed group characteristics in the first and
second quarters of the nineteenth century. What have we then in the
evidence which *Emma* provides? An archetype? I do not know: it
would be impracticable to try to match Highbury with the two thousand or so real market towns and hamlets of the Home Counties in
1815; and only scholar-oafs would either contemplate such an undertaking or dismiss the evidence of *Emma* because its 'typicality' or
otherwise can never be established. A model? In one sense, Highbury
does furnish us with a model. At least, an abstraction of the working
principles of one layer of social order can be constructed from the
book. But Anglo-Saxons – at least, Anglo-Saxon historians – seem
incapable of distinguishing the tin-opener from the contents of the
tin. Instinctively, it seems, they conflate abstraction with general-
ization, and models with large description. Is it then an historical tool
which the social analysis of *Emma* hands us? Again, in one sense, this
is so. But 'tool' is not sufficiently particularizing. The modern historical landscape is littered with 'tools' for its own exploitation, if
one has the imagination to see their potential and the discrimination
to know which may be used for what.

In the end, it is, I think, Scotist language which best expresses the
peculiar value of this novelist's penetrations. Specifically, Duns Sco-
tus's phrases, the 'particular glimpse' and the 'most special image',
seem to me to get closer than 'type' or 'model' or 'tool' to what we
gain. Jane Austen has fixed a stretch of dead reality in a unique, a
'most special image'. How historians use this microscope or clarifier
(which no one else made, and perhaps no one else could have made,
in 1814-15) is doubtless a test of their dexterity in their trade. But
whether or not we employ her 'particular glimpse' in helping to explain pre-industrial England in an industrializing England, or the
workings of the workless middle class, or the nature of an intermediate community between town and country, our ears should be
more finely tuned, our eyes should be sharper, our stock of notions
should be larger – I mean, as historians in every case – because the
novel *Emma* was composed. Nor should historians neglect the chaste
lesson in composition itself. When Harriet Smith tells Emma that
Miss Nash would be surprised to learn that Robert Martin had proposed marriage to her, '"for Miss Nash thinks her own sister very

well married, and it is only a linen-draper"'", and Emma replies,

'"One should be sorry to see greater pride or refinement in the teacher of a school"'" (pp. 55-6), at least three scales of early-nineteenth-century social evaluation are delicately indicated and interwoven in thirty words. How many of us could say as much with thirty thousand?

CHAPTER 7

THE FINAL PHASE:
Sanditon

JANE AUSTEN IS commonly regarded as an artist standing outside her own time. On the one hand, her acknowledged literary masters, Richardson and Johnson, belonged to a bygone age, and even the admired Fanny Burney to an earlier generation. Charlotte Brontë, for one, regarded Jane Austen's work – specifically, *Pride and Prejudice* – as damned by its eighteenth-century formalism and constraints: 'a carefully fenced, highly cultivated garden, with neat borders and delicate flowers; but no glance of bright vivid physiognomy, no open country, no fresh air, no blue hill, no bonny beck'.[1] On the other hand, we have seen that the Austen novels were instantly categorized as radical in conception and treatment by such acute critics of the day as Scott and Whately.[2]

Yet Jane Austen's last, uncompleted piece of work seems to provide not only 'developments' in her writing 'for which there is little hint in the earlier novels',[3] but also a precise response to and particular manifestation of the spirit of the age in which it was composed, the Regency. Her final phase is also that in which she seems most 'contemporary'.

I

Whether we define the Regency period strictly, as 1811–20, or, more loosely, as the first quarter of the nineteenth century, *Sanditon* belongs to it, unquestionably, in date. In fact, it is close to the meridian. The entire fragment of the projected novel, a mere 22,000 words, was written – as Jane Austen was dying – between 17 January and 18 March 1817.[4] These two months have as high a claim as any to represent the climax of the post-war freneticism which the term 'Regency' generally connotes; and in fact it is the scramble for innovation, riches and self-realization, at the expense of duty, integrity and social peace, which engrosses *Sanditon* and constitutes the target in Jane Austen's sights. But is the exactitude of the chronological attribution more than an antiquarian's curiosity? Does *Sanditon* illuminate or improve our image of the Regency? Does the very concept of a 'Regency period' add to our understanding or evaluation of *Sanditon*? Does either help us with the most obvious historiographical issue opened up by such thoughts, the legitimacy and the fruits of historical phasing?

In answer to the last question, one can, I think, say boldly and simply that historians must periodize or perish. They can only avoid the labelling of groups of years or lengths of time by falling to the depths of sightless positivism or the undifferentiated chronicle. Of course, having made the choice, they must next undertake a critique of the chosen periodization, considering its deficiency as an entity; the reproduction, before or after its temporal limits, of some of its supposed idiosyncrasies; and its spatial, even districtal, limitations. But in the end they will either surrender the category as hopelessly riddled by exceptions or continue to employ it, however qualified. What *is* ruled out is the abandonment of the use of labels. 'The Age of Reason', 'the French Revolutionary period', 'the mid-nineteenth century', '*la belle époque*' are indispensable frames of reference – or, if not these, whatever better general titles can be found to serve as an historical shorthand. The tag says *ars longa*, not *ars sine termino*.

'The Regency' is far from secure as a periodization. Strictly, it describes the mere nine years, 1811-20; and these were years, moreover, of extraordinary variations in Britain's international power, level of employment and state expenditure. The Regent himself was to reign, in his own right, for another decade. The dominant Prime Minister of his regency, Liverpool, was to govern for almost as long after 1820 as he had before it. Further, the word 'Regency' is debauched, from the historian's standpoint, by its appropriation by the connoisseurs of furniture and artefacts. They use the word with great chronological licence, moving freely between 1790 and 1830 at least, and are concerned with common forms rather than contemporaneity. None the less, the term has certain important unities and certain special characteristics for historians. Among the more obvious are these: a phase of inflation, extravagance, conspicuous consumption, debt, speculation, joblessness, rising class conflict, speed and speed of change, and a phase in which Coleridge, Wordsworth, Shelley, Byron, Keats, Scott, Cruikshank, Repton, Nash, Constable and

Turner were all producing work of high significance.

Byron – and who had a better claim to do so? – sang the requiem in 1822. In Canto XI of *Don Juan*, composed in the autumn of that year, he wrote:

> Talk not of seventy years as age; in seven
> I have seen more changes, down from monarchs to
> The humblest individual under heaven,
> Than might suffice a moderate century through.
> I knew that nought was lasting, but now even
> Change grows too changeable, without being new...[5]

This points to two definers of the 'Regency'. First, it bore the marks of a post-war burst of relaxation, indulgence and liberation. Literally, such a delimitation would tie it to the years 1814–20 – 1814 rather than 1815 because the Hundred Days ending in Waterloo were an unforeseeable as well as a very brief reversal. But the break following the Peace of Amiens in 1802 had already shown several of these characteristics in the higher ranges of society; and still more important, from about 1808 onwards a generation, which had grown up perpetually embattled in (so far as continental Europe was concerned) an island fortress, was coming to maturity. The well-to-do among them were eager to make good their lifelong deprivations. Secondly, Byron's stress upon the rapidity and totality of change points to the feverish, reckless, jazz-like strain in the concept 'Regency'. No one captured, and posthumously preserved, this quality so well as he.

> Then dress, then dinner, then awakes the world!
> Then glare the lamps, then whirl the wheels, then roar
> Through street and square fast flashing chariots, hurl'd
> Like harness'd meteors...[6]

'Meteor' is of course the master image. The 'Regency', for the upper ten thousand at least, burned brightly but briefly in its swift, hectic passage.

The archetypal standard work covering these years is, I suppose, Steven Watson's volume of the Oxford History of England, *The Reign of George III*; and the relevant section of his book is headed, 'The Restlessness of the Regency'. Nothing could be more apropos *Sanditon*: restlessness is at once its leitmotif and its key stylistic note. The twelve short chapters of the fragment are tense with movement – in the utmost contrast to, say, the pace and circumscription of

Emma's Highbury – and in a sort of mimicry the writing of *Sanditon* is, for the most part, staccato, rushing, impressionistic and elliptical.[7]

Watson selects as the three exemplars of the Regency spirit, building, fashion and what he calls 'the new fad' of the seaside holiday. Regency building, he writes, was distinguishable by its gaiety, lightness and (often) superficial shoddiness. 'The balance of taste was precarious. The success of the regency period was a prelude to a disastrous decline in architecture as novelty and pastiche swamped the sense of form.'[8] He might almost be describing Sanditon New Town. 'Trafalgar House. . . . ', begins a memorable passage of Jane Austen's fragment,

> was a light elegant Building, standing in a small Lawn with a very young plantation round it, about an hundred yards from the brow of a steep, but not very lofty Cliff – and the nearest to it, of every Building, excepting one short row of smart-looking Houses, called the Terrace, with a broad walk in front, aspiring to be the Mall of the Place. . . .
>
> Charlotte having received possession of her apartment, found amusement enough in standing at her ample Venetian window, & looking over the miscellaneous foreground of unfinished Buildings, waving Linen, & tops of Houses. . . .[9]

Mr Parker, the prime mover in *Sanditon* in every sense, has let his solid, comfortable family home. Jane Austen makes clear its respectability by speaking of it as 'well fenced & planted & rich in the Garden, Orchard & Meadows which are the best embellishments of such a Dwelling' (p. 379). Parker is now the owner-occupier of the villa Trafalgar House. He has but one regret, however – his precipitate choice of name; for as he himself observes, '"Waterloo is more the thing now"' (p. 380). At any rate, when he is chided by his wife on the loss of the woods and shade which had surrounded their old country place, he jauntily responds that '"we have the Canvas Awning, which gives us the most complete comfort within doors – & you can get a Parasol at Whitby's for little Mary at any time, or a large Bonnet at Jebb's"' (p. 381). Long-grown grace, we are being told, was not so much lost as thrown away for flimsy novelty.

Raiment followed the same course. Almost to the year, the Regency inaugurated a new epoch. It was about 1810 that female fashion turned towards gauzification and scattered bedeckment, and that the customary layers of petticoats and the high necklines vanished. Even so undemanding a censor as Byron professed (in 'The Waltz') to be disturbed:

> Muse of the many-twinkling feet! whose charms
> Are now extended up from legs to arms...
> Thy breast – if bare enough – requires no shield;
> Dance forth – *sans armour* thou shalt take the field...[10]

Jane Austen, in her annual descriptions of the London modes for the benefit of Cassandra, also marked the reign of frivolity and licence from 1812 on; and in turn, though more obliquely, *Sanditon* made substantially the same comment on the times. '"Look at William Heeley's windows"', exclaimed the delighted Mr Parker, '"Blue Shoes, & nankin Boots! – Who w^d have expected such a sight at a Shoemaker's in old Sanditon!"'. In the New Town, of course, things were still more advanced, with bright displays of 'Straw Hats & pendant Lace', 'smart Trinkets', and 'Drawers of rings & Broches' (pp. 383, 389-90).

As for Steven Watson's third piece of litmus, the rise of the seaside holiday resort, this was the very vehicle chosen by Jane Austen for her satire; while Watson's master categorization, restlessness, is echoed by the heroine, Charlotte Heywood, when she describes one of her encounters at Sanditon as '"Activity run mad!"' (p. 410). Indeed, the stage is set in the opening pages by Mr Parker's

> 'All done in a moment; – the advertisements did not catch my eye till the last half hour of our being in town; – when everything was in the hurry & confusion which always attend a short stay there – One is never able to complete anything in the way of Business you know till the Carriage is at the door....'   (p. 367)

It is certainly striking to find the choices of a modern work of historical summation anticipated so perceptively more than a century and a half before. *Sanditon* was clearly meant to be a lampoon of modernization, and unerringly Jane Austen selected and connected telling features of contemporary life as its exemplars. But she cut more deeply than this. To parody Paine, she not only mocked the plumage, she also anatomized the living bird. Buildings, clothes, pleasure places and motion are all externalities, comparatively easy to track in their new courses, and then to classify. Ideology, temper and frames of mind are much more difficult affairs; but these subtleties also are caught and pilloried in *Sanditon*. Here Jane Austen is not so much anticipating the verdict of posterity upon the last years during which she lived, as furnishing us with fresh and more fundamental definers of the Regency as a separate age. I would select three in particular for special notice, Political Economy, the Romantic mode and the pursuit of the body's health; and I shall try to deal with each of these in turn.

II

We are scarcely launched into the opening chapter of *Sanditon* before the Political Economical debate begins. The first protagonist, the squire Mr Heywood, stands as a type of the old values, and as such deplores the mushrooming of watering-places on his native Sussex coast. Their 'growing the fashion', and his 'wonder' '"*Where* People can be found with Money or Time to go to them!"', are clearly pejorative comments, implying idleness and waste. The gravamen of Heywood's charge however is that the new resorts are inflationary and socially subversive. They were '"Bad things for a Country; – sure to raise the price of Provisions & make the Poor good for nothing"'. The argument between Heywood and the speculating promoter of Sanditon, Mr Parker, is thereafter complicated by the mutual courtesy of two gentlemen strangers. Heywood politely allows that Sanditon (of which he knows nothing) may be exceptional – or at least no worse than any other seaside venture. With similar good manners, Parker grants that Heywood's strictures may be justified in the case of the 'large, overgrown' established places, the Brightons and the Eastbournes. It is true that in his eagerness as drummer, Parker contradicts himself absurdly. In the same sentence in which he speaks of Sanditon's security in being small, he looks forward confidently to '"the growth of the place, the Buildings, the Nursery Grounds, the demand for every thing"'. Similarly, he goes on to describe those who are trying to add to the number of Sussex seaside resorts – a group in which he is patently a leading member – as persons '"excessively absurd, . . . [who] must soon find themselves the Dupes of their own fallacious Calculations"'. None the less, he does present Political Economy's counter to the traditionalists like Heywood. The new Sanditons, Parker contends, would excite '"the industry of the poor and diffuse comfort & improvement among them of every sort"' (pp. 368-9) or, in our jargon, they would increase employment and raise the basic standard of living and levels of consumption.

Later, substantially the same debate takes place, but now with

Parker's confederate in speculation, Lady Denham, arguing the conservative case. Avarice rather than fanaticism has driven Lady Denham to join Parker in promoting Sanditon, and she greets the news that a Creole family will holiday there with some satisfaction initially.

'That sounds well. That will bring money.'
'No people spend more freely, I beleive, than W[est] Indians,' observed Mr Parker.
'Aye – so I have heard – and because they have full Purses, fancy themselves equal, may be, to your old Country Families. But then, they who scatter their Money so freely, never think of whether they may not be doing mischeif by raising the price of Things...and if they come among us to raise the price of our necessaries of Life, we shall not much thank them Mr Parker.'
'My dear Madam, They can only raise the price of consumeable Articles, by such an extraordinary Demand for them & such a diffusion of Money among us, as must do us more Good than harm. – Our Butchers & Bakers & Traders in general cannot get rich without bringing Prosperity to *us*. – If *they* do not gain, our rents must be insecure – & in proportion to their profit must be ours eventually in the increased value of our houses.'
'Oh! – well. – But I should not like to have Butcher's meat raised, though – & I shall keep it down as long as I can.'[11]

Lady Denham is no economist. She understands so little of her own enterprise, or even of her own greed, as later to complain that since Sanditon had become 'a public place',

'Families come after Families, but as far as I can learn, it is not one in an hundred of them that have any real Property, Landed or Funded. – an Income perhaps, but no Property. Clergymen may be, or Lawyers from Town, or Half pay officers, or Widows with only a Jointure. And what good can such people do anybody? – except just as they take our empty Houses – and (between ourselves) I think they are great fools for not staying at home.'(p. 401)

But Parker is a primitive Keynesian, a Keynesian, as it were, before the modern state. For all his folly, he argues consistently for investment, for expenditure, for inflation, for consumerism, and for economic growth as the basis of general prosperity; he even foreshadows, in rudimentary form, Kahn's multiplier! The naïvety of the economic language, and the lilliputian scale and farcical nature of the speculative activity, should not deceive us. By 1817 the great depression of the nineteenth century, so far as Britain was concerned, was well on its way, with mass demobilization, a drastic reduction in public expenditure and in the money supply, catastrophic falls in demand, and galloping unemployment. There were few Mr Parkers and many Mr Heywoods in the consequent economic controversy; but Jane Austen could find at least one reflationist and give him a fair run for his – to say nothing of other people's – money.

We might note in passing that Malthus's *Enquiry into the Nature and Progress of Rent*, which underpinned theoretically his famous *Essay*, was published less than two years before *Sanditon* was composed, while Ricardo's *Principles of Political Economy* first appeared in 1817 itself.

III

It is notorious that Jane Austen ridiculed certain features of the Romantic mode. 'Romantic' has of course its problems, but like 'Regency' we cannot avoid employing it as academic shorthand; there is no better term. At any rate, every schoolboy, or at least every schoolgirl knows that *Northanger Abbey* was a sustained satire upon Gothicism. Most would also have been told that *Sense and Sensibility* was an elaborate indictment of the second quality in the title. There is not much to quarrel with in either view, and indeed *Sanditon*, so far as it goes, continues in both these strains. The note of mockery of the pseudo-picturesque is struck immediately. In the opening scene Parker sprains his ankle but, discerning a delightful little house at a distance, is convinced that it is the dwelling of the surgeon whom he is seeking. '"*There*, I fancy lies my cure", he exclaimed, pointing to the neat-looking end of a Cottage, which was seen romantically situated among wood on a high Eminence' (p. 364). Heywood soon sets him right: '"as to that Cottage, I can assure you Sir that it is in fact – (in spite of its spruce air at this distance -) as indifferent a double Tenement as any in the Parish, and that my Shepherd lives at one end, & three old women at the other"' (p. 366). This is plainly *Northanger Abbey in parvo*, romantic illusion punctured by the hard-following reality.

As to the *Sense and Sensibility* strain, the mock-hero of *Sanditon*, the handsome young baronet, Sir Edward Denham, bids fair to turning out a foolish and even comic version of the villain Willoughby.

Sir Edward has been nurtured on Richardson and his successors as
sentimental novelists, especially those specializing in the conscienceless pursuit and conscientious ruin of young women. Denham's
great object in life, Jane Austen writes,

> was to be seductive. – With such personal advantages as he knew
> himself to possess, & such Talents as he did also give himself credit
> for, he regarded it as his Duty. – He felt that he was formed to be a
> dangerous Man – quite in the line of the Lovelaces.   (p. 405)

Sir Edward's selected victim, Clara Brereton, a poor relation of his
aunt-in-law, Lady Denham, fitted the classic pattern. She was
'young, lovely & dependant', an orphan and practically defenceless,
for Lady Denham's patronage was capricious and would certainly
not extend to inconveniencing herself to protect Clara's honour.
Clara's seduction, the fragment continues,

> was quite determined on. Her Situation in every way called for it.
> ... He [Sir Edward] had very early seen the necessity of the case,
> & had now been long trying with cautious assiduity to make an
> impression on her heart, and to undermine her Principles. ... If she
> could not be won by affection, he must carry her off. He knew his
> Business. ... If he *were* constrained so to act, he must naturally
> wish to strike out something new, to exceed those who had gone
> before him – and he felt a strong curiosity to ascertain whether the
> Neighbourhood of Tombuctoo might not afford some solitary
> House adapted for Clara's reception; – but the Expence alas! of
> Measures in that masterly style was ill-suited to his Purse, & Pru-
> dence obliged him to prefer the quietest sort of ruin & disgrace for
> the object of his Affections, to the more renowned.   (pp. 405–6)

Thus, Jane Austen's customary mockery of the excesses of contemporary Romanticism was thoroughly sustained in *Sanditon*. In
fact, it was carried forward into virtually a new genre, what we
might even term the Fiction of the Absurd. The dignified parody of
place to be found in *Northanger Abbey* – after all, the Abbey itself
could not be faulted either as pile or as gentleman's estate – is practically parodied in itself, as the cottage *ornée* stands revealed as a rural
slum dwelling. The same applies when Mr Parker argues the superiority of the gimcrack New Town to the solidity and settled comfort
of his hereditary home. The point is silently emphasized in the last
paragraph of fiction that Jane Austen ever wrote. Sanditon House,
Lady Denham's manor, approached through grounds of 'Beauty and

Respectability',

> was large & handsome . . . every thing had a suitable air of
> Property & Order. . . . They were shewn into the usual sitting
> room, well-proportioned & well-furnished – tho' it was Furniture
> rather originally good & extremely well kept, than new or
> shewey. . . .   (pp. 426-7)

It seems fitting that Jane Austen's penultimate sentence should have
been partly spent in putting down the 'new or shewey'. Similarly,
where *Sense and Sensibility* presents seduction, actual and potential, in
half-tragic terms, *Sanditon*'s would-be seducer is merely silly, a futile
figure of fun. Jane Austen's final assault on Romanticism turns its
grotesque side upwards.

Now, by 1817, she was also working at a deeper level. Her most
penetrating reworking of the Romantic theme is probably her treatment of the poetry of passion. In the Austen canon proper, she had
dealt with this most fully in the writing of *Persuasion* two years
before. Captain Benwick is a highly respectable devotee of the verse
of feeling. Anne Elliot tries gently to persuade him of the moral
danger of excessive indulgence in literature of this form and tone;
and she later smiles privately at the prospect of the hearty Louisa
Musgrove being metamorphosized into a young lady of sensibility
and sentiment under the influence of love and Captain Benwick's
reading list. But it is only the extravagance of its followers, and not
the substance of the new poetry which *Persuasion* satirizes – and even
that most mildly.

In *Sanditon*, however, the egregious Sir Edward is cast as the ex-
pounder and justifier of Romantic verse. '"Do you remember"', he
begins,

> 'Scott's beautiful Lines on the Sea? – Oh! what a description they
> convey! . . . That man who can read them unmoved must have the
> nerves of an Assassin! – Heaven defend me from meeting such a
> Man un-armed.'
>
> 'What description do you mean? – said Charlotte. I remember
> none at this moment, of the Sea, in either of Scott's Poems.'
>
> 'Do not you indeed? – Nor can I exactly recall the beginning at
> this moment.'

Burns, the erotic Burns, was Sir Edward's hero.

> 'If ever there was a Man who *felt*, it was Burns. – Montgomery has
> all the Fire of Poetry, Wordsworth has the true soul of it – Camp-

bell in his pleasures of Hope has touched the extreme of our Sensations – "Like Angel's visits, few & far between". Can you conceive any thing more subduing, more melting, more fraught with the deep Sublime than that Line? – But Burns – I confess my sence of his Pre-eminence Miss H. – If Scott *has* a fault, it is the want of Passion. – Tender, Elegant, Descriptive – but *Tame*. . . . But Burns is always on fire. – His Soul was the Altar in which lovely Woman sat enshrined, his Spirit truly breathed the immortal Incence which is her Due. –'

'I have read several of Burn's Poems with great delight, said Charlotte as soon as she had time to speak, but I am not poetic enough to separate a Man's Poetry entirely from his Character; – & poor Burns's known Irregularities, greatly interrupt my enjoyment of his Lines. – I have difficulty in depending on the *Truth* of his Feelings as a Lover. I have not faith in the *sincerity* of the affections of a Man of his Description. He felt & he wrote & he forgot.'[12]

It is noteworthy that Sir Edward fails to mention Byron. Yet he is meant to be an up-to-the-moment young man of fashion. Certainly, his conversation is loaded with the latest literary jargon and affectations. Prefixes such as 'hyper-' or 'pseudo-' or 'anti-' were then the vogue – they were to leave a lasting legacy – and Sir Edward speaks dutifully in the current cant. '"It were Hyper-criticism, it were Pseudo-philosophy to expect from the soul of high toned Genius, the grovellings of a common mind"' (p. 398), is a prime example. Elsewhere, he extols the 'anti-puerile' man, this compound being Jane Austen's final substitution for what she originally wrote, 'sagacious'. Yet Sir Edward has apparently read no Byron. The explanation may well be that Jane Austen herself read comparatively little Byron; there is only one – irreverent – reference in the *Letters* to her reading his work: 'I have read the Corsair, mended my petticoat, & have nothing else to do', she wrote to Cassandra on 5 March 1814.[13] After all, Byron had not long burst upon the firmament. The latest-written poetry quoted in *Sanditon* comes from *The Lady of the Lake*, which was published in 1810.[14] Perhaps Jane Austen meant to suggest that Sir Edward's pretence to be up-to-the-moment in poetry was as hollow as much else about him, for both Anne Elliot and Captain Benwick in *Persuasion* are presented as familiar with Byron's 1813 works, *The Giaour* and *The Bride of Abydos*.[15]

At any rate, Jane Austen was well aware that early Byronic man (whether or not she thought of him in some such terms) had recently turned up on the literary scene. He is quite evident in *Sanditon*. Sir Edward has marked, if ludicrous, aspirations in this direction. Not for nothing does he juxtapose '"the soul of high toned Genius"' and '"the grovellings of a common mind"'. The Corsair, as the glorious embodiment of male power, and capability to force the world into the shape he wills, would fill every corner of Sir Edward's fantasies. It is the *Übermensch* mentality, that of the piratical hero standing above and outside all morality, which is (in my view) the target for *Sanditon*'s most deadly shafts.

IV

War is a promoter of health, and of talk and thought about health. At least, one could reasonably invite an undergraduate to discuss such a proposition with relation to (as the examination papers say) the conflicts of 1793-1815. In these years the struggle between France and Britain was in no small degree a trial by medicine. In certain theatres, the Low Countries in 1794-5 or the West Indies at all stages, to take but two examples, the losses in combat were negligible compared with the death-roll from disease. Perhaps the crucial reason for Britain's ultimate success was her mastering, between 1796 and 1802, the problem of keeping tens of thousands of sailors, cooped up for months on end in men-of-war, alive and even fit. Effective sea power, and in particular the critical blockades, rested upon preventive medicine. The long Peninsular campaign was a forcing-ground for other medical advances, chiefly in surgery perhaps, but also in dietary, sanitary and hospital organization. From the beginning, the Revolutionary Wars had vastly increased the demand for medical practitioners: even in 1793 the Army was forced to recognize Scottish and Irish qualifications in order to make up the necessary numbers in its medical corps. Various scandals, and their successor inquiries in 1805-10,[16] changed profoundly the basis of medical training and professional behaviour.

The upsurge in serious medicine was of course accompanied by an upsurge in quackery, as the subject attracted ever more general attention. During these years, the sales of the notorious Dr Solomon's *Guide to Health* (a popular sex manual) were reputed to be running second only to Paine's *Rights of Man*,[17] so much so that by 1817 Solomon could construct his massive Palace of Health in London. Meanwhile the wartime tax on patent medicines had proved unexpectedly remunerative, producing several millions for the exchequer by this time.

Certain of the effects of these advances – good and bad – are taken up for sceptical scrutiny in *Sanditon*. Possibly Jane Austen's own disease directed her attention thither. 'What we have here...', it has been urged, 'is a dying woman treating the subject of illness with amusement and raillery.... Was she trying to cheer herself up by making fun of her condition? Or was she...so absorbed in the subject of ill health, that the subject presented itself irresistibly?'[18] Her letters of 1817 – not to add, her habitual disposition – do not support this view. She wrote calmly, hopefully yet – if need be – resignedly to her family and friends up to a few weeks before she died. On 22 May 1817 (she died on 18 July) she told Anne Sharp,

> I have kept to my bed since the 13 of April, with only removals to a Sopha. *Now*, I am getting well again, & indeed have been gradually tho' slowly recovering my strength for the last three weeks. I can sit up in my bed & employ myself, as I am proving to you at this present moment, & *really* am equal to being out of bed, but that the posture is thought good for me.[19]

A week later she wrote from Winchester.

> I am gaining strength very fast. I am *now* out of bed from 9 in the morn^g to 10 at night – upon the sopha t'is true – but I eat my meals with aunt Cass: in a rational way, & can employ myself, and walk from one room to another. – Mr Lyford [the physician attending Jane Austen] says he will cure me, & if he fails I shall draw up a Memorial and lay it before the Dean & Chapter, & have no doubt of redress from that Pious, Learned, and Disinterested Body.[20]

But who can say with certainty what thoughts of illness or mortality may have lain behind such words? What cannot be questioned is that, having selected the new watering-place as her vehicle for satirizing modernization, Jane Austen was committed also to guying certain aspects of the medical revolution, in particular, the cult of physical well-being, self-doctoring and hypochondria. Orthodox medicine was spared; neither physicians nor criticism of physicians appear in *Sanditon*. It is only imaginary health and sickness which are sent up.

Salubrity was the seaside resort's selling point, in the first instance. Very early in the fragment, Parker gives this the full salesman's pitch.

> He held it indeed as certain, that no person c^d be really well,...

could be really in a state of secure & permanent Health without spending at least 6 weeks by the Sea every year. – The Sea air & Sea Bathing together were nearly infallible, one or the other of them being a match for every Disorder, of the Stomach, the Lungs or the Blood; They were anti-spasmodic, anti-pulmonary, anti-sceptic, anti-bilious & anti-rheumatic. Nobody could catch cold by the Sea, Nobody wanted appetite by the Sea, Nobody wanted Spirits, Nobody wanted Strength. – They were healing, softing, relaxing – fortifying & bracing – seemingly just as was wanted – sometimes one, sometimes the other – If the sea breeze failed, the Sea-Bath was the certain corrective; – & where Bathing disagreed, the Sea Breeze alone was evidently designed by Nature for the cure.   (p. 373)

Conversely, to denigrate a rival resort to Sanditon, Parker points to its '"ridge of putrifying sea weed...most insalubrious Air...[and] Water brackish beyond example, impossible to get a good dish of Tea within 3 miles of the place"' (p. 369). Thus, Jane Austen deals very simply with the claims that the seaside raises the body to its highest pitch, while acting also as a prophylaxis. She allows Mr Parker's faith in his sovereign slogan – '"Saline air & immersion"' (p. 367) – to topple over by the weight of its own absurdity.

But the seaside as speculation depended on more than the craze for fitness and the preventive measure. The invalid was its second clientele. Here again Parker demonstrated the superiority of his economic sense to that of his co-entrepreneur, Lady Denham. He saw the absence of any resident physician as a brake upon Sanditon's development. The ill, the feeble and the convalescent would fight shy of a place unable to provide them with their customary medical attendance. His search for a surgeon was in fact the initial motivator of his adventures. But Lady Denham, still smarting under the memory of ten fees charged by the practitioner who (as she put it) '"sent *him* [her husband] out of the world"' (p. 394), reasoned otherwise.

'It w^d be only encouraging our servants & the Poor to fancy themselves ill, if there was a D^r at hand. Oh! Oh! pray, let us have none of the Tribe at Sanditon'.   (p. 393)

Besides, she herself had two milch asses, whose produce she wished to palm off privately on some consumptives, and a chamber-horse (evidently the Regency equivalent of the exercise bicycle) for hire. But Mr Parker was justified in the event. When at last the West Indian heiress, Miss Lambe, was inveigled to Sanditon, her chape ron, Mrs Griffiths, would have nothing to do with asses' milk or chamber-horses.

'Miss L. was under the constant care of an experienced physician; – and his Prescriptions must be their rule' – and except in favour of some Tonic Pills, which a Cousin of her own had a Property in, Mrs G. did never deviate from the strict Medecinal page. (p. 422)

Until Miss Lambe's arrival, Sanditon appears to have had no success in tapping the invalid market – that is to say, the regular invalid market, for Mr Parker's two sisters and his youngest brother, Arthur, who arrived together, might be described as independent operators. '"Invalides indeed"', exclaimed the dominant sister, Diana; '"I trust there are not three People in England who have so sad a right to that appellation"' (p. 410). But she had worked her way through doctors and was now effectively in practice on her own account.

'We have entirely done with the whole Medical Tribe. We have consulted Physician after Phy^n in vain, till we are quite convinced that they can do nothing for us & that we must trust to our own knowledge of our own wretched Constitutions for any releif.'
(pp. 386–7)

Diagnosis was Diana's forte. When her sister Susan had been suffering from headache and six leeches a day for ten days on end, Diana, on '"being convinced on examination that much of the Evil lay in her gum, ... persuaded her to attack the disorder there"' and to have three teeth extracted. Meanwhile, she pronounced that Arthur was '"more languid than I like, ... I fear for his Liver"' (p. 387). When Diana had first turned up at Trafalgar House it was without Susan and Arthur. She had persuaded them to remain in their hotel for, as she said, Susan had suffered hysterics when she came in sight of '"poor old Sanditon"', while Arthur was assured by her that it would be imprudent for him to expose himself to the elements: '"there is so much Wind that I did not think he c^d safely venture, – for I am *sure* there is Lumbago hanging about him"' (p. 407). Immediately on arrival at the villa she turned her hand, literally, to Mr Parker's ankle – with rather more cheering results on this occasion: '"That's right; all right & clean. The play of your Sinews a *very* little affected... [though] I see by the position of your foot, that you have used it too much already"' (pp. 408, 411).

When Mr Parker and Charlotte paid their return visit to the other

Parkers, there were, Jane Austen writes, 'almost as many Teapots &c [on the supper tray] as there were persons in company'. While the visitors were treated to ordinary fare, Susan Parker drank 'one sort of Herb-Tea & Miss Diana another', and Arthur what was meant to be a 'large Dish of rather weak Cocoa'. Susan, more worn down by medicine (we are told), was in every sense a pale version of Diana. But Arthur struggled hard for a more comfortable form of valetudinarianism. He fought, for example, to be allowed to butter his own toast, with

> His Sisters... declaring he was not to be trusted; – and he maintaining that he only eat enough to secure the Coats of his Stomach. ... Charlotte c^d hardly contain herself as she saw him watching his sisters, while he scrupulously scraped off almost as much butter as he put on, & then seize an odd moment for adding a great dab just before it went into his Mouth.

As Jane Austen drily notes, his invalidism was 'by no means so spiritualized' as his sisters', and Charlotte was surely right in her conclusion that he had adopted it in order to indulge 'an indolent Temper... determined on having no Disorders but such as called for warm rooms & good Nourishment' (pp. 416–18).

It is all summed up in a passage of what Graham Hough has called her 'coloured narrative',[21] that peculiarly Austenesque form in which the thoughts of character and author blend gradually and inextricably.

> It was impossible for Charlotte not to suspect a good deal of fancy in such an extraordinary state of health.... The Parkers, were no doubt a family of Imagination & quick feelings – and while the eldest Brother found vent for his superfluity of sensation as a Projector, the Sisters were perhaps driven to dissipate theirs in the invention of odd complaints.... Some natural delicacy of Constitution in fact, with an unfortunate turn for Medecine, especially quack Medecine, had given them an early tendency at various times, to various Disorders; – the rest of their sufferings was from Fancy, the love of distinction & the love of the Wonderful. They had Charitable hearts & many amiable feelings – but a spirit of restless activity, & the glory of doing more than anybody else, had their share in every exertion of Benevolence – and there was Vanity in all they did, as well as in all they endured. (pp. 412–13)

Thus the wheel of *Sanditon* comes full circle. Imaginary roads to health and imaginary disease are satirized to the edge of farce. But in the end they are caught up and interwoven with the general biting analysis of restless activity, love of distinction and, above all, vanity – that is to say, with the larger indictment of the England of 1817.

V

In many ways, *Sanditon* differs startlingly from Jane Austen's earlier work. No one can say how it would ultimately have developed, although the outcome of her other fragment, *The Watsons*, seems largely predictable and its relationship to various stretches of *Mansfield Park, Emma* and *Persuasion* unmistakable. It is true of course that the manuscript of *Sanditon* was uncorrected, apart from the over-writing of alternative words and phrases. Yet the pitch and tone of the twelve draft chapters are absolutely consistent, *and* consistently extraordinary in the corpus of Jane Austen's work.

The most striking difference between *Sanditon* and the rest is – ironically enough perhaps – its modernity. As Margaret Drabble observes,

> There are plenty of melodramatic trappings – with the beautiful heroine in distress, Clara, and the half mulatto heiress Miss Lambe, we are almost in the romantic atmosphere of Charlotte Brontë, and would be well into it were it not for the irony with which Jane Austen handles her material. But the material attracts her, nevertheless. The future beckons.[22]

In the final chapter, perhaps the most memorable image in *Sanditon*, Charlotte's glimpse over the palings through the mist of 'something White & Womanish in the field on the other side' (p. 426), gives off decidedly Brontëish emanations. Stranger still, I think, is the faint foreshadowing of Dickens. At times, Sir Edward's speech seems almost a pre-echo of Micawber's, and Mr Parker's that of Mr Jingle. What of these jerking sentences of Parker's, for example, '"the dissolution of a Partnership in the Medical Line – in your own parish – extensive Business – undeniable Character – respectable references – wishing to form a separate Establishment – You will find it at full length Sir"' (p. 366), or, '"The finest, purest Sea Breeze on the Coast – acknowledged to be so – Excellent Bathing – fine hard sand – Deep Water 10 yards from the Shore – no Mud – no Weeds"' (p. 369) and so on. It is perhaps easy to make too much of this merely verbal form of resemblance; but two others seem really significant and substantial. One is the unwonted savagery and even coarseness of the irony in *Sanditon*, the other, its systematic use of comic exaggeration. While there is no question of replication, there are undoubted family resemblances between Lady Denham and Lady Catherine de Bourgh, Sir Edward and Willoughby, Mr Parker and Mr Weston, and the younger Parker sister and Mr Woodhouse. But how much harder and harsher, crueller and less delicate, is the mockery of folly and vice in the case of the first character in each coupling. Again, how magnified, how melodramatic, even how grotesque, are not the embodiments of the qualities in *Sanditon* – even to the extent, in the case of Willoughby and Sir Edward, of the novelist repeating her first near-tragedy as farce? If not in exuberance or plotting, at least in certain strategies of attack, is there not some sort of cousinhood between the Austen of 1817 and the young Dickens of two decades later?

None the less, there are crucial differences. The economy of style and composition, the ease of the marksmanship, and the freedom from sentimentality, all distance *Sanditon* from Dickens, Charlotte Brontë and their entire generation. Combined with other qualities of the fragment, these render it, I believe, an exactly contemporary work in a sense beyond that of any of the completed Austen novels. The resultant tone or temper of *Sanditon* seems more akin to some of the greatest literature of the immediate post-war years than to any late-eighteenth-century or early Victorian writing. In reading *Sanditon* one is reminded most of Peacock's *Nightmare Abbey* and Byron's *Don Juan*, both of which were completed within four years of Jane Austen's fragment. The material reasons for the association are different in the two cases. *Nightmare Abbey* – and perhaps *Crochet Castle* should be added, for despite its later date, it is very similar in technique – are akin to *Sanditon* upon the intellectual plane. It is Romantic posturing and the ideological fads, the trends and claptrap of the day, the March of Mind and its accompanying argot and camp-followers, which Peacock excoriates. Conversely, the Byron of *Don Juan* is a moralist, pitilessly gibbeting contemporary vanity and deceit. These two characteristics of the *fin-de*-Regency seem to converge and intersect in *Sanditon*. But the three works meet completely in a special sort of amalgam of wit, economy and ruthlessness. Perhaps we can best 'place' this peculiar genre by describing it – more properly this time – as later Regency in form and temper.

★ ★ ★

What of the writer as witness to the present and – if it is not im-
pertinent to add – the historian as presiding magistrate? First, let us
for the moment invert the relationship and consider how the historian may help in understanding what the writer says. In the case of
Sanditon, he or she can proffer a moderately well-established category, bearing the label of convenience, 'Regency'. Like all other
periodizations, this concept has been forged as a historian's working
tool. That is to say, he or she has bound together a cluster of characteristics and associated them with a particular stretch of time, in order
to describe, analyse and argue more economically and efficiently. In
the special instance of 'Regency' the general connotations are hectic-
ness, levity, restlessness, speculation, conspicuous waste and consumption, and the like. All this is also both symbolized and actual-
ized in the historian's imagination, by specific phenomena such as
those selected by Steven Watson, buildings, dress and manners and
the seaside holiday. With these models, ready-made, before us, we
see *Sanditon* in a new light. The hectic, the restless, the speculative,
the shallow and the vain are epitomized by and concentrated in the
chosen centre-piece, the new watering-place. The device opens the
way to satirizing shady speculation, doubtful building ventures, the
mushrooming leisure industry and more generally the entire New
World of façades, insatiation and display.

In short, the historian's working device, the template which he or
she has selected to clarify and speed up the work, gives us immediate
access to a deeper level of interpretation or at any rate a more complex, and interlocked, reading of Jane Austen's fragment. On the one
hand, our abstraction, 'Regency', serves as a burning-glass, con-
centrating the scattered rays into a new intensity of insight. On the
other – to adhere to the metaphor of optics – it acts also as a prism,
lighting up fresh facets of implication as we twist the piece of writing
this way and that under the exterior illumination.

But an equal concern of this particular book is what *Sanditon* has to
offer the historian. Again, I select three elements for consideration.
First, it renders more vivid and concrete what the historian already
knows. Certain of the conventional characteristics of our image of
post-Napoleonic-war Britain gain in solidity, and begin to take on a
sort of third dimension in our minds, from the happy chance that
they have been particularized by such an observer as Jane Austen.
Next, by a sort of nuclear breeding, this very particularization suggests fresh ranges of historical investigation, precisely because it is so

firmly located in the very day of its composition. Striking the historian's imagination with a new force and freshness, particularities such as *Sanditon*'s start up chains of useful questions. Which were the southern and south-eastern resorts that took off in the early nineteenth century – following the first wave of Weymouth, Hastings, Folkestone, Margate, Ramsgate, Bognor, Lyme Regis and Brighton?[23] Who were the speculators who laid out and – in all senses including the pejorative – developed them? Should we not merely laugh at Mr Parker's puffing of Sanditon's comparative proximity, in travel time, to London, and his ill-fated quest for a seaside doctor, but also see in these the elements of hypotheses to explain the boom? Who has investigated the rise of proprietary pharmaceuticals? Who has investigated the origins of the cult of fitness? Who has considered the seven-eighths of the late Romantic movement which lay beneath the surface but supported its great, exposed expressers? Who has considered the laity to whom the high priests of political economy preached, who – on the evidence of *Sanditon* at least – were by no means mere passive or supine auditors? In short, the seeds of several doctoral dissertations or revisionary books may be scattered through the pages of the fragment, awaiting perhaps the right reader to set them in generation.

Finally, *Sanditon* refines the periodization with which this chapter opened. It would be foolish to claim that the *Zeitgeist*-manifestations which I have discerned in the fragment – early economic, literary and salubrietary forms of modernization – are the only ones to be discovered, or perhaps even the most important. But they are certainly there: and once we distinguish and define them, correspondences with actualities in the second half of the second decade of the nineteenth century begin to crowd in on us. In other words, our piece of historical shorthand, the phrase, 'Regency period', is enriched and sensibly enlarged. The calibration of the historian's reference frame is finer, the range of his preliminary calculator multiplied.

Unluckily, the actual term 'Regency novel' has become attached, for half a century or more, to a certain genre of 'historical' romances. But even if the tag itself is bedraggled after years of such appropriation, *Sanditon* has earned it in its proper, chronological sense. It is an epitome of its epoch. To say that *Sanditon* is the fragment of a Regency novel is, I believe, to throw light on both what was written and the exact time of writing. Of course, Jane Austen left behind her no more than the opening of a once-corrected draft, only one-fifth or one-sixth, perhaps, of the projected whole. But it was she who wrote. To invoke the motto of the Moscow Arts Theatre – whatever Jane Austen herself might have thought of such a reference – there are only small actors, there are no small parts.

REFERENCE NOTES
BIBLIOGRAPHICAL NOTE
INDEX

CHAPTER 1   [JA = Jane Austen]

1. JA to Cassandra Austen, 24 and 29 Jan 1813, *Jane Austen's Letters to her Sister Cassandra and Others*, ed. R. W. Chapman (London, 1952; hereinafter cited as *Letters*), pp. 294, 298. For detailed discussion of this point see J. F. Burrows, 'Jane Austen's *Emma*: A Study of Narrative Art' (Ph. D. dissertation, University of London, 1967), App. A, pp. 284-7. See also *Jane Austen's Manuscript Letters in Facsimile*, ed. Jo Modert (Carbondale and Edwardsville, Ill., 1990; hereinafter cited as *Manuscript Letters*), pp. 32-3.

2. See generally N. Sykes, *Church and State in England in the Eighteenth Century* (Cambridge, 1934); G. F. A. Best, *Temporal Pillars: Queen Anne's Bounty, the Ecclesiastical Commissioners, and the Church of England* (Cambridge, 1964); A. D. Gilbert, *Religion and Society in Industrial England: Church, Chapel and Social Change, 1740-1914* (New York, 1976); W. R. Ward, *Religion and Society in England 1790-1850* (London, 1972); I. C. Bradley, *The Call to Seriousness: the Evangelical Impact on the Victorians* (London, 1976); and F. K. Brown, *Fathers of the Victorians: the Age of Wilberforce* (Cambridge, 1961).

3. W. and R. A. Austen-Leigh [*Jane Austen. Her Life and Letters*], revised and enlarged by Deirdre Le Faye as *Jane Austen: a Family Record* (London, 1989; hereinafter cited as Le Faye, *Family Record*), pp. 43, 66-7, 78. See also M. Lane, *Jane Austen's Family: Through Five Generations* (London, 1984), pp. 94-5. In the late-eighteenth-century and early-nineteenth-century church the incomes and expectations of performance of curates were so

low that a considerable number of them were in effect pluralists or non-residents or both.

4. Caroline Austen, *Reminiscences of Caroline Austen* (Jane Austen Society, 1986), pp. 18-19.

5. J. E. Austen-Leigh, *Memoir of Jane Austen* (Oxford, 1926), p. 81.

6. A. G. L. Haig, *The Victorian Clergy* (Sydney, 1984), pp. 256, 298, 314-15.

7. R. W. Chapman, *Jane Austen. Facts and Problems* (Oxford, 1948; hereinafter cited as Chapman, *Facts and Problems*), p. 39.

8. Ibid., p. 95. The then anonymous 'Biographical Notice' of the author was prefixed to the posthumous edition of *Northanger Abbey* and *Persuasion* (London, 1818) and was slightly expanded as an introduction to Bentley's collected edition (London, 1833): Chapman, *Facts and Problems*, p. 169.

9. Ibid., p. 95.

10. JA to Francis Austen, 25 Sept 1813, *Letters*, p. 340.

11. JA to Philadelphia Walter, 8 Apr 1798, *Letters*, p. 19.

12. JA to Cassandra, 24 Oct 1808, *Letters*, pp. 225, 227.

13. JA to Cassandra, 30 Jan 1809, *Letters*, p. 261. Earlier she had written to Cassandra, 'It is well that Dr Moore [a clergyman] was spared the knowledge of such a son's death' (24 Jan 1809, *Letters*, p. 258).

14. JA to Francis Austen, 3 July 1813, *Letters*, pp. 313-14.

15. JA to Martha Lloyd, 2 Sept 1814, *Letters*, p. 507.

16. Ibid., p. 508.

17. JA to Fanny Knight, 18 Nov 1814, *Letters*, p. 410.

18. J. Austen, *Mansfield Park* (London, 1933), p. 21 (subsequent page references appear

in the text). All my quotations from and references to the novels come from R. W. Chapman's edition of *The Works of Jane Austen*.

19. '"This is not my idea of a chapel. There is nothing awful here, nothing melancholy, nothing grand"': *Mansfield Park*, p. 85.

20. J. Austen, *The Watsons* (London, 1933), pp. 343-4. The specific question of whether or not *Mansfield Park* is an 'evangelical' novel has been much debated (see P. Garside and E. McDonald, 'Evangelicalism and *Mansfield Park'*, *Trivium*, vol. x [May 1975], pp. 34-50, and D. Monaghan, '*Mansfield Park* and Evangelicalism: a Reassessment', *Nineteenth-Century Fiction*, vol. xxxiii [Sept 1978], pp. 215-30, for arguments on either side). There would seem to be no evidence to support the view that either the novel or Jane Austen herself was 'evangelical' in the sectarian sense. The utmost that can be said for the first is that characteristically Evangelical language is often employed in *Mansfield Park* (cf. Brown, *Fathers of the Victorians*, p. 394). But though the Evangelicals themselves may have used the word 'serious' to mean 'evangelically committed', it was, as has been said above, in no sense their special property. Other Anglicans used it freely in the much larger and looser sense of taking their religion seriously, and of practising it devoutly. As to the author, she once specifically observed, 'I do not like the Evangelicals' (JA to Cassandra, 24 Jan 1809, *Letters*, p. 256), and later that 'We do not much like Mr Cooper's new Sermons; – they are fuller of Regeneration and Conversion than ever – with the addition of his zeal in the cause of the Bible Society' (JA to Cassandra, 8 Sept 1816, *Letters*, p. 467). Respect for total commitment was certainly compatible with distaste – theological, moral and social alike – for the ideas and conduct which were manifested by Evangelical zealots.

21. Haig, *Victorian Clergy*, pp. 2-4, 351-6.

22. Ibid., pp. 358-60.

23. T. Love Peacock, *Nightmare Abbey*, Halliford edn. (London, 1924), p. 41.

24. JA to Cassandra, 14 June 1814, *Letters*, p. 389.

25. D. Lodge, *Changing Places: a Tale of Two Campuses* (Harmondsworth, 1978), p. 46.

CHAPTER 2

1. B. C. Southam, *Jane Austen's Literary Manuscripts: a Study of the Novelist's Development through the Surviving Papers* ([London], 1964), p. 45.

2. Ibid., p. 53. Cassandra's dating, probably made in 1817 or 1818, places the commencement at October 1796 and the conclusion at August 1797.

3. In that year she wrote, jokingly, 'I would not let Martha [Lloyd] read "First Impressions" again upon any account. . . . I saw through her design; she means to publish it from memory, and one more perusal must enable her to do it'; JA to Cassandra Austen, 11 June 1799, *Letters*, p. 67.

4. J. Austen, *Lady Susan* (London, 1933), Mrs Vernon to Mr De Courcy, letter 6, p. 251 (subsequent page references appear in the text). The inspiration for Lady Susan may have been the Lloyds' grandmother, 'the cruel Mrs Craven . . . a most courteous and fascinating woman in society' but fiercely acquisitive and possessed of 'a stern tyrannical temper': C. Austen, *Reminiscences*, pp. 7-9. Jane would have heard the story from the Lloyd girls.

5. Mary Lascelles has suggested in *Jane Austen and Her Art* (Oxford, 1939), pp. 13-14, that the conclusion may have been added when Jane Austen was making a fair copy of *Lady Susan* in or after 1805; but she allows that this is 'mere guesswork'.

6. J. Austen, *Northanger Abbey* (London, 1933), p. 243.

7. *The Watsons*, p. 326 (subsequent page references appear in the text).

8. J. E. Austen-Leigh, *Memoir of Jane Austen*, 2nd edn. (1871), p.364.

9. J. Austen, *Pride and Prejudice* (London, 1933), p. 18 (subsequent page references appear in the text).

10. *Letters*, pp. 1-2.

11. Ibid., p. 3.

12. [14] Jan 1796, *Letters*, pp. 5-6.

13. P. Honan, *Jane Austen: Her Life* (London, 1987), p. 107.

14. W. and R. A. Austen-Leigh, *Jane Austen. Her Life and Letters. A Family Record*, 2nd edn. (New York, 1965; hereinafter cited as Austen-Leigh, *Life and Letters*), p. 89.

15. J. A. P. Lefroy, 'Jane Austen's Irish Friend', *Proceedings of the Hugenot Society of London*, vol. 23 (1979), pp. 148-65.

16. JA to Cassandra, 17 Nov 1798, *Letters*, p. 27.
17. Honan, *Jane Austen*, p. 110.
18. Le Faye, *Family Record*, pp. 96-7.
19. JA to Cassandra, 17 Nov 1798, *Letters*, p. 28.
20. JA to Francis Austen, 3 July 1813, *Letters*, p. 317.
21. Austen-Leigh, *Life and Letters*, p. 93.
22. Honan, *Jane Austen*, p. 193.
23. J. Austen, *Persuasion* (London, 1933), p. 243.
24. Fanny Knight, quoted in Honan, *Jane Austen*, p. 195.
25. Honan, *Jane Austen*, p. 197; F. C. Lefroy, 'Family History', quoted in Le Faye, *Family Record*, p. 122.
26. *Pride and Prejudice*, p. 125.
27. Catherine Hubback, 1 Mar 1870, quoted in Chapman, *Facts and Problems*, p. 62.
28. Letter from Caroline Austen to Amy Austen-Leigh, 17 June 1870, quoted in Le Faye, *Family Record,* p. 122.
29. J. Austen, *Sense and Sensibility* (London, 1933), pp. 369, 374.
30. *Persuasion*, pp. 246-7.

CHAPTER 3

1. G. H. Treitel, 'Jane Austen and the Law', *Law Quarterly Review*, vol. C (1984), p. 586.
2. G. H. Treitel, 'Legal Puzzles in Jane Austen's Works', *Magdalen College Record* (1987), p. 60. Correspondingly, Jane Austen makes it clear that both Mr Collins in *Pride and Prejudice* (p. 64) and Henry Tilney in *Northanger Abbey* (p. 25) are above twenty-four years of age.
3. *Sense and Sensibility*, p. 295.
4. Treitel, 'Legal Puzzles', p. 59.
5. *Collected Reports of the Jane Austen Society 1949-65* (London, 1967), p. 61.
6. Frank received £40 as late as 1795-6, when he was a lieutenant, and Charles £49 as late as 1796-7: ibid.
7. *Letters*, p. 37.
8. Ibid., p. 47.
9. JA to Cassandra Austen, 24 Dec [1798], *Letters*, p. 45.
10. JA to Cassandra, 9 Jan 1796, *Letters*, p. 3.
11. JA to Cassandra, [14] Jan [1796], *Letters*, p. 4.
12. 2 June 1799, *Letters*, p. 63.
13. 11 June 1799, *Letters*, p. 69.
14. 15 Oct 1808, *Letters*, p. 222.
15. Letter from Lady Knatchbull (Fanny Knight) to Marianne Knight, 23 Aug 1869, quoted in Le Faye, *Family Record*, p. 253.
16. JA to Cassandra, 21 May 1801, *Letters*, p. 133.
17. JA to Cassandra, 12 May 1801, *Letters*, p. 126.
18. Henry Austen to Francis Austen, 28 Jan 1805, R. A. Austen-Leigh, *Austen Papers, 1704-1856* (London, 1942; hereinafter cited as *Austen Papers*), pp. 233-4.
19. James Austen to Francis Austen, 30 Jan 1805, *Austen Papers*, p. 236.
20. JA to Cassandra, *Letters*, p. 174.
21. Her expenditure for 1807 (to the nearest pound in each case) was: clothes and pocket money £14, washing £9, presents for others £6, charities £6, letters and parcels £4 and hire of pianoforte £4: Jane Austen's Diary for 1807, quoted in Le Faye, *Family Record*, p. 145.
22. JA to Fanny Knight, 13 Mar [1817], *Letters*, p. 483.
23. *Letters*, p. 117.
24. JA to Cassandra, *Letters*, p. 209.
25. JA to Cassandra, 26 June 1808, *Letters*, p. 199.
26. *Sense and Sensibility*, p. 4.
27. 6 Apr 1817, *Letters*, pp. 491-2.
28. *Letters*, p. 276.
29. [Nov or Dec 1814], *Letters*, p. 423.
30. JA to Cassandra, 15 June 1808, *Letters*, pp. 188-9.
31. JA to Cassandra, 26 June 1808, *Letters*, p. 203.
32. 18 Apr 1811, *Letters*, p. 271.
33. 30 Nov 1814, *Letters*, pp. 419-20.
34. *Letters*, p. 317.
35. Ibid., p. 425.
36. Draft letter from Henry Austen to John Chapman, late Oct 1815 (F-362), *Manuscript Letters*, p. 51.
37. JA to Caroline Austen, *Letters*, p. 511.
38. *Sense and Sensibility*, p. 4 (subsequent page references appear in the text).
39. *Mansfield Park*, p. 3.
40. M. Sadleir, *Trollope: a Commentary*, revised edn. (London, 1945), p. 240 n. 1. Hawthorne wrote of Trollope's novels as 'just as real as if some giant had hewn a great lump out of the earth and put it under a glass case, with all its inhabitants going about their daily business, and not suspecting that they were made a show of'.
41. JA to Cassandra, 25 Apr [1811], *Letters*, p. 273.

42. *Sense and Sensibility*, Notes, p. 383.
43. The great Victorian problems of 'surplus' women and the lack of other occupations for those who did not marry were not new. Unfortunately, the first British censuses, of 1801 and 1811, did not distribute the sexes according to age group. But that of 1821 did so, giving a female numerical superiority of 51.26, 56.47 and 52.24 per cent for the age groups 15-20, 20-30 and 30-40 years respectively (House of Commons Papers, 1822, vol. XV, p. 543). This return is incomplete and also omits members of the armed forces, all of whom would have been male, and a substantial proportion of whom would have been English. It is however the best data we have on the likely composition of the population during Jane Austen's adulthood. If the ratios were the same in 1801 and 1811, females would probably have been slightly preponderant in all the post-15 years categories, and most markedly in the 15-40 age groups. Although the 'surplus' may have been very small, any excess would have been telling given the comparative absence of alternative employment for women.

    Middle- and upper-middle-class women were probably at most disadvantage. Governessing and school-teaching were their only major sources of work outside the household. There was some ambiguity in Jane Austen's attitude to these employments. She made a friend of Anne Sharp, for a time governess to her brother Edward's children; and in *Emma* both Mrs Weston, who had been a governess, and Mrs Goddard who was a schoolmistress, are spoken of with approbation. But on balance Jane's references, in her fiction and correspondence alike, to these occupations suggest that she regarded them as demeaning, if not positively wretched as a mode of living. It is interesting that neither she nor Cassandra nor any of the women in her own outer family or circle, however poor, appears to have considered working in either branch of child instruction.

CHAPTER 4

1. Philadelphia Walter to James Walter, 23 July 1788, *Austen Papers*, p. 131.
2. Eliza de Feuillide to Philadelphia Walter, 26 Oct 1792, *Austen Papers*, p. 148.
3. The notorious second-hand comment on Jane Austen as a girl which Mary Russell Mitford reported – 'Mama says she was then the prettiest, silliest, most affected husband-hunting butterfly she ever remembers' – seems unreliable. There is no evidence that 'Mama' even saw Jane Austen after she was seven or eight years of age. Living about fifteen miles from Steventon thereafter, she was probably within range of local gossip, but it would be mere speculation to suppose that there was any such gossip about Jane. See *A Life of Mary Russell Mitford, related in a selection of letters to her friends,* ed. A. G. L. L'Estrange (London, 1870), I. 305.
4. JA to Fanny Knight, 13 Mar 1817, *Letters*, p. 484.
5. JA to Cassandra Austen, 20 June 1808, *Letters*, p. 194.
6. JA to Cassandra, 25 Apr [1811], *Letters*, p. 275.
7. JA to Cassandra, 6 June 1811, *Letters*, p. 289.
8. JA to Cassandra, 3 Nov 1813, *Letters*, p. 367.
9. *Letters*, p. 416.
10. Quoted in C. Hill, *Jane Austen: her Homes and her Friends* (London, 1902), pp. 194-5.
11. *Letters*, p. 481.
12. 15 June 1808, *Letters*, p. 187.
13. 7 Oct 1808, *Letters*, pp. 216-17.
14. JA to Cassandra, 24 Jan 1809, *Letters*, p. 256.
15. JA to Fanny Knight, 18 Nov [1814], *Letters*, pp. 408-9.
16. *Letters*, pp. 409-11.
17. JA to Fanny Knight, 30 Nov [1814], *Letters*, pp. 417-18.
18. *Letters*, Notes, p. 481. Anna's parents refused at first to countenance her engagement to Michael Terry and she was 'banished' in November 1809 for some months to Godmersham. In March 1810 her father reluctantly consented to the match, but soon after a brief visit to Dummer Anna decided against marrying Terry, and James 'put an end to the engagement'. Anna was again 'banished', this time to Chawton Cottage, for nearly three months: Fanny Knight's Diaries for 1808 and 1809, and F. C. Lefroy, 'Family History', quoted in Le Faye, *Family Record*, pp. 161-2.
19. JA to Cassandra, 29 May 1811, *Letters*, p.

282.

20. JA to Francis Austen, 25 Sept 1813, *Letters*, pp. 340-1.
21. JA to Cassandra, 26 Oct 1813, *Letters*, p. 363.
22. JA to Cassandra, 3 Nov 1813, *Letters*, p. 367.
23. JA to Fanny Knight, 18 Nov [1814], *Letters*, p. 411.
24. *Sense and Sensibility*, pp. 378-9.
25. JA to Cassandra: 17 Nov, 1 Dec 1798, *Letters*, pp. 29, 35.
26. Elizabeth Austen had appeared to be doing well after the birth of her eleventh child (in less than fourteen years), but on 10 October 1808 'she was taken *violently* ill and *expired* (may God have mercy upon us) in ½ an hour!!!!': Fanny Knight's Diary for 1808, quoted in Le Faye, *Family Record*, p. 150. Elizabeth had been very unwell during the preceding pregnancy.
27. JA to Fanny Knight, 20 Feb 1817, *Letters*, p. 480.
28. JA to Fanny Knight, 23 Mar [1817], *Letters*, p. 488.
29. 13 Mar 1817, *Letters*, p. 483.
30. JA to Fanny Knight, 23 Mar [1817], *Letters*, p. 488. In fact, Anna was not pregnant on this occasion.
31. JA to Cassandra, 25 Apr [1811], *Letters*, p. 272.
32. [Dec 1815], *Letters*, p. 449.
33. JA to Fanny Knight: 30 Nov [1814], 20 Feb 1817, 13 Mar [1817], *Letters*, pp. 417, 479, 483.
34. JA to Cassandra, 26 Nov [1815], *Letters*, p. 437.
35. JA to Fanny Knight, 20 Feb [1817], *Letters*, p. 479.
36. JA to Cassandra, 30 Nov [1814], *Letters*, p. 418.
37. JA to Martha Lloyd, *Letters*, p. 504.
38. *Northanger Abbey*, p. 20.
39. *Pride and Prejudice*, p. 236.
40. *Sense and Sensibility*, p. 112.
41. *Persuasion*, p. 4.
42. 11 Dec 1815, *Letters*, p. 443.
43. *Northanger Abbey*, p. 18.
44. JA to Cassandra, 8 Apr [1805], *Letters*, p. 151.
45. J. Austen, *Emma* (London, 1933), pp. 21-2.
46. *Pride and Prejudice*, p. 39.
47. J. Austen, *Catharine, or The Bower* (London, 1933), pp. 197-8 (subsequent page references appear in the text).

48. *Northanger Abbey*, p. 13 (subsequent page references appear in the text).
49. Hill, *Jane Austen: her Homes and her Friends*, p. 18.
50. *Pride and Prejudice*, pp. 37, 93 (subsequent page references appear in the text).
51. JA to Cassandra, 29 Jan [1813], *Letters*, p. 297.
52. *Pride and Prejudice*, pp. 135-6.

CHAPTER 5

1. R. Simpson, unsigned review of the *Memoir, North British Review*, vol. 52 (Apr-July 1870), p. 139.
2. *Northanger Abbey*, pp. 197-8.
3. *Persuasion*, p. 37 (subsequent page references appear in the text).
4. *Quarterly Review*, vol. XIV (1815), p. 193.
5. T. S. Eliot, *Notes Towards the Definition of Culture* (London, 1948), p. 43.
6. *Letters*, pp. 513-14.
7. Ibid., p. 514.
8. Austen-Leigh, *Memoir of Jane Austen*, p. 16.
9. *Persuasion*, p. 125.
10. JA to Cassandra Austen, 12 May 1801, *Letters*, p. 129.
11. JA to Cassandra, 20 Nov 1800, *Letters*, p. 91.
12. JA to Cassandra, 14 Oct 1813, *Letters*, p. 350.
13. JA to Cassandra, 27 Oct 1798, *Letters*, p. 24.
14. 29 July 1817, *Letters*, p. 517.
15. JA to Cassandra, 3 Jan 1801, *Letters*, p. 102.
16. *Letters*, p. 17.
17. On 1 Nov 1797 Mr Austen, after describing briefly *First Impressions*, asked Cadell, 'What will be the expence of publishing at the Author's risk; & what will you venture to advance for the Property of it, if on a perusal, it is approved of?': Austen-Leigh, *Memoir of Jane Austen*, p. 137. Cadell declined, by return of post, to consider the manuscript.
18. Lane, *Jane Austen's Family*, p. 114.
19. 21 Jan 1805, *Letters*, p. 144.
20. JA to Francis Austen, 22 Jan [1805], *Letters*, pp. 145-6.
21. Lane, *Jane Austen's Family*, p. 136.
22. *Letters*, p. 358.
23. JA to Cassandra, 23 Sept [1813], *Letters*, pp. 329, 334.
24. JA to Cassandra, *Letters*, p. 1.
25. JA to Cassandra, [14] Jan [1796], *Letters*,

p. 5.

26. Mrs Cassandra Austen to Mary Lloyd, 30 Nov 1796, *Austen Papers*, p. 228.

27. JA to Cassandra, 7 Jan 1807, *Letters*, p. 173.

28. Elizabeth Chute to her sister, 22 Feb 1797: M. A. Austen-Leigh, *James Edward Austen-Leigh* (privately printed, 1911), p. 17.

29. Lane, *Jane Austen's Family*, p. 109.

30. JA to Anne Sharp, 22 May [1817], *Letters*, p. 494.

31. JA to Cassandra, *Letters*, pp. 107-8.

32. JA to Cassandra, 14 Jan 1801, *Letters*, p. 111.

33. Ibid., pp. 111-12. About this time Jane Austen wrote brusquely of the marriage anniversary party which James and Mary were to hold, 'I was asked, but I declined it', JA to Cassandra, 8 Jan 1801, *Letters*, p. 106.

34. JA to Cassandra, *Letters*, p. 173.

35. JA to Cassandra, 27 Dec [1808], *Letters*, p. 241.

36. *Letters*, p. 181.

37. JA to Anne Sharp, 22 May 1817, *Letters*, p. 494.

38. Cassandra Austen to Fanny Knight, [20] July 1817, *Letters*, p. 515.

39. *Letters*, p. 121.

40. Lane, *Jane Austen's Family*, p. 113.

41. Ibid., p. 115.

42. JA to Cassandra, 3 Jan 1801, 8 Apr [1805], *Letters*, pp. 99, 152.

43. JA to J. Edward Austen, 16 Dec [1816], *Letters*, p. 468.

44. *Letters*, p. 431.

45. 2 Mar, 5 Mar [1814], *Letters*, pp. 376, 377-8, 381.

46. JA to Cassandra, 15 Sept [1813], *Letters*, p. 320.

47. JA to Francis Austen, 25 Sept 1813, *Letters*, p. 340.

48. *Letters*, p. 487.

49. 3 July 1813, *Letters*, p. 315.

50. Henry Austen to Frank Austen, 28 Jan 1806, *Austen Papers*, p. 235.

51. It is certainly possible that Jane Austen drew on the letter to make an addition or substitution when revising *Sense and Sensibility* for publication in 1811.

52. C. Austen, *Reminiscences*, pp. 48, 57.

53. 21 Jan [1799], 26 Nov [1815], *Letters*, pp. 57, 438.

54. 26 May 1801, *Letters*, p. 137.

55. JA to Cassandra, 26 Nov [1815], *Letters*, p. 438.

56. Ibid., pp. 438-9.

57. Ibid., p. 438.

58. JA to Cassandra, 5 Mar [1814], *Letters*, p. 382.

59. 26 July 1809, *Letters*, p. 265.

60. JA to Cassandra, 7 Jan [1807], *Letters*, p. 173.

61. JA to Cassandra, 8 Feb 1807, *Letters*, pp. 178-9.

62. *Manuscript Letters*, F-354.

63. JA to Francis Austen, 3 July 1813, *Letters*, p. 316.

64. 14 Oct 1813, *Letters*, p. 351.

65. *Letters*, p. 473.

66. JA to Cassandra, 30 Jan 1809, *Letters*, p. 260.

67. 11 Oct 1813, *Letters*, p. 344.

68. JA to Cassandra, 8 Sept [1816], *Letters*, p. 466.

69. JA to Cassandra, 30 June 1808, *Letters*, p. 206.

70. JA to Cassandra, 13 Oct 1808, *Letters*, pp. 219-20.

71. According to Anna Lefroy, however, both Elizabeth and her children preferred Cassandra Austen to Jane. 'They [the children] liked her [Jane] indeed as a play-fellow, & as a teller of tales, but they were not really fond of her. I believe that their Mother was not: at least that she very much preferred the elder Sister': D. Le Faye, 'Anna Lefroy's Original Memories of Jane Austen', *Review of English Studies*, NS vol. xxxix, no. 155 (1988), p. 419. In the case of Elizabeth, at least, Anna Lefroy was probably reporting what her mother had told her. Her comments may also have been coloured by her sense of her own (and her aunt Jane's) intellectual superiority to the Godmersham Austens/Knights, for she goes on to say, 'A little talent went a long way with the Goodneston Bridgeses [Elizabeth was a Bridges] of that period, & much must have gone a long way too far'.

72. 13 Oct 1808, *Letters*, p. 220.

73. *Letters*, p. 336.

74. *Persuasion*, p. 43.

75. JA to Francis Austen, 25 Sept 1813, *Letters*, p. 339.

76. L. Davidoff and C. Hall, *Family Fortunes: Men and Women of the English Middle Class, 1780-1850* (London, 1987), p. 12.

77. C. Austen, *Reminiscences*, p. 48.

78. *Letters*, pp. 493, 495.

79. JA to ——, [end of May? 1817], *Letters*,

pp. 497-8.

80. 27 May 1817, *Letters*, p. 497.

81. JA to J. Edward Austen, 27 May 1817, *Letters*, p. 496.

82. JA to Cassandra, 8 Jan 1799, *Letters*, p. 51.

83. JA to Cassandra, 14 Oct 1813, *Letters*, p. 354.

84. *Letters*, p. 391.

CHAPTER 6

1. For a complete list of the characters in *Emma*, see G. Leeming, *Who's Who in Jane Austen and the Brontës* (London, 1974), pp. 3-81. The exact total depends upon the number of children allocated to certain 'multi-child' families.

2. R. Blythe, in his Penguin edition of J. Austen, *Emma*, (Harmondsworth, 1966), p. 469.

3. *Letters*, p. 401.

4. *Emma*, p. 233 (subsequent page references appear in the text).

5. *Emma*, p. 456. A little earlier in the same conversation, Mrs Elton is speaking of 'the magistrates': ibid., p. 455.

6. Ibid., p. 136. Emma's earlier comment, while she was still hoping to marry Mr Elton to Harriet, 'quite the gentleman himself, and without low connections; at the same time not of any family that could fairly object to the doubtful birth of Harriet', is not really contradictory in terms of rank, but rather the adulatory, as against the critical, expression of the same social evaluation: ibid., p. 35.

7. Ibid., p. 236. Cf. the comment of the contemporary Scottish novelist, Susan Ferrier, on *Emma*, 'There is no story whatever but the characters are all so true to life . . . that it does not require the adventitious aids of mystery and adventure': *Memoir and Correspondence of Susan Ferrier*, ed. J. A. Doyle (London, 1898), p. 128.

8. 17 Nov 1798, *Letters*, p. 30.

9. *Emma*, p. 207; for the composition of their dinner-party, p. 214.

10. G. Hough, 'Narrative and Dialogue in *Emma*', *Critical Review*, vol. XII (1970), p. 223; cf. also R. Williams, *The Country and the City* (London, 1973), pp. 115-17.

11. See above, pp. 106-8.

12. K. Kroeber, '*Pride and Prejudice*: Fiction's Lasting Novelty', in *Jane Austen: Bicentenary Essays* (London, 1975), p. 150, ed.

J. Halperin.

13. P. Teilhard de Chardin, *Man's Place in Nature: the Human Zoological Group*, Fontana edn. (London, 1971), pp. 97-8.

14. M. Elwin, *Lord Byron's Wife* (London, 1962), p. 159.

15. R. Whately, unsigned review of *Northanger Abbey* and *Persuasion, Quarterly Review*, vol. XXIV (1821), p. 362.

16. This was the 'common fare' of all three London-Winchester coach lines, Mountain's, Boulton's and Collyer's.

17. Le Faye, *Family Record*, p. 145.

18. *Letters*, pp. 291-305.

19. Ibid., pp. 292, 298.

20. White was a nephew of the celebrated Revd Gilbert White of Selborne, yet another nearby parish.

21. *Letters*, pp. 292-4. For further information on the Benn family, see *Ordained in Powder: the Life and Times of Parson White of Crondall*, ed. R. P. Butterfield (Farnham, 1966), p. 73.

22. JA to Cassandra Austen, 24 Jan 1813; JA to Martha Lloyd, 29 Nov 1812: *Letters*, pp. 295, 501.

23. *Letters*, pp. 504-5.

24. JA to Cassandra, 24 Jan 1813, *Letters*, p. 295.

25. *Letters*, p. 294.

26. JA to Cassandra, 29 Jan [1813], *Letters*, p. 297.

27. JA to Cassandra, 4 Feb [1813], *Letters*, p. 300. That not merely the existence but also the authorship of the book was revealed is implicit in the warning Jane gives to Cassandra not to rely on the secrecy observed at their brother James's house in Steventon (where Cassandra was then staying), as 'the means of saving you from everything unpleasant'.

28. Jane Austen does not specifically say that she attended this dinner-party, or describe it after it (presumably) took place. But it is almost certain that she was a guest, given the established pattern of Chawton dining interchange. The Austens themselves gave dinner-parties. At one of theirs a little earlier (1 December 1812), the guests included Captain and Mrs Clement, Miss Benn and Mrs Digweed. Mr Digweed was unable to dine with the Austens on 1 December 1812 because he was shooting rabbits at Steventon on that day: JA to Martha Lloyd, 29 Nov [1812], *Letters*, p. 500.

29. JA to Cassandra, 9 Feb [1813], *Letters*, p.

305.

30. Ibid. The Edgeworth work was probably the Second Series of *Tales from Fashionable Life* (1812). That by Mrs Grant was almost certainly *Letters from the Mountains, being the real correspondence of a Lady, between the years 1773 and 1807* (1807).

31. JA to Cassandra, *Letters*, p. 300.

32. JA to Cassandra, 24 Jan 1813, *Letters*, p. 293.

33. Horace and James Smith, *Rejected Addresses or the New Theatrum Poetarum* (London, 1812), is a collection of parodies or pastiches. These imaginary addresses to celebrate the re-opening of the Drury Lane Theatre on 12 Oct 1812 were supposed to be entries in the prize competition which marked the occasion. The relevant lines in the Crabbe parody are:

Hark! the check-taker moody silence breaks,
And bawling "Pit full!" gives the check he takes;
Yet onward still the gathering numbers cram,
Contending crowders shout the frequent damn,
And all is bustle, squeeze, row, jabbering, and jam.
See to their desks Apollo's sons repair –
Swift rides the rosin o'er the horse's hair!
In unison their various tones to tune,
Murmurs the hautboy, growls the hoarse bassoon . . . ,

(*Rejected Addresses*, new edn. [London, n.d.], p. 141)
Crabbe was, incidentally, one of Jane Austen's favourite poets.

34. *Letters*, p. 293.

35. JA to Cassandra, 27 Dec [1808], *Letters*, p. 243.

36. JA to Cassandra, 24 Jan 1813, *Letters*, p. 293.

37. JA to Cassandra, 4 Feb [1813], *Letters*, p. 299. For a discussion of the tensions of domestic life with Mrs Austen, see G. Gorer, *The Danger of Equality* (London, 1966), pp. 248-64.

38. *Letters*, pp. 280-91.

39. M. Laski, *Jane Austen and Her World* (London, 1969), p. 90.

40. Ibid., p. 121. This niece, Eleanor Jackson, is mentioned in Jane Austen's letter of 24 January 1813 as one of the admirers of *Rejected Addresses*, with the appended comment, '*She* looks like a rejected addresser': *Letters*, p. 294.

41. O. MacDonagh, *The Nineteenth Century Novel and Irish Social History: Some Aspects* (Dublin, 1970), p. 19.

CHAPTER 7

1. Charlotte Brontë to G. H. Lewes, 12 Jan 1848, *The Brontës: Lives and Correspondence* (London, 1932), II. 179-80.

2. See above, pp. 105, 136-7.

3. Southam, *Jane Austen's Literary Manuscripts*, p. 103.

4. Ibid., pp. 101-2. Southam estimates the length of the fragment a little higher, at 'about 24,000 words'.

5. *Byron's Poems*, ed. V. de Sola Pinto (London, 1963), III. 344.

6. Ibid., III. 340.

7. B.C. Southam argues persuasively against Chapman's contention (*Facts and Problems*, p. 208) that 'a certain roughness and harshness of satire' in the draft of *Sanditon* would have been smoothed out in the final revision. Southam points out that, although so many passages are so 'energetic and elliptical' in style as to suggest hasty writing, these passages were not materially altered by Jane Austen in the revisions which she did make, and also that the staccato manner fits the character or situation being described. There are other passages in the draft where, suitably to the person or action, 'typical features of her developed style in the mature novels' are repeated: Southam, *Jane Austen's Literary Manuscripts*, pp. 107-9.

8. J. Steven Watson, *The Reign of George III, 1760-1815* [The Oxford History of England, vol. XII] (Oxford, 1960), p. 547.

9. J. Austen, *Sanditon* (London, 1933), p. 384 (subsequent page references appear in the text).

10. *Byron's Poems*, I. 295.

11. *Sanditon*, pp. 392-3. For convenience of reading, I have paragraphed the conversational exchanges in this and other quotations from *Sanditon*, although the manuscript runs them together in single passages.

12. *Sanditon*, pp. 396-8. Tony Tanner observes that apart 'from the odd reference to the "distant Tweed" and "Sweet Teviot"' he, like Charlotte, 'cannot re-

member any descriptions of the sea in Scott's poems': T. Tanner, *Jane Austen* (Cambridge, Mass., 1986), p. 275.

13. *Letters*, p. 379. *The Corsair* had been published less than two months earlier.

14. When Charlotte Heywood spoke of 'either of Scott's poems', the reference was probably meant to be to *Marmion* (1808) and *The Lady of the Lake*.

15. *Persuasion*, p. 100. Jane Austen's implied comment on these poems, when she refers to 'all the impassioned descriptions of hopeless agony' and 'various lines which imaged . . . a mind destroyed by wretchedness', seems disapproving.

16. The first relevant inquiry was set afoot under 45 Geo. III c.47 on 5 June 1805 and the last, into the Scheldt expedition, in 1810. The reformed Army Medical Board was appointed during 1810.

17. F. Barry Smith, 'Sexuality in Britain 1800-1900 : Some Suggested Revisions', in *A Widening Sphere: Changing Roles of Victorian Women*, ed. M. Vicinus (London, 1977), p. 194.

18. Margaret Drabble in her introduction to J. Austen, *Lady Susan; The Watsons; Sanditon*, Penguin edn. (Harmondsworth, 1974), p. 24.

19. *Letters*, p. 493.

20. JA to J. Edward Austen, 27 May 1817, *Letters*, p. 496.

21. See above, ch. 6, n. 10.

22. Drabble, introd., *Lady Susan; The Watsons; Sanditon*, p. 30.

23. J. Walvin, *Beside the Seaside* (London, 1978), p. 20.

———————— BIBLIOGRAPHICAL NOTE ————————

The principal sources for this book are Jane Austen's novels and other fictional work and her correspondence and other personal writings. In quoting from her fiction, I have used throughout R. W. Chapman's editions (London, 1933), with further reference to B. C. Southam, *Jane Austen's Literary Manuscripts* (Oxford, 1964). My quotations from her letters are drawn from R. W. Chapman, ed., *Jane Austen's Letters to her Sister Cassandra and Others*, 2nd edn. (London, 1952), supplemented by Jo Modert, ed., *Jane Austen's Manuscript Letters in Facsimile* (Carbondale and Edwardsville, Ill., 1990).

On Jane Austen's own and her family's background, I have followed the usual track of recollections and memoirs: Henry Austen, 'Biographical Notice of the Author' (Preface to the first edition of *Northanger Abbey* and *Persuasion*, 1818, revised for the Bentley edition of the novels, 1833); J. E. Austen-Leigh, *A Memoir of Jane Austen* (London, 1870, and subsequent editions); Caroline Austen, *My Aunt Jane Austen* (Jane Austen Society, 1952) and *Reminiscences* (Jane Austen Society, 1986); J. H. and Edith C. Hubback, *Jane Austen's Sailor Brothers* (London, 1906); W. and R. A. Austen-Leigh, *Jane Austen: Her Life and Letters: A Family Record* (London, 1913); and R. A. Austen-Leigh, *Austen Papers, 1704-1856* (London, 1949).

The revision and enlargement of the Austen-Leighs' *Life and Letters* by Deirdre Le Faye, under the title *Jane Austen: a Family Record* (London, 1989), has proved of the utmost help, and I have also profited from Maggie Lane, *Jane Austen's Family through Five Generations* (London, 1984). The proceedings (*Collected Papers*) of the Jane Austen Society contain various valuable contributions on personal, family and relevant contemporary history. Constance Hill, *Jane Austen: her Homes and her Friends* (London, 1904), provided me with some interesting material, particularly on topography; and I found Penelope Bryde, *A Frivolous Distinction: Fashion and Needlework in the Works of Jane Austen* (Bath, 1979), an illuminating source on the topic of dress.

Various biographies and biographical pieces were very helpful to me, in particular, the first and the latest substantial modern 'lives': Elizabeth Jenkins, *Jane Austen: A Biography* (London, 1938) and Park Honan, *Jane Austen: Her Life* (London, 1988).

With kind permission, I have also drawn freely on my own papers published in *Historical Studies*, vol. xviii, no. 70, *Sydney Studies in English*, vol. xii (1986-7), and in Tom Dunne, ed., *The Writer as Witness* (Cork, 1987), for Chapters 1, 6 and 7 respectively.

Other material used directly in the book is acknowledged in the Reference Notes.

Characters in Jane Austen's novels are indexed as sub-headings under the
novels in which they appear.

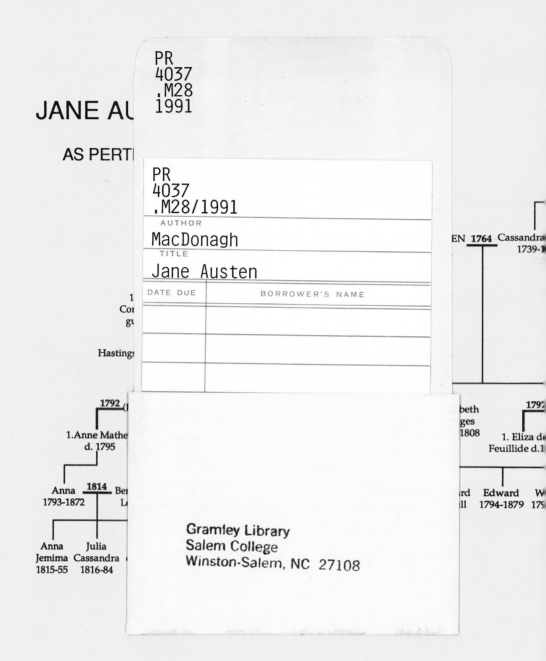

JANE AU

AS PERT

EN **1764** Cassandra
1739-

1
Cor
gu

Hastings

1792
1.Anne Mathe
d. 1795

Anna **1814** Ben
1793-1872 L

Anna Julia
Jemima Cassandra
1815-55 1816-84

beth
ges
1808

179
1. Eliza d
Feuillide d.1

rd Edward W
ll 1794-1879 179